Communicate!

Contributing Author

Dom Saliani

NELSON / EDUCATION

NELSON / EDUCATION

Communicate!

Contributing Author: Dom Saliani

Director of Publishing
David Steele

Publisher
Carol Stokes

Program Manager
Leah-Ann Lymer

Developmental Editors
Norma Kennedy
Su Mei Ku
Todd Mercer
Jessica Pegis

Contributing Author, Chapter 9
Maryrose O'Neill

Senior Managing Editor
Nicola Balfour

Senior Production Editor
Carol Martin

Copy Editor
Dianne Broad

Proofreader
Maraya Raduha

Indexer
Noeline Bridge

Editorial Assistant
Georgina Tresnak

Cover Design
Peter Papayakanis

Cover Photo/Illustration
Peter Papayakanis

Art Direction
Suzanne Peden

Composition
Visutronx Services

Production Coordinator
Julie Preston

Permissions
Karen Becker
Vicki Gould

Printer
Transcontinental Printing Inc.

Reviewers
The publishers gratefully acknowledge the contributions of the following educators:

Brenda Badger
New Brunswick

Sandy Brown
Alberta

Mary Dunnigan
Alberta

Angela Ferguson
Ontario

Doug Gregory
Alberta

Ruby Hardiman
Newfoundland

Keli Jo Healey
Newfoundland

Colleen Lindsay
British Columbia

Hugh MacKinnon
Alberta

Regina Maher
Saskatchewan

Anne Manning
Newfoundland

Carol Murray
British Columbia

Vincent O'Brien
Ontario

John Rogers
Ontario

Carolyn Sheffield
Ontario

Allison Sullings
British Columbia

Terry Swift
Manitoba

Mary Lou Tollis
Ontario

**National Library of Canada
Cataloguing in Publication Data**

Saliani, Dom
    Communicate!

(Nelson English)
Includes index.
ISBN 0-17-619717-6 (bound)
ISBN 0-17-619716-8 (pbk.)

1. English language – Problems, exercises, etc. 2. Communication – Problems, exercises, etc. I. Title. II. Series.

PE1112.S215 2001   428'.0076
C2001-930256-8

Table of Contents

TO THE STUDENT viii

UNIT 1: Take It In! 1

CHAPTER 1: Reading Strategies 2
Reading Short Stories 3
   General Strategies for Reading Short Stories 3
   How to Read a Short Story 3
Reading Poetry 7
   General Strategies for Reading Poetry 7
   How to Read a Poem 7
Reading Plays 11
   General Strategies for Reading Plays 11
   How to Read a Play 11
Reading Novels 17
   General Strategies for Reading Novels 17
   How to Read a Novel 18
Reading Newspapers 22
   Why Do People Read Newspapers? 22
   "Leads" and Newspaper Articles 22
   Newspaper Opinion Pieces 23
   How to Read a Newspaper Opinion Piece 24

CHAPTER 2: Viewing Strategies 27
Editorial Cartoons 28
   How to View an Editorial Cartoon 28
Visual Aids: Charts and Graphs 30
   How to View a Visual Aid 30
Photographs 33
   How to View a Photograph 33
Advertising 36
   Posters 36
   How to View a Poster 36
   Print Advertisements 39
   How to View a Print Advertisement 39
Brochures 42
   How to View a Brochure 42
Feature Films and Television 46
   How to View a Feature Film 46
Web Sites 49
   How to View a Web Site 49

UNIT 2: Express Yourself! 53

CHAPTER 3: The Writing Process 54
The Writing Process: An Overview 55
Prewriting 56
    Find and Limit Your Topic 56
    Define Your Purpose and Your Audience 57
    Choose a Form 58
Drafting 59
    Organize Your Thoughts 59
    Write a First Draft 61

CHAPTER 4: Improving a Draft 65
Revising and Editing 66
    Revising 66
    Editing 69
Editing Style, Grammar, and Usage 75
    Transitions 76
    Sentence Variety 78
    Clauses 80
    Participles and Gerunds 81
    Prepositional and Gerund Phrases 82
    Sentence Fragments 83
    Run-On Sentences 84
    Modifier Mistakes 85
    Awkward Sentences 86
    Parallelism 87
    Subject-Verb Agreement 88
    Discriminatory Language 90
    Active and Passive Voice 93
    Precise Pronouns 94
    Redundancy 97
    Repetition 97
    Vocabulary and Writing 98
    Comparative and Superlative Adjectives and Adverbs 100
    Double Negatives 100
    Commonly Confused Words 101
    Literary and Rhetorical Devices 103
    Language to Avoid in Your Writing 104
Strategies for Fixing Writing Problems 106
    Writing Groups 106

CHAPTER 5: Presenting Your Work 111
Presenting Written Work 112
   Proofread for Spelling, Capitalization, and Punctuation 113
   Spelling 114
   Hyphenated Words 118
   Abbreviations 119
   Numbers and Metric Units 121
   Capital Letters 123
   Punctuation 125
   Italics and Underlining 132
Formatting 133
   Formatting Your Final Draft 133
   Formatting on the Computer 134
Adding Front and Back Matter 138
   Front Matter 138
   Back Matter 141
   Formatting Checklist 142

CHAPTER 6: Writing Essays 143
Applying the Writing Process 144
The Three Parts of an Essay 145
   The Introduction 145
   The Body 146
   The Conclusion 148
Structuring Your Essay 149
   Keywords in Essay Topics 149
Model Essays 150
   Model Essay #1: Literary Essay 150
   Model Essay #2: Persuasive Essay 154
   Model Essay #3: Research Essay 156

CHAPTER 7: Researching 161
Making a Research Plan 162
Using the Library 163
   Locating Books 163
   Reference Resources 163
   Magazines and Newspapers 165
   Special Library Resources 166
   Sources Outside the Library 167
   Narrowing Down Research Resources 170
Using Questions to Focus Research 172

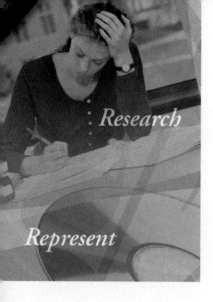

Research

Represent

Evaluating Research Information 173
Taking Notes 174
Giving Proper Credit to Sources 177
The Style of Your Acknowledgments 177
Acknowledging Sources in the Text of Your Research Report 177
Acknowledging Sources Using Footnotes 178
Bibliography and Works Cited 179
Plagiarism 181

CHAPTER 8: Business and Technical Writing 183
Applying the Writing Process 184
Preparing to Communicate for Business Purposes 185
The Business Audience 185
The Structure of Business Writing 185
Communicating in the Business Setting 187
Business Letters 187
Other Types of Business Writing 196
Communicating to Get a Job 200
The Letter of Application 200
The Résumé 202
The Job Interview 205
The Follow-Up Letter 209
Reports 211
Progress Reports 212
Evaluative Reports 215
Proposals 218
Checklist for Writing Reports 222
Communicating Technical Information 223
Understanding Technical Information 223
Presenting Technical Information 223
Defining Terms 224
Explaining a Process or Procedure 226

CHAPTER 9: Representation Strategies 229
The Design Process: An Overview 230
Predesigning/Planning 230
Drafting/Designing 231
Revising and Editing 232
Publishing/Production 232
Photographs 233
How to Create a Photograph 233
Posters 235
How to Create a Poster 235
Visual Aids 238
How to Create a Visual Aid 238

Brochures 241
  How to Create a Brochure 241
Videos 244
  How to Create a Video 244
Web Sites 248
  How to Create a Web Site 249

UNIT 3: Speak Out! Listen Up! 251

CHAPTER 10: Speaking and Listening 252
Effective Public Speaking 253
  Thinking About Public Speaking:
  What, Who, Why, How, Where, and When 253
  Writing an Effective Speech 255
  Using Audio-Visual Aids 257
  Giving an Effective Presentation 257
Effective Listening 261
  Preparing to Listen: What Are Your Expectations? 261
  Listening: Concentration and Active Participation 263
  Taking Notes in Lectures or Discussions 265
Effective Group Work 266
  Roles 266
  Working Together 267
Types of Groups 271
  Groups That Form to Achieve a Task and Solve a Problem 271
  Groups That Form to Explore Ideas 273
  Groups That Form to Argue Viewpoints 274
Think More About It 276

APPENDIX: STUDY SKILLS 277
Managing Your Time 278
  Planning 278
  Scheduling 278
Effective Studying 279
  Reading 279
  Taking Notes 281
Tests and Exams 282
  Preparing for an Exam 282
  Writing an Exam 282

GLOSSARY 285

INDEX 289

ACKNOWLEDGMENTS 294

To the Student

At any given moment, you are taking in or giving out information through listening, reading, viewing, speaking, writing, and/or representing. Although you may take these skills for granted, there is always room for improvement. Think of skills you use in any sports or musical activities. Do you constantly practise to get better? *Communicate!* will help you to practise and use your communication skills more effectively.

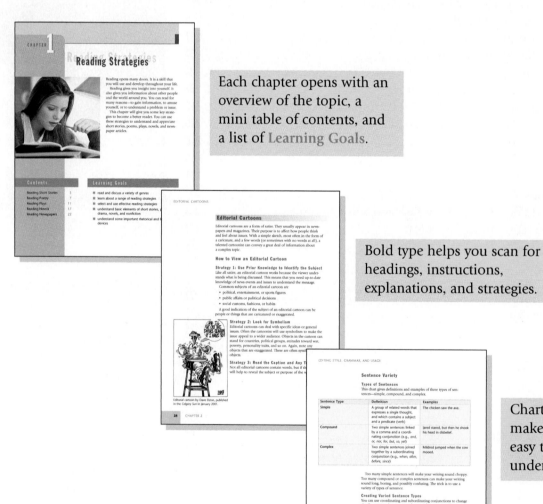

Each chapter opens with an overview of the topic, a mini table of contents, and a list of Learning Goals.

Bold type helps you scan for headings, instructions, explanations, and strategies.

Charts and lists make information easy to find and understand.

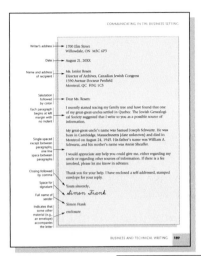

Models provide real-life examples of different types of writing, visuals, and media.

Try It! notes give related hints and activities to try inside or outside the classroom.

Cross-References tell you where to find more information on a topic.

Troubleshooting sections provide tips to help you work through difficult concepts or tasks.

An **Apply It!** box appears at the end of each main section. It includes

- activities that help you to apply what you have just learned
- a **Checklist** to make sure you've followed all the steps or suggestions
- a **Think About It** activity to help you to reflect on your learning strategies

You will also find a **Glossary** of terms and an **Index** at the back of the book.

Here are some ways to use *Communicate!*

An Assigned Text for Your English Class
For each assigned chapter:

- Read the first page to get an overview of the content.
- Skim the chapter (or a small section at a time), noting headings, models, examples, graphics, margin notes, and the general organization.
- Read a section of text, then work on the related Apply It! activities. Be sure to use the Checklist to check your work.
- Keep a journal to record your response to the Think About It activities.

A Reference for Your Other Classes
Communicate! can help you with assignments from other subject areas. For specific assignments:

- Examine the table of contents of *Communicate!* and skim each chapter so that you know what information is available and where to find it when you need it.
- Make note of chapters that could be particularly useful. For example, Chapter 7 (Researching) could help you with a history assignment.
- Complete Apply It! activities related to your assignment for practice, and use the Checklists to check your understanding.
- When you get an assignment back, note areas of weakness and re-read appropriate sections of *Communicate!*

A Career Planning Tool
Think about the career path or college program that you would like to pursue when you leave high school.

- Make a list of all the communication skills you think you will need for your chosen career or college program.
- While you work through *Communicate!*, note when you are working with each skill on your list. Jot down relevant page references in your journal, and comment on whether you feel you need more practice with the skill. Talk to your teacher about how he or she can help you.
- When you have finished working through *Communicate!*, refer to page 276 to find out what to do next.

Take It In!

Every single day you take in information through reading and viewing. Although you have already had years of practice, there are ways to become an even better reader and viewer. Now is a good time to become an expert!

Analyze

Interpret

Appreciate

Evaluate

Contents

Chapter 1
Reading Strategies 2

Chapter 2
Viewing Strategies 27

Reading Strategies

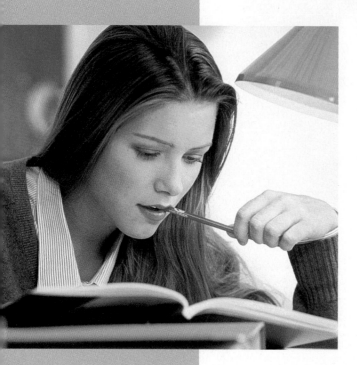

Reading opens many doors. It is a skill that you will use and develop throughout your life.

Reading gives you insight into yourself. It also gives you information about other people and the world around you. You can read for many reasons—to gain information, to amuse yourself, or to understand a problem or issue.

This chapter will give you some key strategies to become a better reader. You can use these strategies to understand and appreciate short stories, poems, plays, novels, and newspaper articles.

Contents

Reading Short Stories	3
Reading Poetry	7
Reading Plays	11
Reading Novels	17
Reading Newspapers	22

Learning Goals

- read and discuss a variety of genres
- learn about a range of reading strategies
- select and use effective reading strategies
- understand basic elements of short stories, poetry, drama, novels, and nonfiction
- understand some important rhetorical and literary devices

Reading Short Stories

The short story, like the novel, is part of the fiction genre. Short stories share many basic elements with novels such as

- setting
- characters
- plot
- conflict

However, because a short story is brief, these key elements are usually set early within the story. Here are some strategies that work well when reading short stories.

General Strategies for Reading Short Stories

1. Read the story a few times. The first time, just try to understand what is going on. On your second reading, focus more on important story elements such as setting, characters, conflict(s), theme, and any literary devices such as symbols.

2. As you read, jot down notes about the story. What is your first impression of the characters—their dialogue and behaviour? Write down your predictions about the plot. Do you have any questions about the deeper meaning of the story and the story's purpose?

3. Write down any words you do not understand. Consider the context in which these words appear to help you predict their meaning. Then, check in a dictionary to see if your prediction was accurate.

How to Read a Short Story

Strategy 1: Consider Title, Author, Nationality, and Date

- Before reading the story, look closely at the title. Often, writers give important information, such as a symbol, in the title. Now make predictions about story content.
- Research and read background information about the author. Editors often provide biographical information on the book sleeve or at the back of the book. If not, use literary resources or the Internet to find author information.

  What conclusions can you draw based on the author's name and nationality? Where and when did he or she write the short story?

Cross-Reference

See Reading Novels, page 17.

Cross-Reference

See the Glossary to learn about symbols and theme.

Cross-Reference

See Chapter 7 for information on how to research.

Knowing where and when might suggest historical and cultural ideas that relate to story content and meaning.

Strategy 2: Make Predictions Based on the Story's First Paragraphs

Read the first 20 or 30 lines of the story very carefully. Often, the first few paragraphs contain important information that establishes setting and character. Setting descriptions can reveal story atmosphere and tone.

Strategy 3: Make Personal Connections with the Story

How does the story relate to you and your experience? The following questions will help:

Do the characters remind you of people you know?

- **Personal:** Do the characters remind you of people you know? How? In what ways can you identify or sympathize with the main characters? Do the situations or conflicts remind you of something that has happened to you or to someone you know? How?

- **Literary:** What stories have you read or seen (e.g., in movies) that have similar characters, events, and writing styles? In what ways are these stories similar and different?

- **Senses:** As you read, take time to imagine how the characters and settings appear. What would the setting sound or smell like?

Strategy 4: Identify the Story's Purpose

Decide if the story was written to entertain or to say something important about life. Ask yourself:

- Are the characters shown realistically or are they exaggerated?
- Do the characters and conflict just make me laugh, or do they make me think more deeply about issues and themes?

Strategy 5: Discuss Your Ideas with Others

In a small group, discuss your responses to the short story and listen to other students' responses and questions.

Strategy 6: Appreciate the Author's Craft

Consider how the story is told—the language and word choices the author makes; this is sometimes called the author's style. Ask yourself:

- What effect does the author create through his or her choice of a particular word, symbol, or metaphor?
- Does the author use contrast? How? What is the author's tone?
- How does the tone add to the effect?

Using the six strategies you've just learned, read the following excerpt from a short story. A student's ideas are written in the margin and refer to the colour codes in the excerpt.

Cross-Reference

See Tone, pages 62 to 63. See the Glossary to learn about metaphor and irony.

Blood Knots
(excerpt)
by Mallory Burton

I have neglected to tie the wading boots properly, to pull the braided laces tight against the metal grommets, to fasten them securely with a double knot. This is partly due to lack of effort and partly because the boots are much too big for me. They belong to my father. Belonged to my father. I suppose they are mine now. Neither my mother nor my sister fishes. I am the only one.

The boots are full of fine gravel, which chafes between my thick, outer wading socks and the lightweight fabric of these summer waders. I should get out of the river to empty the boots, but it doesn't seem worth the effort of battling the current all the way back to the bank.

A mosquito buzzes close to my temple. I can hear its thin whine over the rushing of the stream, see the dark fluttering blur out of the corner of my eye. The insect lands, and I feel its sting, such a tiny prick that I wonder why I have always made such a fuss about them, slapping at myself and smearing poisonous oil all over my face and limbs.

The Internet says a blood knot is used in fly-fishing.

Why is the narrator wearing the father's boots? Does "blood" in the title mean "family"?

Sounds like the father died. Is this why the narrator has neglected to tie up the boots properly?

Is the narrator lonely?

Must be uncomfortable!

Why not kill the mosquito?

Apply It!

With the help of your teacher, choose a short story to read, then try these activities.

1. Consider the title of the short story, the author's name and nationality, the copyright date, and any other background information about the author and story. Use this information to make predictions about the story's content.

2. As you read, make notes about what you are reading. Use the notes included with the excerpt from "Blood Knots" on page 5 for ideas about the kinds of information to record and the questions to ask.

3. In a small group, discuss the story's purpose. Was it written to entertain, to present an important insight about life, or both? Provide evidence to support your views.

Checklist

✓ Did I check the title, the author's name and nationality, the copyright date, and any other background information that could help me understand the story?

✓ Did I make notes and ask questions while I read the story?

✓ Did I discuss the story's purpose with my classmates?

✓ Did I conclude what the story's purpose was?

✓ Did I support my conclusion with evidence from the story?

Think About It: Which short-story reading strategies did you find most useful? Note any strategies you could see yourself using again. Jot down a few reasons.

Reading Poetry

From earliest history, people have created poetry to express their most important thoughts, feelings, beliefs, stories, and dreams.

Much of poetry's power comes from the way in which poets use language. In poetry, the fewer words, the better. Poets also use powerful images to appeal to our senses, and create beauty through rhythm and other poetic sound devices.

Poetry demands special reading strategies.

General Strategies for Reading Poetry

1. Read the poem more than once. Every time you read it, you will learn something new.

2. Read slowly, paying careful attention to punctuation. Don't stop at the end of a line unless there is a reason to do so.

3. Read the poem aloud. Poems are meant to be heard as well as read.

How to Read a Poem

Strategy 1: Consider Title, Author, Nationality, and Date

- Pay attention to the title. A poem's situation, purpose, or theme may be suggested by its title.
- Check to see if information about the poet is included with the poem. If it isn't included, research it. Research also when and where the poem was written. This information can help you understand the events described, or why the poet used certain types of language.

Strategy 2: Make Personal Connections with the Poem

- As you read, record your first impressions and responses to the poem. What are your thoughts and feelings about the poem? What parts affected you most? What questions do you have about the poem?
- Do you identify with the feelings expressed in the poem? Think about when and where you had similar feelings or experiences. How were those feelings and experiences similar?

Strategy 3: Identify the Poem's Purpose

Poems are written for different purposes. For example:

- A lyric poem expresses powerful emotions.
- A narrative poem tells a story.
- Light verse is intended to amuse an audience.

As you read any poem, ask yourself what the poet is trying to accomplish. After reading the poem, ask: Did the poet accomplish his or her purpose?

Strategy 4: Discuss Your Ideas with Others

Discuss your responses, ideas, and questions with classmates. Often, their observations and ideas can help you see the poem in a fresh way.

Strategy 5: Appreciate the Poet's Craft

As you read the poem, note the words and phrases the poet uses, and the effects these words and phrases create. For example:

- Literary devices are used to appeal to the reader's imagination. Metaphors and similes are common devices. When the poet uses a metaphor such as: "The moon was a ghostly galleon sailing the broad dark seas," the reader creates a mental picture based on the poet's words.
- Personification—giving non-human things human qualities—is another effective device, because humans always understand human emotions. For example: "The wind made the trees moan."
- Imagery is vivid description that appeals to our five senses. For example, imagery in a poem that describes the smell of freshly baked bread takes us right into the scene.
- Poetic sound devices are words and phrases that appeal directly to the ear. Rhyme is the device you are most familiar with. Alliteration, assonance, and consonance are other devices that enhance the sound of poetry.

Using the five strategies you've just learned, read the following poem.

Cross-Reference

See the Glossary to learn about metaphor, simile, personification, alliteration, assonance, consonance, and rhyme.

How Do I Love Thee?

by Elizabeth Barrett Browning

How do I love thee? Let me count the ways.

I love thee to the depth and breadth and height

My soul can reach, when feeling out of sight

For the ends of Being and ideal Grace.

I love thee to the level of everyday's

Most quiet need, by sun and candlelight.

I love thee freely, as men strive for Right;

I love thee purely, as they turn from Praise.

I love thee with the passion put to use

In my old griefs, and with my childhood's faith.

I love thee with a love I seemed to lose

With my lost saints,—I love thee with the breath,

Smiles, tears, of all my life!—and, if God choose,

I shall but love thee better after death.

Apply It!

Read the poem "How Do I Love Thee?" and complete these activities.

1. Paraphrase the poem. When you paraphrase a poem, you summarize it in your own words. Share and discuss your paraphrase with some classmates.

2. Which of the following did you find in this poem? Share evidence of your findings with a partner.

   - metaphor
   - simile
   - personification
   - rhyme
   - assonance
   - consonance
   - alliteration

3. As a group, prepare a multimedia presentation of this poem. Your work might include any combination of the following media in the presentation:

   - audio- or videotape
   - computer
   - music
   - visuals (e.g., original artwork or magazine photos)

   See Chapter 9 for ideas on how to create your presentation.

Checklist

✓ Did I include all important details of the original poem in my paraphrase? Did I keep the tone as well?

✓ Did I look for metaphors, similes, personification, rhyme, assonance, consonance, and alliteration in the poem?

✓ Did I share my findings with my partner?

✓ Did I work well with other group members throughout the planning and presentation stages of the multimedia project?

Think About It: How did discussing the poem with classmates and sharing ideas with others help you improve your understanding of the poem?

Troubleshooting: Be Positive

Some students think poetry is difficult to understand. Do you? It may help to remember that

1. poetry helps you better understand your thoughts and feelings
2. poetry is found in the lyrics of all your favourite songs

Reading Plays

Plays have many of the same elements as short stories and novels. For example, plays, like short stories and novels,

- have settings
- involve various characters in conflict
- develop important themes

General Strategies for Reading Plays

1. Scan the play to get a sense of its length, organization of scenes, and the length of dialogue and speeches.

2. Read the *Dramatis Personae* (Cast of Characters) carefully. Note the relationships between characters. As you read the play, review the *Dramatis Personae* to help you keep track of characters and their relationships.

3. Read the opening stage directions. Here the playwright provides important information about what the stage should look like and how the characters should appear.

How to Read a Play

Strategy 1: Research the Playwright and Play History

Find out if the play is based on a real event. Knowing this information can help you understand possible historical, political, and social meanings of the play.

Drama has changed over time. Plays from different periods in history generally use styles and language suited for the audience of that period.

Strategy 2: Think About the Title and Characters' Names

The title may hold a clue about the play's theme. The names of characters may also give clues about their personalities and purpose.

Strategy 3: Draw a Diagram of the Stage

As you read the stage directions, sketch what you think the stage will look like. The drawing need not be too detailed. Use boxes and lines to show furniture and doors. Label important furniture and props.

Play the part.

Strategy 4: Read the Play Aloud

Whether you are reading aloud as a large group, with a partner, or alone, remember that plays are meant to be heard and seen. When you are reading a character's part, use the tone and emotion suited to that character and his or her dramatic situation. Check the level of your voice. Can you be heard? Are you shouting?

Strategy 5: Appreciate the Playwright's Craft

As you read the play, think about dramatic elements and writing techniques the author uses to help you see and respond to characters and their situation(s). Here are a few dramatic elements, techniques, and questions to consider when you read plays. You might use the questions in a group discussion about the play.

- *The purpose of the play and the audience for whom it was written.* Is the play meant to entertain, amuse, inform, shock, or affect our emotions in some other way? Who is the play's audience? For example, is it a play for children?

Cross-Reference

See the Glossary to learn about suspense and atmosphere, or mood.

- *Techniques the playwright uses to maintain interest and create suspense.* What elements and writing techniques in the play encourage you to find out more about a character, situation, or theme?

- *How relationships between characters are established by the blocking.* Blocking is the purposeful movement and positioning of actors on stage. How does the blocking of a play reveal or suggest any conflict?

- *The use of lighting and any music or sound effects.* What mood or atmosphere do these elements create?

Using the five strategies you've just learned, read the following excerpt from a play.

Trifles
(excerpt)

by Susan Glaspell

CHARACTERS
GEORGE HENDERSON, County Attorney
HENRY PETERS, Sheriff
LEWIS HALE, a neighbouring farmer
MRS. PETERS
MRS. HALE

SCENE: *The kitchen in the now abandoned farmhouse of* JOHN WRIGHT, *a gloomy kitchen, and left without having been put in order— unwashed pans under the sink, a loaf of bread outside the breadbox, a dish towel on the table—other signs of incompleted work. At the rear the outer door opens and the* SHERIFF *comes in followed by the* COUNTY ATTORNEY *and* HALE. *The* SHERIFF *and* HALE *are men in middle life, the* COUNTY ATTORNEY *is a young man; all are much bundled up and go at once to the stove. They are followed by the two women—the* SHERIFF's *wife first; she is a slight wiry woman, a thin nervous face.* MRS. HALE *is larger and would ordinarily be called more comfortable looking, but she is disturbed now and looks fearfully about as she enters. The women have come in slowly, and stand close together near the door.*

COUNTY ATTORNEY (*rubbing his hands*): This feels good. Come up to the fire, ladies.

MRS. PETERS (*after taking a step forward*): I'm not—cold.

SHERIFF (*unbuttoning his overcoat and stepping away from the stove as if to mark the beginning of official business*): Now, Mr. Hale, before we move things about, you explain to Mr. Henderson just what you saw when you came here yesterday morning.

COUNTY ATTORNEY: By the way, has anything been moved? Are things just as you left them yesterday?

SHERIFF (*looking about*): It's just the same. When it dropped below zero last night I thought I'd better send Frank out this morning to make a fire for us—no use getting pneumonia with a big case on, but I told him not to touch anything except the stove—and you know Frank.

COUNTY ATTORNEY: Somebody should have been left here yesterday.

SHERIFF: Oh—yesterday. When I had to send Frank to Morris Center for that man who went crazy—I want you to know I had my hands full yesterday. I knew you could get back from Omaha by today and as long as I went over everything here myself—

COUNTY ATTORNEY: Well, Mr. Hale, tell just what happened when you came here yesterday morning.

HALE: Harry and I had started to town with a load of potatoes. We came along the road from my place and as I got here I said, "I'm going to see if I can't get John Wright to go in with me on a party telephone." I spoke to Wright about it once before and he put me off, saying folks talked too much anyway, and all he asked was peace and quiet—I guess you know about how much he talked himself; but I thought maybe if I went to the house and talked about it before his wife, though I said to Harry that I didn't know as what his wife wanted made much difference to John—

COUNTY ATTORNEY: Let's talk about that later, Mr. Hale. I do want to talk about that, but tell now just what happened when you got to the house.

HALE: I didn't hear or see anything; I knocked at the door, and still it was all quiet inside. I knew they must be up, it was past eight o'clock. So I knocked again, and I thought I heard somebody say, "Come in." I wasn't sure. I'm not sure yet, but I opened the door—this door (*indicating the door by which the two women are still standing*) and there in that rocker—(*pointing to it*) sat Mrs. Wright.

(*They all look at the rocker.*)

COUNTY ATTORNEY: What—what was she doing?

HALE: She was rockin' back and forth. She had her apron in her hand and was kind of—pleating it.

COUNTY ATTORNEY: And how did she—look?

HALE: Well, she looked queer.

COUNTY ATTORNEY: How do you mean— queer?

HALE: Well, as if she didn't know what she was going to do next. And kind of exhausted.

COUNTY ATTORNEY: How did she seem to feel about your coming?

HALE: Why, I don't think

she minded—one way or other. She didn't pay much attention. I said, "How do, Mrs. Wright, it's cold, ain't it?" And she said, "Is it?"—and went on kind of pleating at her apron. Well, I was surprised; she didn't ask me to come up to the stove, or to set down, but just sat there, not even looking at me, so I said, "I want to see John." And then she— laughed. I guess you would call it a laugh. I thought of Harry and the team outside, so I said a little sharp: "Can't I see John?" "No," she says, kind o' dull like. "Ain't he home?" says I. "Yes," says she, "he's home." "Then why can't I see him?" I asked her, out of patience. "'Cause he's dead," says she. "*Dead*?" says I. She just nodded her head, not getting a bit excited, but rockin' back and forth. "Why—where is he?" says I, not knowing what to say. She just pointed upstairs— like that (*himself pointing to the room above*). I got up, with the idea of going up there. I walked from there to here—then I says, "Why, what did he die of?" "He died of a rope round his neck," says she, and just went on pleatin' at her apron. Well, I went out and called Harry. I thought I might—need help. We went upstairs and there he was lyin'—

COUNTY ATTORNEY: I think I'd rather have you go into that upstairs, where you can point it all out. Just go on now with the rest of the story.

HALE: Well, my first thought was to get that rope off. It looked … (*stops, his face twitches*) … but Harry, he went up to him, and he said, "No, he's dead all right, and we'd better not touch anything." So we went back downstairs. She was still sitting that same way. "Has any-body been notified?" I asked. "No," says she, unconcerned. "Who did this, Mrs. Wright?" said Harry. He said it busi-nesslike—and she stopped pleatin' of her apron. "I don't know," she says. "You don't *know*?" says Harry. "No," says she. "Weren't you sleepin' in the bed with him?" says Harry. "Yes," says she, "but I was on the inside." "Somebody slipped a rope round his neck and strangled him and you didn't wake up?" says Harry. "I didn't wake up," she said after him. We must 'a' looked as if we didn't see how that could be, for after a minute she said, "I sleep sound." Harry was going to ask her more questions but I said maybe we ought to let her tell her story first to the coroner, or the sheriff, so Harry went fast as he could to Rivers' place, where there's a telephone.

COUNTY ATTORNEY: And what did Mrs. Wright do when she knew that you had gone for the coroner?

HALE: She moved from that chair to this one over here (*pointing to a small chair in the corner*) and just sat there with her hands held together and looking down. I got a feeling that I ought to make some con-versation, so I said I had come in to see if John wanted to put in a telephone, and at that she started to laugh, and then she stopped and looked at me—scared. (*The* COUNTY ATTORNEY, *who has had his note-book out, makes a note.*) I dunno, maybe it wasn't scared. I wouldn't like to say it was. Soon Harry got back, and then Dr. Lloyd came, and you, Mr. Peters, and so I guess that's all I know that you don't.

COUNTY ATTORNEY (*looking around*): I guess we'll go upstairs first—and then out to the barn and around there. (*To the* SHERIFF) You're convinced that there was nothing important here—nothing that would point to any motive?

SHERIFF: Nothing here but kitchen things.

(*The* COUNTY ATTORNEY, *after again looking around the kitchen, opens the door of a cup-board closet. He gets up on a chair and looks on a shelf. Pulls his hand away, sticky.*)

COUNTY ATTORNEY: Here's a nice mess.

(*The women draw nearer.*)

MRS. PETERS (*to the other woman*): Oh, her fruit; it did freeze. (*To the* COUNTY ATTORNEY) She worried about that when it turned so cold. She said the fire'd go out and her jars would break.

SHERIFF: Well, can you beat the women! Held for murder and worryin' about her preserves.

COUNTY ATTORNEY: I guess before we're through she may have something more serious than preserves to worry about.

HALE: Well, women are used to worrying over trifles.

(*The two women move a little closer together.*)

Apply It!	Checklist
Read the excerpt from the play *Trifles* and complete these activities.	✓ Did I use the Internet or the library for my research?
1. Use the Internet or the library to find information about the author and the play. See Chapter 7 for more on researching.	✓ Did I note important background information that could help me understand the play?
2. Read the stage directions carefully and make a sketch of the stage. Label the important props, doors, and stairs.	✓ Did I sketch the stage and label all important elements?
3. In groups, plan, rehearse, and produce a presentation of the excerpt.	✓ Did we rehearse our parts and present lines using appropriate tone of voice and volume?
4. Write another scene based on what you've seen of the characters and conflict. Perform the scene with a group.	✓ Did I focus on important character traits revealed in the excerpt when developing characters in my new scene?

Think About It: Which strategy for reading a play did you find most helpful? How did it work for you?

Troubleshooting: Be the Director

When you read a play, take on the role of director. Ask yourself:

1. What should the stage look like?

2. How should the actors deliver their lines?

3. How should the actors move and react?

Reading Novels

The novel is much longer than the short story, yet it shares several elements with shorter fiction such as setting, atmosphere, plot, characters, conflict, point of view, and theme. There are many different types of novels. These are just a few:

- literary
- historical
- adventure
- romance
- science fiction

Novels have some unique features, which require special reading strategies. For example, a novel can take place over a long period of time. Novels can also show conflict at many levels among major and secondary characters.

General Strategies for Reading Novels

1. Scan the novel. Get a sense of the overall organization and length of the chapters. If the chapters have titles, predict what each might be about and how the chapters could be related.

2. Set a reading schedule. Decide how long it will take to read the novel. To do this, time how long it takes you to read one page. Multiply the time by the number of pages. Next, create a reading log in which you record realistic reading goals. Check regularly to see how well you are meeting your goals so that you finish the novel on schedule.

3. Choose a quiet spot for reading. A comfortable seat with good lighting and few distractions is ideal.

4. Read with a pen in hand. Use sticky notes to mark important information about the novel. On the notes, write your comments and ideas. Later, when you need to prepare for a group discussion or write a literary essay on the novel, much of your work is already done.

Read a novel today.

How to Read a Novel

Strategy 1: Preview the Book's Features

- Read the front and back covers of the book. They may contain quotations from the book, summary comments, or critics' remarks that tell you more about the novel.
- Look at the copyright page to find out when the book was published. Look at the back page of the book. Sometimes author information is included here.
- Based on your preview, predict the subject of the novel.

Strategy 2: Read Slowly at First

- Read the opening paragraphs slowly and carefully. Often while describing the setting, the author establishes the tone and atmosphere of the work.
- Ask yourself, what does the author want me to think and feel at the beginning of the novel?

Strategy 3: Record Your Responses and Questions

- Record your emotional responses to events and characters. Ask questions such as:
  - What is it in the novel that touches, angers, or surprises me? Do I feel sympathetic or identify with a particular character or characters? Why?
- Write questions that focus on key novel elements such as character motivation, conflict, and theme. You may not be able to answer all these questions right away, but they offer topics for future essays.

Strategy 4: Discuss Your Ideas with Others

In a small group, share your responses to questions you've asked. Discuss your responses to the novel and any issues it raises. You'll probably need to meet several times while reading the novel. Hold these discussions at important points in the novel's plot.

Strategy 5: Reread the Novel

Good novels need to be read at least twice. What you may have thought unimportant during your first reading often becomes more important on your second reading. You will probably read the novel faster the second time.

Using the five strategies you've just learned, read the following excerpt from a novel by a Canadian author.

Fish House Secrets
(excerpt)

by Kathy Stinson

Friday

Chad

I don't know where to start. Should I tell you about Jill coming to the Fish House that first time? Or should I tell you about the accident? Or about what I saw on the beach before the night of the storm?

The beginning. That's what Billy J. always says. He was my English teacher last year in Grade Ten. Why not start at the beginning?

I was born in Toronto. My parents are—were—Emily Merrill, painter—maybe you've heard of her, and Gordon Merrill, professor of mathematics. Please note that I did not say my father is a math prof, or a professor of math. He is a "professor of mathematics." My father is very particular about that.

Somehow I don't think this is the beginning that Billy J. was talking about. Even though my father *is* a very particular kind of guy. Worse since the accident.

There it is again. The accident last fall. Maybe that's the beginning. Except for my mom. For her it was the end.

It was slippery. It started to rain when we were cheering for the winning touchdown. Mom was on her way to pick me and a couple of other guys up after the game. This truck skidded on a curve. You know how the roads get slick when it first starts to rain? Well, this truck coming toward her just slid right over the curve and creamed her through the guardrail into a ditch.

Usually me and my friends took the bus home from games, but it would have taken about three transfers to get back from this game because of where it was, and it didn't start till late, so my mom said she'd pick us up. I guess I don't need to tell you I wish we'd taken the bus. It's probably not very cool to say so, but I miss her. A lot.

But what's almost worse is how my dad has been since then. It's like all of a sudden he thinks he's got to be two parents. And it's not like we were exactly pals before. We didn't hate each other or anything. Don't get me wrong. We've just never had all that much to do with each other, that's all. We might talk about the Blue Jays and spring training and who was getting traded, stuff like that. We've been to the odd game too. And he gives me fifty bucks every term I keep up a B+ average, as long as "mathematics" isn't one of the subjects that slips below a B. He's a nice guy. We've just never been what you'd call close.

But when mom died, he got different. Like fathers on TV. You know, wanting to do things with their kids all the time, talking serious with them. And it's like he wants to take care of me. I'm fifteen years old. I don't need to be taken care of. I guess he thinks he's making up for me not having a mother any more, I don't know. All I know is after three days cooped up in the car and two nights in motels getting to Gran and Gramp's summer place where the rugged hills overlook the sea, he's really bugging me.

And I'm not prepared for how being there again brings her back.

Jill

God, am I stupid. There's no way I can get to Sheila's before it gets dark. Not now.

I should've known something was wrong when I passed that tired-looking old house with the rusted old shell of a car out front, and the cracked pot of weeds and geraniums beside the step. Why didn't I turn back then?

It's that lady in the store's fault. She told me the Merritts' place was down this road. That's why I kept going. Okay, maybe I should've got better directions from Sheila, but I didn't know then I was definitely coming. And I left in kind of a hurry.

Besides, I wasn't dead sure it was the wrong road till it kind of petered out to this grassy track. By then, these gulls were circling around and the sea was calling to me. I had to come down here. Just for a few minutes. The ground to the right of the path falls away to a tumble of rocks. The waves are washing the shore, it's almost hypnotic,

and I stay longer than I mean to, poking along, collecting shells and a few stones. It's heaven to be down by the sea again. Like a dream.

The lonesome squawk of a gull snaps me out of it. It raises its wings, and soon it's only a speck. It reminds me how far I have to go, back to the highway to try the other road, the one we passed just before this one, me and the guy I hitched a ride with out of Halifax this morning. At least I guess that's the road I was supposed to take.

But there's no way I can get back to the highway before dark, never mind find Sheila's cottage. What am I going to do? Curl up for the night under one of the old fish boxes that the sea's tossed up on the rocks? Or under the bushes back by the path? No, wait.

Out at the end of the point where that seagull disappeared there's a house. At the edge of the rock beach. From here it looks like there's no glass in its windows. It must be empty.

I climb back to the path. I'm sure the house is empty. I can stay there for the night and try for Sheila's again in the morning.

Apply It!

Read the excerpt from the novel *Fish House Secrets* and complete these activities.

1. The first paragraph establishes the first-person point of view. It is not clear who the "you" refers to in the first paragraph. In groups, suggest whom the narrator is talking to. Which possibility do you think is the strongest? Why?

2. There are two narrators in the novel—Chad and Jill. Write a well-organized paragraph explaining why you think the author has chosen these two voices to tell the story.

3. Based on what you've read of this novel so far, predict what will happen next.

4. Do you want to read the whole novel? Explain why or why not.

Checklist

✓ Did we suggest whom the narrator might be addressing?

✓ Did we support our suggestions with evidence?

✓ Did I carefully read the novel excerpt to understand the two narrative voices?

✓ Did I write a paragraph explaining why the author used these two voices?

✓ Did I predict what might happen next in the novel?

✓ Did I explain why I want to or don't want to continue reading?

Think About It: How will using some or all of the novel-reading strategies help you "get into" the next novel you read?

Reading Newspapers

We live in a rapidly changing world, where yesterday's newspaper is old news. It is hard to believe that news used to take months or even years to travel from one location to another!

Many people depend on newspapers for their information, which may be printed on paper or delivered electronically on the Internet. This section will help you brush up on your newspaper reading skills.

Why Do People Read Newspapers?

People read newspapers for many reasons. The reasons are reflected in the types of stories newspaper editors choose to print. Here are some reasons a story might be considered newsworthy.

1. Timeliness: The story has just happened.

2. Location: The story deals with events in the reader's community, province, or country.

3. Personal importance: What has happened affects the reader, or his or her family or friends.

4. Name recognition: The event involves well-known people.

5. Drama: The story is exciting.

6. Human interest: The story is about a person's life and can touch readers deeply.

7. The unusual: The story is out of the ordinary and might shock, surprise, impress, or amuse.

Why do you read the newspaper?

"Leads" and Newspaper Articles

The lead is the first paragraph of a newspaper article. The lead often answers who, what, when, where, why, and how. Its purpose is to give the reader key information quickly so that he or she will want to read further.

Type of Lead	Example
Summary lead: Briefly summarizes the most important details in the story.	At 9:37, Monday night, an explosion caused by a leaky gas line rocked a residence in downtown Winnipeg, causing $100 000 damage.
Narrative lead: Describes what an eyewitness saw, heard, smelled, and/or felt.	As the wind blew and the rain fell, frightened homeowners stood by helplessly while flames surrounded their homes.
Question lead: Asks questions that are answered in the article.	What would you do if you had to turn in your own sister? A 10-year veteran of the police force was faced with this predicament late last night.
Dramatic or shocking statistic lead: Immediately grabs the reader's attention.	Experts predict that over a lifetime, today's average Internet user will spend close to 24 years online.
Anecdotal lead: Begins with a story about a specific person but soon develops into a larger issue.	Despite the fact that she hates nothing more than a needle, Sharon Clarke endured the annual ordeal of getting a flu shot.

Apply It!

1. In groups, discuss the ways in which each type of lead appeals to readers. Create a chart to summarize your group's conclusions.

2. Ask each group member to scan local, provincial, or national newspapers to find examples of each type of lead. Divide responsibility equally among group members. See Chapter 10 for how to work effectively in a group.

Checklist

✓ Did we state how each type of lead could appeal to readers?

✓ Did we summarize our conclusions in a chart?

✓ Did we skim local, provincial, or national newspapers to find examples of each type of lead?

✓ Did we divide up responsibility among group members equally?

Think About It: Write your own definitions for each of the five types of leads.

Newspaper Opinion Pieces

Opinion pieces express the opinions of newspaper editors or columnists on issues relating to the news. Opinion pieces might take the form of

- editorials
- columns
- opinion piece articles, sometimes called op-ed pieces

How to Read a Newspaper Opinion Piece

Strategy 1: Read the Headline/Title and Lead

Cross-Reference

See Chapter 6 to learn about thesis statements.

Read the headline and lead to get a sense of what the opinion piece is about and whether the topic interests you. Often you can identify the author's viewpoint or thesis in the title or opening lines of an opinion piece.

Strategy 2: Read Critically

- As you read an opinion piece, question the author's opinion, arguments, ideas, and information. Does the author support his or her arguments using accurate facts, examples, expert opinions, and sound logic? If in doubt, check facts.
- Does the author consider different viewpoints or arguments? The author shows bias if he or she offers arguments and opinions to support only one side of an issue. When you read an opinion piece, decide whether the author has been fair and balanced.

Strategy 3: Read Actively to Form Your Own Opinions

Once you've identified the author's position, note your own opinion on the issue or topic. After reading the entire opinion piece, ask yourself:

- Did the opinion piece change my opinion on the issue or topic? If so, how?
- What arguments and persuasive writing techniques did the writer use to change or affect my thinking?

Use the above strategies to read the following opinion piece that appeared in *The Globe and Mail* in March 2001.

Pilfering Music

The Globe and Mail, March 6, 2001

Napster users had a busy weekend. With a legal boom about to be lowered on the free-music Web site, many of them spent hours frantically downloading songs from the Internet before it was too late.

Some, such as "Web entrepreneur" Matt Goyer of Waterloo, Ontario, plotted to get around the coming end of Napster by setting up an offshore clone of the system. Others tried to organize a boycott of the recording companies that have fought Napster in court….

It's always ugly when a free lunch comes to an end. For many months now, music lovers have been able to get recordings for free by visiting the Napster site, typing in the name of their favourite songs, and having the music appear, as if by magic, in their computers. Now that U.S. court rulings are about to cut off their supply, they are acting as if they have been robbed of a right.

But, of course, it is they who have been doing the robbing. Downloading music from Napster without the creators' permission is no different from walking into a music store and slipping a CD into your pocket without paying for it. Musical recordings, like books, are protected by copyright. That means they belong to the musicians and the recording companies that work with them. When someone downloads a song without paying, he is stealing from the composer who wrote it, the singer who performed it and the company that produced and distributed it.

Yet many Napster users have managed to convince themselves that what they are doing is perfectly harmless. Some even claim they are doing the world a favour by battling the greedy music industry, promoting free expression, and pioneering on the frontier of the Internet.

It's not harmless. Copyright is a vital safeguard for musicians, as it is for writers and artists. Without it, the works they produce can be reproduced and traded at will, undermining their livelihood. That recording companies are big and some musicians are rich does not make stealing their music any more excusable. For all their posing, those who use Napster to download unauthorized music are not rebels or pioneers or crusaders against censorship. They are thieves.

They may not be the sort of people who will steal your car or break into your house, but they are the sort who file fake welfare claims or refuse to repay their student loans. This sort of thievery is every bit as destructive as the smash-and-grab kind, perhaps more so. Our society works better than most because most people respect and obey the law. Once one kind of cheating becomes socially permissible, as downloading music has become, other kinds are sure to follow.

It's an ethical slippery slope. As long as "everyone's doing it," it becomes easier to cheat on your taxes or pad your expenses or bilk the credit-card company.

Internet music theft is worrisome enough because of the damage it does to the music industry and the threat it poses to honest commerce on the Net. But what's really disturbing is what it says about the ethics of the Internet generation.

Is the Internet generation becoming unethical?

Apply It!

1. With a partner, list all persuasive writing techniques and arguments the author uses to give his or her opinion. List the techniques and arguments from most persuasive to least persuasive.

2. Review the opinion piece for bias. Explain why you think it is or is not biased.

3. Write a letter to the editor giving your opinion about the piece. See Chapter 8 for how to write a letter to the editor.

4. Skim a recent newspaper to find other opinion pieces. Choose one and write your own opinion piece from an opposing viewpoint.

Checklist

☑ Did we make a thorough list of all techniques and arguments?

☑ Did we provide good reasons for our ranking decisions?

☑ Did I evaluate the article for bias?

☑ Did I list arguments supporting my opinion and organize them in a logical and persuasive way?

☑ Did I check the guidelines for letters to the editor and make sure my letter met all guidelines?

☑ Does the title or opening lines of my opinion piece identify my viewpoint?

☑ Does my opinion piece use accurate facts, examples, sound logic, and show both sides of the issue?

Think About It: Which of the strategies introduced in this section did you find most helpful when completing activities? How could you add to, or improve upon, the strategies so they better meet your own reading needs?

CHAPTER 2

Viewing Strategies

Seeing comes before words. The child looks and recognizes before it can speak.

—John Berger

You are surrounded by media. Every day, you are bombarded with photographs, advertisements, magazines, books, posters, charts, graphs, TV, films, and Web sites. You probably have information overload! Some of this information is presented well, and some of it isn't.

To survive in today's information age, you must be able to judge the quality of information. In this chapter you will learn the skills to view and interpret visual material critically and effectively.

Contents

Editorial Cartoons	28
Visual Aids: Charts and Graphs	30
Photographs	33
Advertising	36
Brochures	42
Feature Films and Television	46
Web Sites	49

Learning Goals

- respond personally, analytically, and creatively to different visual media
- develop the ability to analyze and interpret visual material
- develop an appreciation of the work of image makers
- work with, support, and encourage classmates when exploring visual media
- reflect on strengths and preferences in the visual media

Editorial Cartoons

Editorial cartoons are a form of satire. They usually appear in newspapers and magazines. Their purpose is to affect how people think and feel about issues. With a simple sketch, most often in the form of a caricature, and a few words (or sometimes with no words at all), a talented cartoonist can convey a great deal of information about a complex topic.

How to View an Editorial Cartoon

Strategy 1: Use Prior Knowledge to Identify the Subject

Like all satire, an editorial cartoon works because the viewer understands what is being discussed. This means that you need up-to-date knowledge of news events and issues to understand the message.

Common subjects of an editorial cartoon are

- political, entertainment, or sports figures
- public affairs or political decisions
- social customs, fashions, or habits

A good indication of the subject of an editorial cartoon can be people or things that are caricatured or exaggerated.

Strategy 2: Look for Symbolism

Editorial cartoons can deal with specific ideas or general issues. Often the cartoonist will use symbolism to make the issue appeal to a wider audience. Objects in the cartoon can stand for countries, political groups, attitudes toward war, poverty, personality traits, and so on. Again, note any objects that are exaggerated. These are often symbolic objects.

Strategy 3: Read the Caption and Any Text

Not all editorial cartoons contain words, but if they do, they will help to reveal the subject or purpose of the work.

Editorial cartoon by Dave Elston, published in the *Calgary Sun* in January 2001.

Strategy 4: Consider All The Elements Together

Ask yourself:

- What do the drawing, words, and captions add up to?
- What point is being made about the object of criticism or subject of comment?
- Did the cartoonist achieve his or her purpose by making me laugh? How?
- Has the cartoon affected my opinions or feelings in any way? Has it made me look at the topic in a new way?

Apply It!	Checklist
1. In a small group, answer the following questions about Dave Elston's cartoon.	✓ Did I conclude what the cartoon was about? Did I consider all the details in the cartoon?
• Who or what is being criticized? How do you know? List the details that helped you to reach this conclusion.	✓ Did I identify the person or group shown in the cartoon?
• List any part of the cartoon you do not understand.	✓ Did I look for symbolism?
• Is this cartoon humorous? Is the humour successful? How do you know?	✓ Did I research any element that I did not understand?
• Could the cartoonist have made the same point using different details? Which ones?	✓ Did I respond to the humour in the cartoon? If not, do I know why?
2. Over the next few months, note in your journal how two editorial cartoonists treat a high-profile person or event. Then note whether this treatment changes over time. Share your findings with the class.	✓ Did I list other details about the person or event that could have been used to make the same point?

Think About It: How will the process you just learned help you to interpret editorial cartoons in the future? Write down some notes.

Troubleshooting: Finding the Subject

If you have trouble identifying the subject of the editorial cartoon, try reading the section of the newspaper that is likely to deal with the subject. If you still have trouble, use the cartoon as part of a discussion with friends or family.

Visual Aids: Charts and Graphs

Cross-Reference

For information on how to create a visual aid, see pages 238 to 240.

Visual aids, such as charts and graphs, can be found in almost every type of printed material. Visual aids are useful tools because they present complex information in a simple format. Instead of reading a lot of text, you get an instant "information snapshot." However, visual aids are effective only if you can understand the information provided.

How to View a Visual Aid

Strategy 1: Determine the Purpose and Audience

- Read the title/caption. It may reveal the purpose of the information.
- Identify what point within the text the graphic is meant to support.
- Identify the intended audience. Who would be interested in this information?
- Consider the type of graphic that is being used. For example, different types of graphs serve various purposes.

Circle or Pie Graphs

These graphs are used to make comparisons or show ratios in terms of percentages.

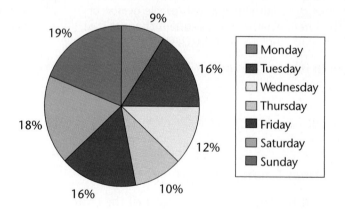

Percentage of Ticket Sales on Different Week Days, April 2000
Source: MovieHouse Cinema

Line Graphs

These graphs are usually used to show trends or developments over time.

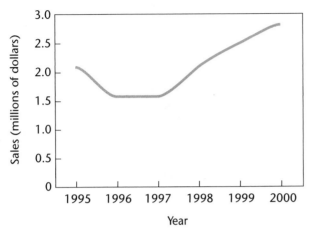

Ticket Sales from 1995–2000

Source: MovieHouse Cinema

Bar Graphs

These graphs use horizontal or vertical bars mainly to make comparisons.

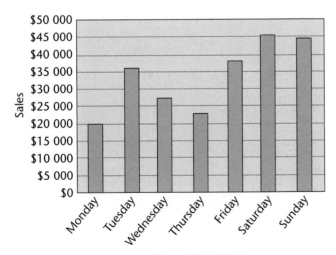

Ticket Sales, December 1–14, 2000

Source: MovieHouse Cinema

Argyll Centre
6859 - 100 Avenue
Edmonton, AB   T6A 0G3

Strategy 2: Identify the Units of Measure

You must understand what units of measure are being used. Only then will you be able to interpret what the information means. Ask yourself if very large or very small units of measure are being used to make something look bigger or smaller on purpose. Go back to the source of the information. Does that person or organization have a known bias?

Strategy 3: Consider the Source

- Does the visual aid clearly show who gathered the data and how this was done? This information is important when deciding if the data is valid.

- Consider who could benefit through sharing this information. Will the general public benefit? Or could this information benefit a private business firm or special interest group?

Apply It!	Checklist
In pairs: Find a chart or graph in a magazine or newspaper (or use one of the graphs on pages 30–31). Consider using a chart or graph that appears in an advertisement since these will make claims that are meant to convince you of something. **a)** Consider what type of information you are probably looking at based on the type of chart or graph used. **b)** Make as many observations about the chart or graph and the information as you can. Remember that observations are objective statements. **c)** Draw some conclusions. Is enough information provided for you to draw valid conclusions? Can different conclusions be drawn from the information? Do your conclusions have implications for everyone, or are they of interest to just a particular group or segment of society? **d)** Is the type of chart or graph used appropriate for the kind of information being presented?	✔ Did we locate a chart or graph in a magazine or newspaper? ✔ Did we try to find a graph or chart used in an advertisement? ✔ Did we make a number of objective statements about the chart and the information? ✔ Did we form a conclusion about the type of information presented? ✔ Did we draw valid conclusions from the chart? Did we determine if the conclusions had narrow or general implications for society? ✔ Did we conclude that the chart was a suitable or unsuitable format for this information?

Think About It: If you often avoid charts or graphs, jot down a few reasons why. Then note how the process you have just read about and practised might help you in the future.

Photographs

In 1839, Louis Daguerre created a new way of presenting information when he invented the camera. Since then, photographs have become popular in all types of media.

Photography is a great way to sell products and express ideas. However, photographs are no more "real" than paintings. Remember that the photographer chooses exactly what you get to see. He or she uses images to convey a message much like a writer uses words. As an effective viewer, you need to be able to "read" this message critically.

Can you imagine life without photographs?

How to View a Photograph

Strategy 1: Identify the Subject

- Is the picture of a person, place, thing, or event?
- Has the photographer used action, colour, pattern, or focus to move your eye to a particular object or person?
- Try to make a personal connection with the subjects in the photograph and the caption.

Strategy 2: Describe How the Subject Is Framed

- What is in or out of focus? Does this create emphasis? Does it create relationships?
- What surrounds the subject? What is in the foreground or background? This is called "context."
- What are the suggested relationships between different objects and/or people in the picture? Consider the direction the subjects are facing. Why are they facing that way?
- What is beyond the edges of the photo? Has the photographer chosen *not* to show you something?

Strategy 3: Consider the Angle of the Shot

The positioning of the camera has a great effect on how you feel about the subject.

- A low-angle shot, looking up at the subject, often emphasizes its size, strength, or power. A high-angle shot, aiming down, can suggest smallness, weakness, and vulnerability.

> **Cross-Reference**
>
> For information on how to create a photograph, see pages 233 to 234.

The Walk to Paradise Garden by W. Eugene Smith. Smith once said of his photos: "I like the light coming from the dark. I like pictures that surmount the darkness."

- A shot from above can also provide a sense of power.
- Close-ups suggest a more intimate relationship between the subject and the camera (audience).
- A long shot suggests being distanced from the subject, and so gives a sense of objectivity.

Strategy 4: Consider How the Photographer Creates Mood and Atmosphere

- How much colour and light is in the photo? Lighting and colour allow us to "feel" the picture rather than just see it.
- Is there action or movement in the photo or is there stillness? How does this movement or stillness make you feel?

Apply It!	Checklist
1. Using the strategies outlined in How to View a Photograph, analyze the photograph on page 34. What thoughts, feelings, or impressions does the photograph convey to you? Support your response with specific reference to details in the photograph. 2. Does this photograph move you to words? Create a poem or short story to accompany it. Be sure to include the title of the photograph in your work.	✓ Did I determine the subject of the photo? ✓ Did I identify things that stood out in the photograph and determine how these things are related? ✓ Did I consider the positioning and context of the subjects? ✓ Did I think about why this particular angle was used? ✓ Did I consider the mood and atmosphere of the photograph? ✓ Did I consider the emotion the photograph evoked in me? ✓ Did I use the title of the photograph in my poem or short story?

Think About It: When you first pick up a book or open a newspaper, is your eye drawn to pictures or photographs first? Explore some reasons this might be the case, based on what you have learned in this section.

Advertising

Advertising has become so much a part of our daily lives that it is almost impossible to imagine life without it. Everywhere we look, there is advertising. It used to arrive mostly by print, radio, and TV. Today it comes through fax machines, electronic scoreboards, e-mail, and the Internet.

Advertising affects much more than just our spending. It often influences what we consider important, and even how we live our lives. Advertisers are geniuses at combining words and images to spark interest and action in the viewer. Since advertising has this power, it is important that we understand how it works and how it affects us.

Posters

Cross-Reference

For information on how to create a poster, see pages 235 to 237.

Posters come in all shapes and sizes. They can be hand-made and mounted on a bulletin board with thumbtacks. Or they can be posted on billboards and viewed from the street. Posters are effective in delivering their message when they combine aggressive colours, attractive or appealing models, eye-catching artwork, and clever slogans.

How to View a Poster

Strategy 1: Determine What Attracted Your Attention

What first drew your attention to the poster? Was it

- the bright colour(s)?
- the artwork?
- the model?
- the words or slogan?

Strategy 2: Identify the Emotion Created

Cross-Reference

Think back on what you learned about creating emotions through photography. See pages 33 to 35.

To work, advertising must create an emotional response in the viewer. The advertisement's job is to link the product with the fulfillment of a human need. Consider how

- the poster makes you feel
- the image helps create this emotion
- the caption creates emotion

Where would you see a poster like this one?

Strategy 3: Consider the Location

Posters are placed in strategic locations. Consider why a particular poster is found where it is. Is the poster placed so that it

- is exposed to a particular audience?
- is seen at a particular time of day?
- gives easy access to the product or service?

Strategy 4: Consider the Desired Action

Ask yourself:

- How do the emotions and the message come together to create action in the viewer?
- What does the advertiser hope you will do as a result of reading the poster?
- Is the poster effective? Does it make you feel like taking a particular action?

Apply It!	Checklist
Study the StudentCounsellor.com poster and then write your reaction to it in your notebook. Reflect on • what first attracted your attention • what you found appealing or clever about the poster • how the poster made you feel • whether you were affected by the poster • whether you found anything wrong with the way the poster presents its message	✓ Did I determine why the poster drew my attention? ✓ Did I decide what was appealing or clever about the poster? ✓ Did I explain how the poster made me feel? ✓ Did I determine if this poster influenced me? ✓ Did I analyze the poster and decide if it was effective in the way it presented the message?

Think About It: Reflect on the process of critically examining a poster. How might these steps help you become more skilled at interpreting a poster's unspoken message as well as its obvious message? Jot down a few ideas.

Print Advertisements

Generally, print advertisements work in much the same way as posters. The people who create print advertising have more control over who views their material. If their advertisement will appear in a magazine, they can "pitch" the message to the audience of that magazine.

Like posters, print advertisements must work fast—within seconds—to grab the viewer's attention. An advertiser's message can be lost in the flip of the page.

How to View a Print Advertisement

Strategy 1: Determine What Attracted Your Attention

Which feature of the ad first captured your attention?

- the caption or slogan?
- the colours and settings?
- the artwork and models?
- the text?
- the brand name and logo?

Strategy 2: Focus on the Visual Appeal

- What was your first response to the ad?
- What is the main colour in the ad? Colours affect our moods and even our behaviour. Some colours have a calming effect while others make us feel uneasy. What mood do you think the colours in the ad evoke?
- What effect does the artwork have on you? Does it shock or surprise you? Does it give you pleasure or make you feel anxious?
- People in ads are carefully selected. They are chosen based on who the advertiser thinks will have an effect on the audience. Are the people in the ad models, celebrities, or everyday people?
- What are the people in the ad doing? Are they just posing or are they in the middle of a story? Is the advertisement suggesting a particular lifestyle?

Strategy 3: Consider the Text and the Claims That It Makes

- Are any words printed bigger than others are? Usually the headline, often called a "hook line," will be placed in larger type. It usually poses a striking question or presents clever word play. This line is meant to grab your attention so that you will read the smaller text.

- What need, want, or fear is the advertisement playing on? How does the text suggest that the product or service will help?

- Find any words that limit the claim. These are called "qualifiers." Words or phrases such as "many" or "some," or "they say ..." don't really say much. Qualifiers allow the advertiser to "weasel out" of any complaints made by the consumer. Be particularly suspicious of qualifiers that appear in small print!

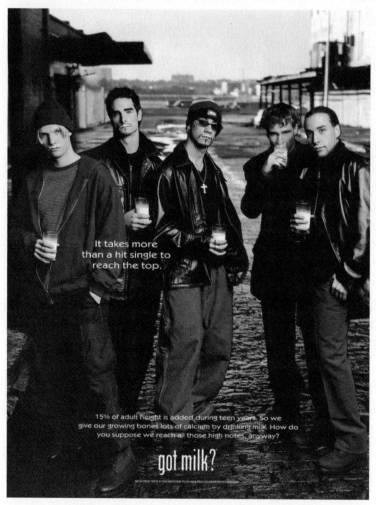

A print advertisement for milk, featuring the Backstreet Boys.

Strategy 4: Consider the Subtext

It is often interesting to "step back" from an ad and consider some of the other messages found in it. For example:

- What does the ad say in terms of what we value or believe as a society?

- According to what is shown in the advertisement, what does our society consider important?

- What does the good life look like? How do we attain happiness? Does the advertisement reflect reality? Do you agree with the values presented in the advertisement?

Apply It!	Checklist
1. Using the strategies outlined in How to View a Print Advertisment, analyze the Got Milk ad. On a sheet of paper, sketch the features of the ad and write your comments in talk bubbles pointing to each feature. Post your analysis in the classroom for others to read.	✓ Did I deal with my first impressions? ✓ Did I consider the content of the text? ✓ Did I analyze the visual appeal? ✓ Did I consider the choice of models? ✓ Did I consider what this ad promises the buyer?
2. With a partner, find an ad that you both consider effective. Write a brief analysis of it and be prepared to share your ideas with the class.	✓ Did I look for the subtext and its relationship to society's values and my values? ✓ Did we locate an ad we consider effective, analyze it, and present our ideas to the class?

Think About It: How has reading this section changed your view of advertising? Do certain steps in the process of analyzing an advertisement seem more useful than others? What would you analyze first if you came across an eye-catching ad this afternoon? Why?

Troubleshooting: Completing an Analysis

One of the most important aspects of analysis is observation. To complete an analysis, it is helpful to brainstorm or make a long list of all your observations and reactions. Then you can narrow down the list and focus on the more insightful comments.

Brochures

Cross-Reference

For information on how to create a brochure, see pages 241 to 243.

Brochures come in all shapes and sizes. Some are informational, while others are product or service advertisements. Some are simple one-colour, folded leaflets. Others have many pages and lots of colour and "gloss."

Brochures are available in many different places—a doctor's office, a hotel lobby, or a school counsellor's office. They can be requested through the Internet, or mass-mailed by a company. Regardless of its format, a brochure is still advertising. You as a viewer must understand what is being said and how this information affects you.

How to View a Brochure

Many of the same strategies for developing advertising and photographs are used to develop a brochure. So, you can use many of the same strategies for viewing them.

Strategy 1: Identify the Intended Audience

Look at the content.

- Review the title to find out what the brochure is about.

- Look at the amount and type of information. Is the reading level quite high? Are there many details and statistics? Is there much jargon? If so, then the developers had an audience in mind that is familiar with the material. If the language level is lower with less text, the message will be for a more general audience.

Look at the design.

- If the design is "flashier" and uses brighter colours, it is probably aimed at a younger audience.

- Is the design "balanced" or asymmetrical? A balanced design is more conservative and suits an older audience.

- Look at the font. Is it funky, conservative, blocky? The style of font projects an image and, as a result, suits different messages and audiences.

- What size is the font? It would be foolish to send a message to an older audience using a very small font. They would have difficulty reading it! The size of font also suggests a level of friendliness. Have you ever noticed that text written for professionals, such as doctors, lawyers, and engineers, tends to be set in smaller type? This projects an image of authority and knowledge. The opposite is true of larger typefaces.

A brochure produced by Canada Post.

Strategy 2: Consider the Use of Images

Often, you can tell a story from just looking at the picture on the brochure. The image will set the tone for the message and will attract a particular audience. Ask yourself:

- What does the number of images suggest about the audience?
- Does the brochure use detailed pictures? Cartoon characters? Shocking photos? What does the style of images say about the content and the intended audience?

Strategy 3: Read the Material That Stands Out

Developers of brochures want to make sure that readers see all the important information before putting the brochure away.

- Read all captions and headings. If the brochure has been well thought out, you should know why you need to read the brochure and what it offers even before you reach the details.
- Read all bold type.
- Read all bulleted and numbered items.

Strategy 4: Determine the Purpose

Designers of brochures want their audience to take some kind of action. Even in an informational brochure, the designer wants you to reach some conclusion and take action. Consider these questions:

- How am I being led through this document? The images, colour, design elements, and captions are all designed to lead you through the information. How are you being led to a conclusion? What is that conclusion?
- What action does the developer of the brochure want me to take? Does he or she want me to visit something? Sign up for something? Buy something?
- What information has been included on the last page? Usually the last page includes a call for action. Sometimes it even provides a self-mailer to get you to respond.

Apply It!

Study the brochure from Canada Post, and write down your observations using the strategies above.

Discuss each panel separately, commenting not only on the text and artwork, but also why you think the information is presented as it is.

- Do you think that this is an effective brochure?

- What improvements can you suggest?

Be prepared to share your ideas with the class.

Checklist

✓ Did I consider the intended audience and purpose of the brochure?

✓ Did I consider the colours that are used and the words that are emphasized?

✓ Did I consider the visual elements, including pictures and graphics?

✓ Did I consider why the information is presented as it is?

✓ Did I suggest improvements to the brochure?

✓ Did I share my ideas with others?

Think About It: Now that you've read this section, what is the first thing you notice when you look at a brochure?

Feature Films and Television

Like other media, film and television deliver messages that affect you in subtle but important ways. If you have critical viewing skills, you can interpret these messages and decide which ones you will accept or reject.

These skills will also allow you to discuss television and movies more effectively. Some viewers have difficulty explaining what they like or dislike about a movie. Sophisticated viewers usually enjoy defending their opinions.

How to View a Feature Film

Cross-Reference

For information on how to create a video, see pages 244 to 247.

Strategy 1: Pre-screen the Movie

Predict what you can expect based on

- the title of the movie
- the movie's poster, if there is one, or the cover of the box, if it's a video or DVD
- any reading you can do about the movie

Strategy 2: Use Your Knowledge of Genre to Make Predictions

Feature films and TV programming can be grouped according to genre. Some examples of genres are comedy, drama, action, adventure, science fiction, mystery, and romance. Knowing the genre of a movie is helpful because each genre has its own style and conventions. Whenever you make a prediction about the plot, you are usually making use of information about that genre.

Strategy 3: Identify the Audience and Purpose

Not all movies or TV programs share the same purpose and audience. If a movie reaches its intended audience, whether young or old, it has been successful in accomplishing its purpose. As a result, it can be considered a "good" movie. So, when watching a movie, ask yourself:

- Did the producers of this movie have a particular message?
- How realistic was the movie meant to be?
- Is the movie aimed at a specific audience?
- Are the story, language, and setting appropriate to the intended audience and purpose?

Strategy 4: Interact with the Movie

Don't just sit back and "let the movie happen." Here are some tips for viewing a movie.

- Focus actively on the screen. Look at the composition of different scenes just as you would analyze a photograph.
- Note how the important elements of the work come together to tell a story, reveal character, and express emotions and ideas.
- Note how elements such as music, lighting, and camera angles help to create setting, character, and mood.
- Watch for different objects of symbolism. This can include the use of colour.

Strategy 5: Look for Emphasis and Repetition

Very little in a movie is accidental. Directors choose their shots carefully, actors speak their lines and move in purposeful ways, music and costumes are thoughtfully chosen, and the final product is carefully edited for maximum effect. As a viewer, you should be looking for important clues that hint at the director's purpose. What kinds of things or images are repeated? What does the director emphasize?

Strategy 6: Consider the Characters

Ask yourself:

- Who are the main characters?
- What is their relationship to each other?
- What challenges do they face? Personal challenges? Social challenges? Do the characters solve them?
- How do the characters change throughout the movie? Does the social group or society change as a result of the action? Does this surprise you or is it expected?
- Are the characters, their situation, and their development believable?

Strategy 7: Consider the Message

Movies project messages that we may or may not recognize or agree with. Look at what the movie says about people and about life and ask yourself if you agree with these ideas and values.

- Does the movie show an optimistic or pessimistic view of life?
- Is the movie realistic or idealistic?
- Is the movie trying to present a social lesson or message?

What challenges face the main characters of the 1997 movie *Titanic*?

- Is the message clear, or has the director relied on symbolism and metaphor to get the message across?

Strategy 8: Evaluate the Movie

These are some general questions to ask yourself about a movie.

- How well was the plot developed and suspense maintained?
- How appropriate was the choice of cast?
- How effective were the music and special effects in creating mood?
- How important was the topic or theme that the movie dealt with?
- What was the quality of the camera work and cinematography?
- To what extent were you emotionally moved by the story? Why?

Apply It!

1. Choose a movie from a genre other than your favourite. Research the movie before watching it. Then predict how it will end and what you may or may not like about it. After viewing the movie, prepare a two-minute oral presentation about what you learned through your research, your predictions, and how this process affected your enjoyment of the movie.

2. Choose a video that you have not seen before and view it actively. Prepare a report that comments on

   - the effects created by the opening credits
   - any impression that is created by the first appearance of the major characters
   - the casting choices
   - the use of music and special effects
   - the believability of the locations and sets
   - the purpose and audience of the movie
   - the ideas developed

Checklist

- ✓ Did I research a movie, predict its ending, and present my findings to the class?
- ✓ Did I consider the impact of the video credits?
- ✓ Did I notice the impression created by the first appearance of the main characters?
- ✓ Did I consider whether the actors were appropriately cast?
- ✓ Did I note the role of music and special effects?
- ✓ Did I find the location and the sets believable?
- ✓ Did I conclude that the movie reached its audience and achieved its purpose?
- ✓ Did I grasp the ideas presented?

Think About It: Which strategies did you already use in the past when you watched movies? Which ones will improve your viewing experiences?

Web Sites

Web literacy, or the ability to access and evaluate Internet resources and services, is an essential skill in the twenty-first century. Most commercial, government, and educational establishments have Web sites. At these sites, you can buy or sell products and services, research and download information, play games, and even chat with friends and family.

Read on to learn how to become a savvy Internet user.

Cross-Reference

For information on how to create a Web site, see pages 248 to 250.

How to View a Web Site

Strategy 1: Identify the Primary Purpose

Sometimes Web sites are not easily categorized. Some sites that may first appear to be informational or educational are actually e-commerce sites. Information and learning are becoming big business. When looking at a site, consider whether it is

- an informational site
- a promotional site
- an educational site
- an e-commerce site
- a portal site, which is meant to be a "jumping off" point to other types of sites on the Internet

Look at the site's "domain," which is the last part of the Web address or the URL (Uniform Resource Locator). This might give you some information about the purpose of the site. Here are some common domains you should know.

Domain	Type of Site
.com	commercial, for-profit company
.edu	post-secondary educational institute
.org	non-profit institute
.gov	government agency
.net	Internet-related network
.ca	Canada
.uk	United Kingdom
.jp	Japan

Strategy 2: Navigate Through the Site

A Web site is usually made up of a group of Web pages that are linked to each other. It should be simple to find the information you need and to navigate through the site. Look for the following:

- Are the navigation tools—buttons, scroll-bars, and so on—found in the same place on each page?
- Is it clear what is a link and what is not?
- Are common elements or colours found on all pages? On a well-designed Web site, it is always clear that you are still on the site.
- Can you always reach the home page?
- Is contact information provided on every page?
- Is a link to a site map available at all times?
- Do you ever have to go through more than two links to reach the information you are looking for?
- Has the Web-site creator provided you with helpful navigation tools such as a site-search option?

Strategy 3: Consider the Quality of the Content

One of the dangers of the Internet is that there is no standard for its contents. The greatest challenge that users of the Net will face is deciding if the material is trustworthy. Here are some tips.

- Look for tools that make finding information easy. One such tool is a list of Frequently Asked Questions (FAQ). If a site has this feature, it shows that the Web designer has tried to anticipate the kinds of questions that users will have.
- Determine the quantity and quality of links on the site. The quality of links that a site has indicates how knowledgeable the site owners are in their area of expertise.
- Assess the quality of information on the site itself. Does the information seem authoritative? Has it been researched and well developed? Have outside sources been cited? Does the site offer a list of "further readings"?
- Does the site indicate how current the information is? Is it clear when the page was last updated?

Cross-Reference

See Evaluating Research Information, page 173.

- Is the information presented in a professional manner? Does the page have spelling or grammatical errors? Do the graphics and animations load quickly? Is the page attractive or unappealing to look at? These types of considerations may not seem important, but you can often tell a lot about the people behind a Web site by how much care they have taken in developing it.

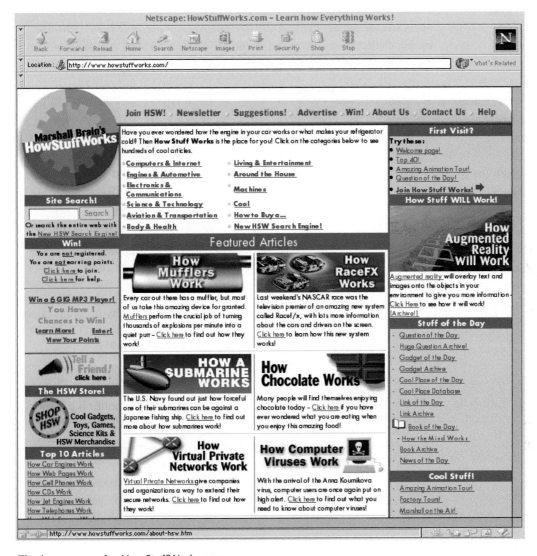

The home page for HowStuffWorks.com.

Strategy 4: Consider Security and Confidentiality

You should always consider what steps a Web site's creators have taken to protect your interests.

- How do they protect your credit card information?
- Do they offer the choice of ordering by phone or by regular mail?
- How easy is it for you to place an order?
- How much personal information must you provide? Be wary of Web sites that ask for a lot of personal data since this information may be sold to mailing list brokers. A site should only ask for enough information to fulfill the order.
- What is the site privacy policy? Most legitimate sites will have one.

Apply It!

1. Log on to the HowStuffWorks Web site. Using the suggestions in Strategy #1, *view* the Web site. Without actually following any links, determine which features of the site you would like to visit first. Why? What other features would you also link to?

2. Explore more thoroughly what the HowStuffWorks Web site has to offer. Follow links. Use the Search function to locate information on something you know well. Consider the quality of the information you received. Now do a search for something that you are not as familiar with but are curious about. Write a paragraph in which you evaluate the quality of the site. Was the information you received helpful?

3. Determine how the Web-site creators pay their bills. Study the Web site carefully and look for advertisements. What conclusions can you draw about how the site produces revenue?

4. Find a poorly designed Web site. Print off the first page of the site and write a short report discussing why you think this is an inferior Web site.

Checklist

- Did I find the site and determine what I would like to look at first?
- Did I skim the entire page and anticipate what I might find at each link?
- Did I consider all the navigation tools available to me?
- Did I test the links?
- Did I evaluate the quality of information both on the site, as well as on the sites that I was able to link to?
- Did I analyze how the site generates revenue?
- Did I find a poor site, print off a sample page, and note why it is inferior?

Think About It: How does comparing a good Web site with a bad Web site help you understand more about the Internet and the value of Web sites in general? What will you do the next time you link to a new site? How does this differ from what you have done in the past?

UNIT 2

Express Yourself!

Taking in information is important. But you also have to express your own knowledge, feelings, and requests—often through writing and representing. Here you can apply easy-to-follow steps to learn how to write like a pro!

Draft

Edit

Research

Represent

Contents

Chapter 3
The Writing Process   54

Chapter 4
Improving a Draft   65

Chapter 5
Presenting Your Work   111

Chapter 6
Writing Essays   143

Chapter 7
Researching   161

Chapter 8
Business and
Technical Writing   183

Chapter 9
Representation Strategies   229

CHAPTER **3**

The Writing Process

When you want to go somewhere, you need to know where you want to end up, what you'll use to get there, and which route you'll take. It also helps to have a map. The process of writing is like taking a trip—your destination being a piece of writing worth the effort.

This chapter gives you an overview of stages of the whole writing process. Then it focuses on the first and, for many writers, most difficult part of this process—getting started.

You will learn how to

- identify and focus writing topics
- identify a writing purpose and audience
- organize your ideas

so you can write an effective first draft.

As you read the chapter and apply skills, ask yourself: How can I use the strategies and tips provided to develop and improve my own writing process?

Contents

The Writing Process:
An Overview   55

Prewriting   56

Drafting   59

Learning Goals

- select and use strategies to generate ideas for writing assignments
- select and use strategies to limit and focus the scope, or size, of a writing assignment topic
- identify the purpose and audience for a piece of writing, and make writing choices to suit the purpose and audience
- develop a clear outline structure that will help you to write a good first draft
- reflect on writing successes and pinpoint the ones that need improvement

The Writing Process: An Overview

Few people can sit down and write well without a good deal of thought and preparation beforehand and revising and editing afterward. In fact, writing is really a process. The five main stages in the writing process are as follows:

- prewriting
- drafting
- revising
- editing
- presenting

Which stages are now part of your writing process? On which stage(s) do you spend the most time when writing? Why?

This chapter focuses on the first two stages of the writing process: prewriting and drafting. Within each of these two stages are important steps.

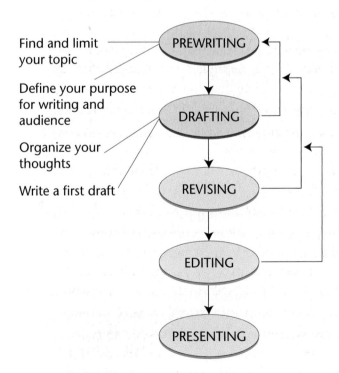

Prewriting

In the prewriting stage, you need to

- find and limit (focus) your topic
- identify your purpose for writing and your audience

Find and Limit Your Topic

Finding Writing Ideas

Start by listing subjects that interest you. Then use one or more of the following strategies to generate more specific topics related to those subjects.

Strategy 1: Clustering

Begin by writing a keyword or topic. Then write down words and ideas associated with the keyword. Connect these new ideas to the keyword and to each other using circles and lines. Let your mind wander to explore as many connections as possible.

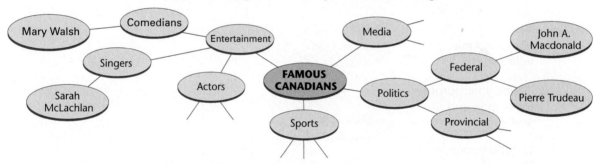

Strategy 2: Freewriting

Start with a general subject in mind. Write freely for a set period of time—say, five minutes—about your subject. Then review what you have written and try to see any patterns, topics, or ideas that look interesting.

Strategy 3: Brainstorming or Listing

Brainstorm ideas for writing assignments with a group of four or five classmates. Have one person record all the suggested ideas. The goal is to list many ideas, not to worry about quality. Later, you can weed out less useful suggestions.

Strategy 4: Making Journal Entries

Keep a journal over time to record your thoughts and ideas. When you need to find a writing topic, review your journal entries for patterns and ideas that suggest promising writing topics.

Cross-Reference

See also Brainstorming, pages 267 to 268.

Strategy 5: Reading

If you are stuck for a writing subject, skim magazines, newspaper articles, pamphlets, comic books, and other written materials, or browse the Internet. Photographs in these media can also suggest writing topics.

Need ideas? Read, read, read!

Limiting an Assigned Writing Topic

Suppose your teacher assigns a writing topic such as "A baby-sitting experience." To get writing ideas, use any of the five strategies you've just learned about and follow this method.

1. Look for a word or phrase in the assignment that gives the general subject area. In this example, the general subject is baby-sitting.

2. Use the keyword to freewrite, make a cluster diagram, brainstorm, or simply list anything related to baby-sitting.

3. Cross out any possibilities that do not interest you.

4. Look back at the assignment for other words that may help you limit your topic. Cross out any possibilities that do not relate to these words. For this assignment, think about the word "experience."

5. Look at the smaller topics under baby-sitting, and decide which and how many you could cover in the space and time your teacher has assigned.

A baby-sitting experience?

Apply It!

1. Use the strategies you have just learned about to generate writing ideas on the topic: local heroes.

2. Imagine you have to write a one-page assignment on: "Explain why one particular person is a hero in your life." Follow the five-step method under Limiting an Assigned Writing Topic to find, then limit (focus) your writing ideas.

Checklist

 Did I identify subjects, and then topics and related smaller topics that interested me?

 Did my noted ideas all relate to the requirements of the assignment?

Think About It: Which strategies did you find easiest and hardest to use? Why?

Define Your Purpose and Your Audience

Before starting to write an assignment draft, you need to answer these key questions:

1. What is my purpose for writing?

2. Who is my audience?

Your purpose for writing is why you are writing. For example, you might write to explain or describe something, or to persuade or entertain your audience.

Your writing audience is the people who will read your work; for example, a parent, an employer, a teacher, or a friend. When writing, keep in mind your audience's age, interests, and knowledge. The particular audience determines what you include in your writing and how you present it. For example, you wouldn't use the same type of writing for a job application letter as you would for an e-mail to your closest friend.

Choose a Form

When you've defined your purpose and audience, decide what type of writing form will get your message across most effectively. Should you write a poem, a speech, or an essay? Maybe a poster or a brochure is appropriate.

Apply It!	Checklist
1. With a partner, identify the purpose for writing for each of the two pieces of writing shown below.	✔ Did I identify a clear purpose for each piece of writing?
2. Discuss and identify who is the intended audience for each of these two pieces of writing. What might be each audience's age, interests, and knowledge? How can you tell?	✔ Did I identify an audience for each piece of writing?

**Why My Uncle Is a Hero
in My Life**

Shari Wah

English 11
Ms. Whiles
October 2, 20XX

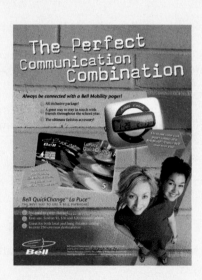

Think About It: Make a few notes on how knowing your purpose for writing and audience might affect the ideas and information you use in your writing.

Drafting

The drafting stage consists of two parts:

1. organizing your thoughts

2. writing the first draft

Organize Your Thoughts

You've identified and narrowed your writing topic, selected your purpose for writing and your audience, and gathered needed ideas and information. Now, how do you organize all this material in the best way possible?

Cross-Reference

See Chapter 7 to learn how to research information.

Step 1: Choose a Style of Presenting Ideas and a Method of Arranging Ideas

Styles of Presenting Ideas

You can either use one of the following presentation styles, or create one that is best suited for your writing topic:

- facts
- examples
- specific incidents
- comparison and contrast
- cause and effect
- definition or description
- reasons or arguments

For example, to convince readers of a character's heroism in an essay, you might use examples of outstanding actions the character has performed.

Methods of Arranging Ideas

Some possible ways of arranging ideas and information in writing assignments are

- by time (chronologically)
- by order of importance
- by features or characteristics
- by location or place

For example, in an essay on heroes, you might decide to arrange your examples from least important to most important, so your strongest point is the last one.

Some methods of arrangement are better suited for certain types of writing. Here are a few guidelines to help you make writing decisions.

Type of Writing	Suggested Arrangement
about someone's life or a series of events	chronological (by time)
describing something (such as a tree)	by features (such as the leaves, the trunk, the roots)
persuasive writing	from most important to least important (or the other way around)

Step 2: Prepare an Outline

Here's how to make a writing outline from ideas and information that you have gathered.

1. Review your list of information and separate the main ideas from the supporting ideas.

2. Decide which details to use to support each main idea.

3. If any of the points from your list do not fit under one of the main ideas, consider whether to cut them or to create another main idea. Always ask yourself: "Does this information suit my topic, purpose, and audience?"

4. Arrange your ideas and details into the outline format, such as the one in the following example.

> I. Main idea (e.g., baby-sitting)
>   A. Supporting idea (e.g., making sure you have discipline)
>   1. detail (e.g., make sure the child goes to bed on time)
>   a) minor detail (e.g., make the child agree to go to bed when the TV show ends)
>   b) minor detail (e.g., threaten to phone the child's parents if that doesn't work)

5. If one of your ideas is not supported by at least two details, you can
   - cut the idea out
   - include the information under another idea
   - find more supporting material to back it up

Try It!

One fact or detail may fit in several different sections. Try various arrangements before choosing the best one.

Apply It!

1. In groups, or with a partner, identify and discuss styles of presenting ideas and methods of arranging ideas for these writing assignments:

   a) a description of your bedroom

   b) a character sketch of a favourite athlete

   c) an application letter for a job, giving your skills and work experience

2. Create an outline for an essay on one of the three topics in Apply It! #1.

Checklist

 Did we select styles of presenting ideas appropriate to the topics, purposes for writing, and audiences?

 Did we decide on a method of arranging the information that fits the topic, purpose for writing, and audience?

 Did I prepare a clear and detailed outline as a writing plan to organize my ideas and information?

Think About It: How did following the steps for organizing your thoughts help you get ready for writing? What will you do differently next time? Why?

Write a First Draft

When writing a first draft, you should be concerned about the following:

1. your general structure

2. the structure of each paragraph

3. the tone of your writing

Try It!

At this point don't worry too much about spelling and grammar—just put your ideas down on paper. Later you can revise, revise, and revise some more.

General Structure

The general structure of your writing should have these key elements.

- A beginning or *introduction* that grabs your reader's interest and attention. The introduction should also explain your reason for writing and prepare readers for what they will find in the rest of the piece. (In some forms of writing, such as essays and research papers, this information is contained in a thesis sentence. For more on how to write a good thesis sentence, see Chapter 6.)

- A *body* where you develop ideas or arguments described in the introduction.

- A *conclusion* that reminds the reader of your writing theme or main idea, draws conclusions from the details or arguments presented in your essay body, calls the reader to action, or makes the reader look ahead to the future.

Cross-Reference

Chapter 6 contains more specific information about the structure of essays. Chapter 8 explains the structure of business and technical writing.

Paragraph Structure

Here are some tips for writing and organizing paragraphs.

- Make sure each paragraph contains one main idea that relates directly to the main idea of the piece.
- Make sure every paragraph also contains a topic sentence that explains the main point of the paragraph.
- Make each sentence within a paragraph relate to the topic sentence.

What's your attitude?

Tone

The *tone* of your writing reveals your attitude toward your subject. For example, in writing, as in speaking, your tone can be humorous, serious, light, sarcastic, sad, angry, friendly, and so on. To get a sense of differences in tone, compare the following two passages.

One of the most common complaints about the Internet is that it is difficult to zero in quickly on relevant material—a mind-boggling glut of information exists on the Net, and people find themselves wading through screen after screen of material that is of no use to them, which is time consuming and frustrating.

—Grant Heckman

A common criticism of the Internet is that it is dominated by the crude, the uninformed, the immature, the smug, the untalented, the repetitious, the pathetic, the hostile, the deluded, the self-righteous and the shrill. This criticism overlooks the fact that the Internet also offers—for the savvy individual who knows where to look—the tasteless and the borderline insane.

—Dave Barry

The tone you choose for your writing usually depends on your purpose and audience. Some writing needs to have a more formal tone than others. For example, you wouldn't use slang in a term history essay. Here are some qualities of formal and more informal writing.

Formal Writing

Usually formal writing has a serious and factual tone. The vocabulary is formal as opposed to slang. Full sentences and standard paragraph structure are used. Contractions are not used in formal writing.

> Steven Spielberg's first films were made at a time when directors were the most important people in Hollywood, and his more recent ones at a time when marketing controls the industry. That he has remained the most powerful filmmaker in the world during both periods says something for his talent and his flexibility. No one else has put together a more popular body of work, yet within the entertainer there is also an artist capable of *The Color Purple* and *Schindler's List*.

There's *formal* …

Informal Writing

Informal writing tends to be more familiar and friendly. It may include contractions and slang expressions. It is more likely than formal writing to be written in the first person ("I") and to address the reader as "you."

> Steve Spielberg's first flicks were made when directors were the big shots in Hollywood, and his more recent flicks at a time when marketing rules the biz. The fact that the guy's still tops in the world as a moviemaker during both periods really speaks volumes about his talent and smarts. Nobody else has strung together so many monster hits. But he's also got the artist's soul with quality stuff like *The Color Purple* and *Schindler's List*.

… and there's *informal*.

Apply It!	**Checklist**
1. Look closely at a piece of writing in your writing portfolio. Make notes on how you could improve the general structure.	✓ Did I improve the general structure of my writing with an effective introduction, body, and conclusion?
2. Rewrite any paragraphs that don't have all the features and organization of a good paragraph.	✓ Does each paragraph within my piece of writing now have a clear topic sentence?
3. Find a short, formal (or informal) piece of writing. Identify its audience and purpose. Explain why you consider it a formal (or informal) piece of writing. Rewrite it as informal (or formal) writing.	✓ Does the tone suit my writing topic, purpose, and audience?
	✓ Did I identify characteristics of formal (or informal) writing?

Think About It: Note one important writing goal for improving your writing, based on what you've learned in this section. List some ways to achieve your goal.

Ready? Run with it!

Ready, Set, Write!

Now it's time to write. Here are some final tips to get you started.

1. Start writing anywhere in your outline; it doesn't have to be the beginning.

2. Write in short spurts of five to ten minutes.

3. If the words are coming easily, don't stop!

Troubleshooting: What to Do If You Have Writer's Block

What happens if you can't get started or get stuck while trying to write the first draft? Here are some good troubleshooting tips to get you writing.

- Look over your prewriting notes, clustering, lists, or whatever else you have done up to this point.

- Make an outline of what you have written so far.

- Complete the following sentence: "The purpose of this paper is to [describe/explain/prove] how [my topic] is [good/bad] because of three things [1, 2, 3]."

- Doodle or draw a sketch of what you want to say.

- Find a willing listener, and explain to him or her what you are trying to say. Explaining your purpose to someone else can help make ideas clearer for you.

- Move on to another section and start writing there.

- Show your writing to someone else. Ask the person to comment on it and tell you what questions it raises for him or her.

- If all else fails, leave your writing aside for a few hours or, if possible, overnight. When you come back to the task, your thoughts will probably be clearer.

CHAPTER 4

Improving a Draft

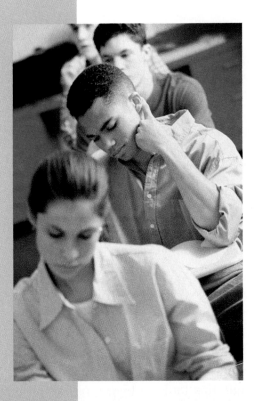

You have finished your first draft, so you're halfway to your goal of a finely polished piece of writing. Now you must tackle two important stages of the writing process—revising and editing.

This chapter will help you to identify writing problems in your first draft and provide strategies to solve these problems. Chapter 4 begins by presenting ideas for revising larger elements of your draft—its organization, content, and focus. It then suggests how to look closely at important details of your writing—your paragraphs, sentences, word choices, and grammar—which you may need to fix through more revising and/or detailed editing.

Contents

Revising and Editing   66

Editing Style, Grammar, and Usage   75

Strategies for Fixing Writing Problems   106

Learning Goals

- ■ revise writing drafts to improve their organization, content, and focus
- ■ edit paragraphs to improve their focus, structure, and flow
- ■ edit sentences to make them correct, clear, and interesting
- ■ improve the language and word choice in a writing draft
- ■ edit a writing draft to make sure that it follows all grammar rules

Revising and Editing

Revising and editing are important stages in the writing process.

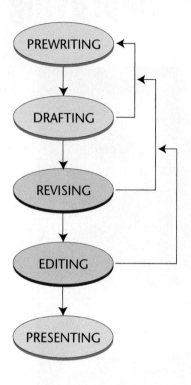

Revising

Revising is making changes to improve your work. When reviewing your first draft, first look for bigger, overall problems. Consider your draft's organization, content, and focus.

Sample Assignment: You have written an essay or research report on how the International Space Station is being built. You've completed the first draft and are reviewing it for any revisions to improve it.

Revising Organization

The organization, or structure, of your draft is how your ideas are arranged. When reviewing any draft the first time, ask yourself: Are my ideas arranged in the best possible way?

Sample Organization Problem: You begin by describing the completed space station. Your final paragraph deals with getting started.

How the International Space Station
Is Being Built

Pierre Gravel

English 11 A
Ms. Olson
March 4, 20XX

Strategies for Solving Organization Problems

1. Create an outline based on the way your draft is organized.

2. Reorganize the outline until the order of ideas or events makes sense.

3. Rewrite the draft following the new outline.

Revising Content

The content of your draft refers to the information and ideas within it. Review the draft again, looking just at the content. As you read, ask yourself:

- Do I need to include more details or background information?

- Are any topics not covered that should be?

- Can I cut anything?

Sample Content Problem: You wrote: "Canada has made and is making important contributions to the construction of the International Space Station." Then you go on to the next step in the space station construction process, without giving the reader any information about Canada's contributions to the project.

Strategies for Solving Content Problems

1. Use your new outline to evaluate the content. Are all your main ideas supported with needed details? If not, add the missing information. Or, you might move the idea to another section of your draft where it fits better.

2. Ask yourself questions about the topic. For example, a reader might ask: What has Canada contributed to the International Space Station?

3. Decide if all the information in each paragraph relates to your topic. Would the paragraph still make its point without the information? If the answer is yes, cut the unnecessary information.

Revising Focus

Your writing focus is how well you keep to your topic. After solving any problems in your draft's organization and content, read the draft a third time to evaluate its focus. Ask yourself: How well does the draft meet my writing purpose (the assignment)? How well does it meet the needs of my audience (the readers—teachers, parents, classmates—who will read my work)?

Sample Focus Problem: Although your assignment is about how the International Space Station is being built, you include unrelated scientific information about what Alan Shepard, the first American astronaut in space, accomplished on his mission. The audience is your fellow classmates.

Strategies for Solving Focus Problems

Read over your draft and answer these questions:

1. Have I accomplished my purpose—to meet the requirements of the writing assignment—without getting sidetracked by including information that doesn't relate to my purpose?

2. Have I thought about my audience (readers) in the writing by considering knowledge they might have or need about the topic? Make revisions until you can answer "yes" to these questions.

General Strategies for Revising

Good authors revise their first draft many times. Every writer has his or her own way of revising. By trying different strategies, you will develop a method that best suits your needs. Here are some strategies to try.

1. Between drafts, let your writing sit overnight or longer if you have time. You will return to it the next day with a clear mind.

2. Revise and rewrite as often as necessary, as long as your deadline permits. Make and use a revising checklist to be sure you have covered all the important points.

Remember ... the key is *constructive* criticism.

3. After you have read through your draft and made some changes, show your work to other people—preferably people from your intended audience. Ask them for a general impression of the writing. Ask them specific questions, based on the problems you have been trying to correct. Use their feedback to make more revisions.

4. If you are working on a computer, print out a hard copy of each draft. If you are writing by hand, recopy your work often. It's often easier to revise on clean pages.

Apply It!	Checklist
Take a first draft of a piece of writing from your writing portfolio. Use some or all of the revision strategies in this section to revise the draft's organization, content, and focus.	✓ Did I create an outline from my first draft? ✓ Did I organize my ideas and information in a logical way? ✓ Did I support each main idea with details? ✓ Did I meet my writing purpose? ✓ Did I cut ideas or information not related to my topic? ✓ Did I consider my audience and include all the information readers will need?

Think About It: What are three ways you have improved your writing from your first draft? Which strategies did you find most useful? Why?

Editing

Once you have revised your first draft so that you are happy with its organization, content, and focus, it's time to improve your writing style. Style has to do with how you write, rather than what you have to say. Style is improved through editing. When you edit, you also correct grammar and usage. (Usage concerns the correct use of words.)

In editing, as in revising, it's best to find and solve the bigger problems first, and then look for and fix the smaller problems. Focus first on your paragraphs, then sentences, and finally on particular words. Otherwise, you could waste time fixing small mistakes on parts of your essay that will need to be changed anyway because of larger problems.

Editing Paragraphs

A paragraph is a unit of information. Here are some characteristics of good paragraphs:

1. *Focus*. Each paragraph should have one main idea that is closely related to the subject of the whole piece. The main idea is often stated in one sentence in the paragraph, called a *topic sentence*.

2. *Structure*. The sentences within a paragraph should be arranged in a logical order that suits the main idea of the paragraph. For example, sentences could be arranged in order of importance. In a history paper, sentences may be arranged in *chronological order*, or order of time.

3. *Flow.* Each paragraph should be linked clearly and logically to those before and after it.

Here is an example from a nonfiction profile that shows the characteristics of good paragraphs.

Plaything of a sports hero.

The Phenomenon

Heroes walk alone, but they become myths when they ennoble the lives and touch the hearts of all of us. For those who love soccer, Edson Arantes do Nascimento, generally known as Pelé, is a hero.

Performance at a high level in any sport is to exceed the ordinary human scale. But Pelé's performance transcended that of the ordinary star by as much as the star exceeds ordinary performance. He scored an average of a goal in every international game he played—the equivalent of a baseball player's hitting a home run in every World Series game over 15 years. Between 1956 and 1974, Pelé scored a total of 1200 goals—not unlike hitting an average of 70 home runs every year for a decade and a half.

Apply It!

1. Edit and rewrite the paragraphs below. Exchange your edited paragraphs with a partner and compare your changes.

2. Take a nonfiction draft from your writing portfolio. Evaluate the first two paragraphs of your draft for focus, structure, and flow. Then make any required editing changes.

Checklist

✔ Did I make sure that each paragraph focuses on one main idea?

✔ Did I arrange the information and ideas in each paragraph in a logical order?

✔ Did I check that the flow between paragraphs is good and the connections clear?

The Great Gretzky

Wayne Gretzky is one of the greatest hockey players ever. Some people think Mario Lemieux is the greatest player, or some players who played earlier in the history of the National Hockey League. Gretzky's accomplishments are truly amazing. In 1980–81 he had 164 points. He was traded to the Los Angeles Kings in 1988 and helped make hockey popular in the United States. In his first season in the NHL, 1979–80, at 17 years of age, he won the league's most valuable player trophy.

Brantford is a city in southwestern Ontario. Gretzky learned to play hockey in Brantford. He was born there in 1961.

Think About It: What specific revisions did you make to the sample or to your own writing? Which element—focus, structure, flow—did you find most difficult to recognize and fix?

Editing Sentences

A sentence is a group of words that expresses a complete thought. Every sentence contains a *subject* and a *verb*. A subject in a sentence is who or what the sentence is about. Here are some things to watch for when you edit your sentences.

Cross-Reference

See Editing Style, Grammar, and Usage, pages 75 to 105.

1. *Clarity.* Check that each sentence expresses a complete thought. It should have a subject and a verb. The subject and the verb must agree in number.

Sample Sentence Problems

- An overhead crane. (The sentence does not express a complete thought. It contains a subject but no verb.)

- An overhead crane *swing* a huge piece of equipment into place. (The subject "an overhead crane" and the verb "swing" do not agree in number. The verb should be "swings.")

2. *Simplicity.* Avoid saying too much in one sentence, which often causes confusion in meaning. If there is a simpler way of saying something, use it. Cut unnecessary words that may get in the way of your meaning.

Sample Sentence Problem

An overhead crane, with workers using power tools, swings a huge block into place on a construction site 402 kilometres up as they work to assemble the million-pound International Space Station that will take five years to complete. (The example packs too much information into one sentence. As a result, the meaning is confused.)

So much to do....

Apply It!	Checklist
Edit these sentences or parts of sentences so they become clear sentences. • Delivers a Russian crane to the International Space Station. • Astronauts will performs more space walk in the next five years than have been conducted since space flight began. • A total of 37 space-shuttle missions, involving the co-operation of 16 nations requiring 160 space walks, are scheduled to assemble, outfit, and begin research use of the station from 1998 to 2005 and so astronauts and engineers are practising all procedures carefully.	✓ Did I make sure that all the sentences have a subject and a verb? ✓ Did I check that the subjects and the verbs agree? ✓ Did I simplify any confusing sentences or wording? ✓ Did I write shorter sentences to replace one that was too long and confusing?

Think About It: If you don't understand these points (e.g., subject-verb agreement, incomplete sentences), how can you get help? List at least three things you can do.

Editing Marks and Strategies

When making improvements to their drafts, editors often use special editing marks to show needed changes.

Editing Marks	
∧ – insert a letter or word	*history* I passed the ∧exam. I passed the histry exam.
ℓ – delete a letter or word	I passed the my exam. I finnished early.
⌗ – begin a new paragraph	⌗ The physics exam is tomorrow.
≡ – change to a capital letter	canada
/ – change to lower case	Physics
⌢⌣ – transpose	She aksed what should we study.
⊙ – insert a period	The movie was too long⊙
∧ – insert a comma	I ate popcorn, licorice, and chips.
∨ – insert an apostrophe	The theatres seats are uncomfortable.
# – insert a space	I almost fell asleep.
.... – leave it as is	I hope never to go there again.

Editing marks have been used in the paragraph below to show editorial changes. Use the chart to figure out what changes have been signalled.

Cloning Express

At the American Fertility Society in Montreal, Jerry Hall reported an extraordinary new experiment in October 1993. He had accomplished something that people only ever dreamed about. Using a new technique, Hall cloned seventeen human embryos into 48. The technique was waiting for the embryo to divide into two, then he stripped the outer coating to seperate the 2 cells, and replaced finally the outer coating with an artificial one. Two embryos with the exact same genetic information were manufactured. Essentially, they were two of the exact same human being. Two humans which could be made into four, eight, sixteen. The very idea that this could be done is overwhelming—even fascinating. It's tempting to imagine all of the possibilities that Hall's experiment exposes, however like a dark cloud looming over a parade, the fact remains that cloning human embryos is completely moraly wrong.

Some Editing Strategies and Tips

These editing strategies and tips will help you to make sure that you don't miss any editing problems as you polish your draft.

1. Go through your draft at least once to improve your paragraphs. Use the checklist on page 70 to focus your editing of paragraphs. Add new checklist items for particular problems you might have with paragraphs.

2. Go through your draft at least once to improve your sentences. Use the checklist on page 72 to focus your sentence editing. Add new checklist items for particular problems you might have with sentences.

3. Use editing symbols to edit your work on paper. If you are working on a computer, be sure to save a copy of your draft before you begin to edit and as you finish each of your editing stages.

4. Remember your audience and purpose as you edit. If you think the material might not interest your reader, or might be confusing, make it more interesting and clearer. Cut any material that doesn't relate to your writing purpose.

5. Ask someone to look over your work after you have edited it. Make changes accordingly.

6. Look for repeated types of mistakes you make in writing. Add items describing these mistakes to your writing problem checklist.

Apply It!	Checklist
1. Copy the passage below into your notebook (double-spaced) and use editing marks to show needed corrections.	Did I use editing marks to show corrections?
2. Use editing strategies and tips you learned in this section to edit a piece of writing in your portfolio. Make some notes on which strategies and tips worked best for you.	Did I refer to the editing strategies and tips presented in this section?

We had a chemstry exam last tuesday and I passed the the test with flying colors. Physics is another story altogether. It has never been one of my strongest subject. I remember when I lived in alberta and it was part of our Science course. It took a lot of work and a lot of pateince but I finally got though I guess it really taughtme that when I put mind to it I'm capable of anything.

Think About It: How will using editing marks make editing an easier task for you? How can you become more familiar with the marks?

Editing Style, Grammar, and Usage

In both the revising and editing stages of the writing process, it's important to solve the big writing problems first and then work your way down to smaller ones—from overall structure and content to paragraphs to sentences to words.

Now we'll look at problems of style, grammar, and usage.

- *Style* has to do with the choices you make in your writing and how well you follow rules of writing.
- *Grammar* is the rules of the forms and uses of words.
- *Usage* deals with the common ways words and phrases are used.

Here are some general rules to follow as you edit for style, grammar, and usage.

1. **Use the right words**. Replace general and unclear words and expressions in your draft with specific and more accurate ones. A dictionary and thesaurus will often help you find the words you want.

2. **Use language that conveys the appropriate tone and meaning for your audience**. Don't use informal language in formal writing. Also, use vocabulary and sentence types and lengths that will allow your audience to clearly understand your meaning.

3. **Write for power**. Try to make your writing fresh by avoiding tired and worn phrases such as clichés. Choose words that create strong impressions and mental pictures for your readers.

Here's an at-a-glance guide to help you find revising and editing information in this book quickly.

Which sign is clearer?

Active and Passive Voice 93
Awkward Sentences 86
Clauses 80
Commonly Confused Words 101
Comparative and Superlative
    Adjectives and Adverbs 100
Discriminatory Language 90
Double Negatives 100
Language to Avoid in Your
    Writing 104
Literary and Rhetorical
    Devices 103
Modifier Mistakes 85
Parallelism 87

Participles and Gerunds 81
Precise Pronouns 94
Prepositional and Gerund
    Phrases 82
Redundancy and Repetition 97
Run-On Sentences 84
Sentence Fragments 83
Sentence Purpose and Tone 79
Sentence Types 78
Sentence Variety 78
Subject-Verb Agreement 88
Transitions 76
Vocabulary and Writing 98

Transitions

Make sure your ideas are linked together.

Transitions are links between paragraphs, sentences, and parts of sentences. They help to show readers the relationships between ideas in your writing. Here are four ways to make transitions. Note that the transitional phrase or word in each strong example appears in italics.

1. *Use a pronoun to refer to a person, thing, or idea just mentioned.*

Weak: Victoria Beach, Manitoba, is a great place to spend a summer. The six beaches are all good for swimming.

Strong: Victoria Beach, Manitoba, is a great place to spend a summer. *Its* six beaches are all good for swimming.

2. *Repeat a keyword.*

Weak: After World War II, Germany was divided into two separate countries by the Berlin Wall. For many, destroying it represented the end of the Cold War.

Strong: After World War II, Germany was divided into two separate countries by the Berlin Wall. For many, destroying *the Wall* represented the end of the Cold War.

3. *Refer directly to the preceding idea using a synonym.*

Weak: Several types of rattlesnakes are found in Canada. Rocky outcrops are a favourite hangout.

Strong: Several types of rattlesnakes are found in Canada. Rocky outcrops are a favourite hangout for *these reptiles*.

4. *Use a transitional expression.*

Weak: I'd love to go out with you tonight. I have a slight case of the flu.

Strong: I'd love to go out with you tonight, *but* I have a slight case of the flu.

Common Transitional Expressions

Here is a list of a few common transitional expressions, arranged by category.

Cause and Effect	Summary	Explanation
as a result	in summary	for example
because	in conclusion	for instance
since	in short	in fact
therefore	in general	namely
Comparison	**Place**	**Purpose**
similarly	beside	for this purpose
likewise	here	for this reason
compare	there	with this in mind
Addition	**Time**	**Contrast**
also, too	eventually	however
in addition	meanwhile	but
furthermore	soon	although
besides	afterward	in contrast
finally	in the future	on the contrary

Apply It!

1. Skim textbooks and newspapers to find at least one other transitional phrase for each category above. Share your findings with the class. Make a class list of as many transitional phrases as you can.

2. Rewrite the following sentences using transitional words or phrases to improve their clarity and show the relationships between ideas.

   a) Care for a crisp, juicy grasshopper for breakfast? In many parts of the world, it is considered perfectly acceptable to eat.

   b) People in North America are often shocked by the thought of eating bugs. Grasshoppers, ants, and bees are considered treats by some people.

   c) Even stink bugs are eaten and enjoyed in some parts of the world. The glands contain a chemical called cyanide, which is poisonous.

Checklist

✓ Did I recognize and record another transitional phrase for each category?

✓ Did I add to the class list of transitional phrases?

✓ Did I refer to the samples in this section to rewrite the sentences?

Think About It: What do you find difficult about applying what you learned about transitions to your writing?

Sentence Variety

Types of Sentences

This chart gives definitions and examples of three types of sentences—simple, compound, and complex.

Sentence Type	Definition	Examples
Simple	A group of related words that expresses a single thought, and which contains a subject and a predicate (verb)	The chicken saw the axe.
Compound	Two simple sentences linked by a comma and a coordinating conjunction (e.g., *and, or, nor, for, but, so, yet*)	Jared stared, but then he shook his head in disbelief.
Complex	Two simple sentences joined together by a subordinating conjunction (e.g., *when, after, before, since*)	Mildred jumped when the cow mooed.

Too many simple sentences will make your writing sound choppy. Too many compound or complex sentences can make your writing sound long, boring, and possibly confusing. The trick is to use a variety of types of sentence.

Creating Varied Sentence Types

You can use coordinating and subordinating conjunctions to change simple sentences into compound or complex sentences. Here are some coordinating and subordinating conjunctions.

Coordinating Conjunctions

and	for	yet	or	but	nor	so

Subordinating Conjunctions

after	if	unless
although	in order that	until
as long as	since	when
because	than	where
before	that	whether
even though	though	while

Sample Sentences

Simple:	The bear growled. I ran.
Compound:	The bear growled *so* I ran.
Complex:	*When* the bear growled, I ran.

Simple:	The dog rolled over. He played dead.
Compound:	The dog rolled over, *and* he played dead.
Complex:	*After* the dog rolled over, he played dead.

Sentence Purpose and Tone

There are different kinds of sentences for the different communication purposes you might have. These allow you to communicate your own special point of view and give tone to your writing. Tone is your attitude, or the way you feel, toward the subject you are writing about. It is part of your writing voice.

Notice how much the sentence purpose changes the writer's tone in the examples below.

Statement: We should definitely adopt a rat as our school mascot. (The writer sees no room for argument.)

Exclamation: How wonderful it would be to adopt a rat as our school mascot! (The writer is thoroughly convinced, an enthusiastic supporter of the change.)

Question: Should we adopt a rat as our school mascot? (The writer may be undecided.)

Command: Help us to adopt a rat as our school mascot. (The writer is convinced and seeking the support of others.)

Try to avoid exclamation marks in more formal writing. Even in your less formal writing, do not overuse exclamation marks. Remember, overuse of any sentence purpose or type can be boring.

Try It!

Read your work out loud to a partner. Ask your audience to listen for choppy parts and sections that are slow moving. Then revise and edit your writing to include sentence variety.

A school mascot.

Apply It!	Checklist
1. Look through books, magazines, and newspapers to find more examples of coordinating and subordinating conjunctions than those provided in this section.	✓ Did I recognize and record more examples of conjunctions?
2. Make the following two simple sentences into one compound sentence and then one complex sentence.	✓ Did I create one compound and one complex sentence from the two simple sentences?
Yesterday dragged on forever. Today has dragged on forever too.	✓ Did I recognize "choppiness" and other sentence problems in the given paragraph?
3. Rewrite the following passage to improve its sentence variety.	✓ Did I combine short sentences to fix the choppiness?
The Jim twins are twin brothers. They were separated at birth. Both boys were adopted into different families. Both were named James by their adoptive parents. They were reunited at the age of 39. Then a string of astonishing similarities was discovered in their lives. Both had been married to women named Linda. They remarried women named Betty. Jim Springer had a son named James Allan. He had an adopted brother named Larry. His twin brother, Jim Lewis, had a son named James Alan.	✓ Did I rewrite the paragraph to use more kinds of sentences?
	✓ Did I use the correct punctuation to end my rewritten sentences?

Think About It: What are three things you learned about sentence variety and conjunctions that you will use in your own writing?

Clauses

A clause is a group of words that contains a subject and a verb. There are three types of subordinate clauses: noun, adjective, and adverb clauses.

Noun Clauses

Noun clauses can function as subjects or objects of sentences. These clauses often begin with one of the following subordinating conjunctions: *that, who, whoever, whom, whomever, what, whatever, how, when, where, whether.*

Example: *Whatever you do* will be fine. ("Whatever you do" is the noun clause.)

Cross-Reference

For information on pronouns, see pages 94 to 96.

Adjective Clauses

An adjective clause modifies a noun or pronoun. Usually an adjective clause answers one of these questions: What kind of? Which one? Adjective clauses begin with a relative pronoun (*who, whoever, whom, whomever, whose, which,* or *that*) or a relative adverb (*when* or *where*).

Example: The car *that has the powerful motor* sits in the garage. ("that has the powerful motor" is the adjective clause. It describes the car and answers the question: which one?)

Adverb Clauses

An adverb clause modifies a verb, adjective, or another adverb. Usually the adverb clause answers one of these questions: Where? When? Why? How? Under what conditions? To what degree? An adverb clause begins with a subordinating conjunction (e.g., *after, although, because, though, since, when, where, while*).

Example: The car ran smoothly *after the tires were balanced*. ("after the tires were balanced" is the adverb clause that answers the question: when?)

Apply It!	Checklist
Copy these sentences. Underline the clause in each. Identify the type of clause and explain what purpose it serves in the sentence. • Whoever enters the door will be the contest winner. • The man who feeds the pigeons sits on the park bench. • When the gas light goes on, we know the car is almost out of gas.	✔ Did I look for a conjunction or a relative pronoun to find the clauses? ✔ Did I identify each as a noun, adjective, or adverb clause? ✔ Did I explain the purpose of each clause?

Think About It: How will you use what you learned about clauses in your own writing?

Participles and Gerunds

Verbals are verbs that are used as a part of speech other than a verb. Two types of verbals you might use in your writing are participles and gerunds.

Participles

A participle is a verbal that modifies a noun or a pronoun. Participles can be in the present or past tense. Present participles end in *-ing*. Past participles usually end in *-ed* or *-d*.

Examples:

The basketball guard is a *captivating* athlete. (The present participle "captivating" modifies the noun "athlete.")

The figure skater gave an *inspired* performance. (The past participle "inspired" modifies the noun "performance.")

No gerunds on *this* sign.

Gerunds

A gerund is a verbal that is used as a noun. Gerunds always end in *-ing*.

Example:

Smoking is forbidden in the building. ("Smoking" is a gerund and the subject of the sentence.)

Prepositional and Gerund Phrases

A phrase is a group of words that acts as one part of speech and doesn't contain both a subject and a verb.

Prepositional Phrases

A prepositional phrase starts with a preposition such as *at*, *by*, *for*, *from*, *in*, *of*, *on*, *to*, or *with*, and ends with a noun or the equivalent of a noun. The noun or noun equivalent is known as the object of the preposition. Usually prepositional phrases function as adjectives or adverbs.

Examples:

She held a large jug *of iced tea*. ("of iced tea" is the prepositional phrase. It serves as an adjective, modifying the noun "jug.")

He stood *by the door*. ("by the door" is the prepositional phrase. It serves as an adverb modifying the verb "stood.")

Gerund Phrases

Gerund phrases always function as nouns. They often function as subjects or objects in sentences.

Examples:

Telling a lie increases the fault. ("telling a lie" is the gerund phrase. It serves as the subject of the sentence.)

She loved *paddling the canoe* across the lake. ("paddling the canoe" is the gerund phrase. It serves as an object of the verb "loved.")

Apply It!

Write your own sentences to show examples of a present participle, a past participle, a gerund, a prepositional phrase, and a gerund phrase. Exchange your sentences with a partner and identify each other's words and phrases.

Checklist

✓ Did I write at least one sample sentence for each example?

✓ Did I exchange sentences with a partner?

✓ Did I identify each type of word or phrase in my partner's sentences?

✓ Did my partner and I help each other revise and correct our examples?

Think About It: What was most difficult about writing your sample sentences? How can you find out more about these elements?

Sentence Fragments

A fragment is a part of a sentence, punctuated as if the words form a complete sentence. Sentence fragments are missing a subject or a predicate (verb) or both and do not express a complete thought. You should not use sentence fragments in formal writing.

Examples:

Problem: Missing Predicate
Big birds. (The fragment has no predicate or verb to complete the sentence.)

Solution:
Big birds swooped across the lead-coloured November sky.

Problem: Missing Subject
Crashed in a fiery blaze. (The fragment has no subject to complete the sentence.)

Solution:
The nose-diving, twin-engine plane crashed in a fiery blaze.

Problem: Complement with No Subject or Predicate
For about 10 seconds. (The complement is a fragment. It has no subject or predicate.)

Solution:
The engine sputtered for about 10 seconds.

When pieces are missing, the picture isn't clear.

When you are editing your formal writing, read each group of words you have started with a capital letter and ended with a period, question mark, or exclamation mark. Examine the word grouping to make sure it has all the elements of a complete sentence. If it doesn't, and is a fragment, use one of the revision strategies above to fix it.

Where Sentence Fragments Are Acceptable

Sentence fragments are sometimes acceptable in informal writing, play dialogue, fiction (e.g., novels and short stories), poetry, advertisements, and everyday speech.

Run-On Sentences

A run-on sentence is made up of two or more complete thoughts that are joined together by only a comma, or simply written as one sentence with no punctuation except the end period.

You can have two complete thoughts in a single sentence. Such a sentence is called a compound sentence or complex sentence. However, you need to join the two thoughts together using either a coordinating conjunction (e.g., *and, or, nor, for, but, so,* or *yet*) or a subordinating conjunction (e.g., *after, because, if, when, as, although, whether*).

Run-on sentence:
Canada is providing a new robotic "Canada hand," the tool consists of two small robotic arms that can do very delicate space-station maintenance jobs.

Compound sentence:
Canada is providing a new robotic "Canada hand," and the tool consists of two small robotic arms that can do very delicate space-station maintenance jobs.

Complex sentence:
After Canada provides the new robotic "Canada hand," the tool, consisting of two small robotic arms, will do very delicate space-station maintenance jobs.

Notice that some wording changes were needed to create a complex sentence.

Here are more examples of how to correct run-on sentences.

Run-on: That man is very wealthy, he owns a fitness clinic.
Acceptable revision: That man is very wealthy. He owns a fitness clinic.
Run-on: We went to Niagara Falls for the day, we enjoyed the mini-golf and wax museums, the Falls were closed for repair.
Acceptable revision: We went to Niagara Falls for the day. We enjoyed the mini-golf and wax museums, but the Falls were closed for repair.

It's much easier to fix a run-on sentence than Niagara Falls.

Apply It!	Checklist
1. Skim newspapers or magazines, a literature textbook, or poetry anthology to find examples of where sentence fragments are used. Record some of these sentence fragments.	✓ Did I find and record examples of acceptable sentence fragments?
2. Rewrite the following passage, eliminating the sentence fragments and run-on sentences.	✓ Did I recognize sentence fragments in the passage?
	✓ Did I find run-on sentences in the passage?
	✓ Did I rewrite the passage so that there were no sentence fragments and no run-on sentences?

   Picnics are no fun. Bugs, dirt, poison ivy. Eating soggy sandwiches. The strawberries get squashed at the bottom of the basket, the juice gets into everything. Wouldn't you really prefer a civilized meal in a civilized restaurant, all the cooking is done for you? No dishes to clean, no pots to scrub. Bugs rarely in evidence. You can always open a window to get a dose of fresh air. If you want fresh air. I prefer air conditioning. So. Next time someone suggests a picnic, take my advice. Run!

Think About It: What strategy or strategies can you use to find and fix sentence fragment problems and run-on sentences in your writing?

Modifier Mistakes

A modifier is a word or phrase that describes another word or phrase in a sentence. There are two common mistakes writers make with modifiers:

1. misplacing them

2. leaving the modifiers dangling

Misplaced Modifiers

Keep modifiers close to the word or phrase they describe. Here are some examples of misplaced modifiers. The arrows show how to correct the sentences.

Elise sat waiting for her boyfriend to arrive *in a black silk dress*.

It hurt so much that I screamed *almost*.

Our apartment was finished *barely* when we first moved in.

"Dangling" is something to avoid.

Dangling Modifiers

A dangling modifier is a descriptive word or phrase that does not modify the noun or pronoun it is intended to modify.

Incorrect: Sailing over the outfield wall, the crowd went wild.
Acceptable: As the ball went sailing over the outfield wall, the crowd went wild.
Incorrect: Driving recklessly, the police gave Jim a ticket.
Acceptable: Because Jim was driving recklessly, the police gave him a ticket.

Awkward Sentences

Awkward sentences make your draft unclear and difficult to read. Here are some strategies to help you solve awkward-sentence problems. Usually the solution involves making sentences simpler.

1. Separate the main thought in the sentence from the less important thoughts.

Awkward: In the end, after many battles, and not before they had used up all legal avenues open to them, with their heads held high, they gave up the fight.
Acceptable: In the end, they gave up the fight, but with their heads held high and not before they had used up all legal avenues open to them.

2. Keep subjects and verbs as close together as possible.

Awkward: This summer, Juan and I, whether we are working or not, will spend a lot of time together.
Acceptable: Juan and I will spend a lot of time together this summer, whether we are working or not.

3. Place modifiers close to the word they modify.

Awkward: In 1987, representatives from 24 countries agreed, gradually, over 10 years, including Canada, to reduce their use of pollutants.
Acceptable: In 1987, representatives from 24 countries including Canada agreed to gradually reduce their use of pollutants over 10 years.

4. Don't try to pack too much information into a single sentence.

Awkward: Intercropping, which involves planting mixed crops in the same field and changing the types of crops every year, and which is a common practice in many developing countries, because planting one crop over and over again can rid the soil of important nutrients, which allows bugs to attack the plants, is an important part of pest control.

Acceptable: Intercropping, which involves planting mixed crops in the same field and changing the types of crops every year, is a common practice in many developing countries. This agricultural method is an important part of pest control, because planting one crop over and over again can rid the soil of important nutrients.

Apply It!	Checklist
Read the following passage and identify sentences that are humorous because of misplaced modifiers and dangling modifiers. Write these sentences on paper and exchange them with a partner. Challenge your partner to name the modifier problem in each sentence, and then to correct it.	✓ Did I refer to the section in the book to review misplaced and dangling modifiers?
Colonel Chris A. Hadfield: Canadian Astronaut	✓ Did I recognize problems with the sentences in the paragraph?
Colonel Chris Hadfield was selected as one of four Canadian astronauts in June 1992. Full of excitement the astronaut training program began at Johnson Space Center in Houston, Texas in August 1992. In November 1995, Colonel Hadfield on a NASA space-shuttle mission to dock with the Russian Space Station *Mir* served as a mission specialist. Focusing on continuing self-improvement, his career has excelled. Colonel Hadfield was the first Canadian to leave a spacecraft and float free in space, on an International Space Station assembly flight. During the flight, he participated in two spacewalks.	✓ Did my partner and I exchange sentences?
	✓ Did I have good ideas of how to solve the problems?
	✓ Did I work on one sentence at a time?
	✓ Did my rewrite make the information clearer and easier to read?

Think About It: Why do you think awkward wording in sentences is so much more noticeable in writing than it is in speech? Which strategies will you use to avoid awkwardness in your writing?

Parallelism

Parallelism means expressing a series of elements within a sentence using a common structure. All items in a series or list within your sentence must match grammatically; for example, all nouns, gerunds, and verbs must match. Here are some examples.

Incorrect/Lacking Parallelism: When I baby-sit, I like baring my teeth, rolling my eyes, and to stick my tongue out to scare the little children. (The three verbs in the series are not parallel in form— "baring" and "rolling" are gerunds; "to stick out" is not.)
Correct/With Parallelism: When I baby-sit, I like baring my teeth, rolling my eyes, and sticking my tongue out to scare the little children.

Incorrect/Lacking Parallelism: Kindness, being physically fit, and a sense of humour are all useful when dealing with young children. (Two of the three items in the series are nouns—"kindness" and "a sense of humour." "Being physically fit" uses a gerund.)

Correct/With Parallelism: Kindness, physical fitness, and a sense of humour are all useful when dealing with young children.

Parallelism with Correlative Conjunctions

Correlative conjunctions are pairs or groups of conjunctions such as "either ... or," "neither ... nor" and "not only ... but also." The grammatical structure following the word or pair of words in the conjunction must match. Here are some examples.

You need parallelism in train tracks and in your writing.

Incorrect/Lacking Parallelism: I was told either to change my train or take the bus.

Correct/With Parallelism: I was told either to change my train or to take the bus. ("To take the bus," which follows "or" must match "to change my train," which follows "either.")

Incorrect/Lacking Parallelism: The curtains were not only too long but also were too wide.

Correct/With Parallelism: The curtains were not only too long but also too wide. (The words "too wide,"—not *were* too wide"—should follow "but also" to match "too long" that follows "not only.")

Subject-Verb Agreement

Every complete sentence has a subject and a verb. For subject-verb agreement, a singular subject takes a singular verb; a plural subject takes a plural verb. Usually, you will easily decide which form of verb to use in a sentence. However, you might run into some possible problem areas.

Plural-Sounding Endings

Some nouns sound as if they are plural because they end in -*s*, but they are really singular, so take a singular verb. Some examples are *news*, *mumps*, *measles*, *physics*, and *mathematics*.

Correct Subject-Verb Agreement: The *news is* not good: *measles is* still the cause of millions of deaths among young children in poor countries.

Compound Subjects

A compound subject can have two or more singular nouns joined together by the word *and*. In this situation use a plural verb.

Correct Subject-Verb Agreement: Her *necklace and bracelet were* a beautiful shade of blue.

Collective Nouns

Collective nouns name a group of people or things; for example, *group*, *army*, *crowd*, *bunch*, and *family*. They usually require a singular verb.

Correct Subject-Verb Agreement: A *bunch* of *grapes was* glued to her hat.

Indefinite Pronouns

Indefinite pronouns ending in *-one*, *-body*, and *-thing* always take a singular verb. Here are some of these pronouns used in sentences, showing the correct verbs to use.

Correct Subject-Verb Agreement:
Everyone loves my pet rat.
Nobody knows the trouble I've seen.
Something is better than nothing.

The indefinite pronouns *some*, *more*, *all*, *none*, *most*, and *any* can be either singular or plural, depending on their use in a specific sentence.

Correct Subject-Verb Agreement:
All of the apple pie *is* gone.
All of the apple pies *are* gone.

Some of the pie *is* gone.

Apply It!	**Checklist**

Apply It!

1. Rewrite these sentences, changing words or phrases to correct faulty parallels.

   a) The only way to calm him down was to give him food, read him a story, or letting him watch TV.

   b) My dog is not only the cutest dog alive, but also he's very smart.

   c) Being outdoors, feeling the soil, and to smell the warm air are what I like about gardening.

   d) To get in shape, either I can join a gym or walk every day.

2. Complete each of these sentence beginnings, using a verb form that agrees with the subject.

   a) When you have a calculator in front of you, mathematics …

   b) Not everyone …

   c) Most geniuses …

   d) My family …

   e) When they are feeling playful, my dog and cat …

   f) The pages of my notebook …

Checklist

✔ Did I recognize the parts of sentences that did not have parallel structure?

✔ Did I correct the non-parallel parts?

✔ Did I complete the sentences with verbs that agree with the subjects?

✔ Did I refer to the relevant sections of the book for help?

Think About It: Write your own definition of "parallelism," with a good example that will help you to identify parallelism problems in your own writing.

Discriminatory Language

Discriminatory language unfairly presents a group or person. The following are some types of discriminatory language.

Gender Bias

Gender bias occurs when people are treated differently in writing because they are male or female. Here's an example of gender bias.

Incorrect: The two mayoral candidates appeared in an all-candidates meeting last night. Ms. Karkov, a pretty blonde, wore a yellow blouse and black skirt and pledged to encourage more industries to locate in the area. Mr. Dressler spoke impressively about his commitment to better housing within the city. (*Ms. Karkov's physical appearance and dress are mentioned. This is not done for Mr. Dressler, so the presentation is unfair or biased.*)

Acceptable: The two mayoral candidates appeared in an all-candidates meeting last night. Ms. Karkov pledged to encourage more industries to locate in the area. Mr. Dressler spoke impressively about his commitment to better housing within the city.

Sexist Words

Here are some sexist words to avoid in your writing, along with words you could use to replace them.

Words to Avoid	Suggested Replacements
man, mankind	humanity, human beings, humankind, people, the human race
policeman, fireman	police officer, fire fighter
stewardess	flight attendant
workman	worker, employee

Many words that end in *man* can be made non-sexist by adding *person* or *employee*. For example, "chairman" can be revised to "chairperson" and "mailman" to "letter carrier."

Pronouns and Gender

In English, we do not have a personal pronoun (like "he" or "she") to cover both sexes. The lack of such a pronoun can be a problem when a personal pronoun refers back to an indefinite singular pronoun (e.g., "whoever") or when the gender of the person is not important.

Incorrect: Whoever parked *their* bike against the telephone pole is in for an unpleasant surprise: only the lock is left!
Correct: Whoever parked *his* or *her* bike against the telephone pole is in for an unpleasant surprise: only the lock is left!

Try It!

Start a chart of your own, showing sexist words to avoid and suggested replacements. Add to it whenever you come across examples in your reading.

The "before" photo of his or her bike.

Strategies for Solving Problems with Pronouns and Gender

Using "his" and "her" too often can be awkward. Here are some strategies to solve this problem.

- *Change the sentence from singular to plural.*
  Avoid: In Japan, a visitor should leave his shoes at the door before entering a house.
  Acceptable: In Japan, visitors should leave their shoes at the door before entering a house.

- *Replace the pronoun with "one" or "you."*
  Avoid: When a client uses a debit card to pay for his purchases, he simply punches his PIN number into a machine, and the money is automatically taken from his bank account.
  Acceptable (only in formal writing): When one uses a debit card to pay for one's purchases, one simply punches a PIN number into a machine, and the money is automatically taken from one's bank account.
  Acceptable: When you use a debit card to pay for your purchases, you simply punch a PIN number into a machine, and the money is automatically taken from your bank account.

- *Reword the sentence so you do not need a personal pronoun.*
  Avoid: A true birdwatcher never forgets his binoculars.
  Acceptable: A true birdwatcher is never without binoculars.

- *In longer pieces of writing, alternate using male and female personal pronouns. That is, use she (or her) in one instance and he (or him) the next time the problem arises. Do not alternate genders within the same sentence.*
  Incorrect: If a teenager is treated fairly by her parents, he will respond reasonably.
  Correct: If a teenager is treated fairly by her parents, she will respond reasonably.

Do you detect a redundancy in the term "PIN number"? (See Redundancy, page 97.)

Apply It!	Checklist

Apply It!

1. Rewrite these sentences to avoid gender bias and sexist words.

   a) Mr. Delvecchio, I'd like you to meet Mr. Hamid, Mr. Dawson, and Sophie, our secretary.

   b) We will give a new car to the businessman who makes the greatest contribution to his community.

   c) He likes that restaurant because his favourite waitress works there.

   d) They will present a gold statue to the salesman who sells the most houses in a year.

2. Look in newspapers and magazines for examples of sexist language. Rewrite them to show how the problem could be solved.

Checklist

✓ Did I recognize gender bias and sexist words in the sentences?

✓ Did I rewrite the sentences to avoid such language?

✓ Did I find examples in print materials of sexist language?

✓ Did I find ways to correct or avoid it?

Think About It: Where do you hear or see examples of sexist language most often? What can you do to correct the situation?

Active and Passive Voice

In the active voice, the subject of the sentence performs the action.

Examples:

Jaffra sniffed the pepper. (Who sniffed? Jaffra did.)

Josh thought about lawn chairs. (Who thought? Josh did.)

Mariko caught the criminal. (Who caught? Mariko did.)

In the passive voice, the subject receives the action.

Examples:

My wallet has been stolen! (The wallet didn't steal; a thief did.)

The baby was found on the steps of the church. (The baby did not find; someone else did.)

I was taught by my mother never to drink milk and laugh at the same time. (I didn't teach; my mother did.)

When writing your draft, try to use the active voice wherever possible. The active voice makes your writing simpler, more direct, and more lively.

Try It!

Look at a sample of your own writing to find examples of the passive voice. Rewrite the sentences in the active voice if possible. Read each version out loud to see which one sounds better.

Guidelines for Using the Passive Voice

There are times where passive voice should be used:

- when you do not know who performed the action
- when the person or thing that received the action is more important than who did the action
- when you do not want to reveal who performed the action

Precise Pronouns

Pronouns are words that can replace nouns. Here are some common trouble spots to watch out for when using pronouns in your writing.

Pronoun Antecedents

An antecedent is the noun that the pronoun replaces. Make sure your reader can tell who or what the antecedent of a pronoun is.

Example:

Unclear: Erica and Marianne went to *her* mother's house. (It is unclear whose mother's house they went to.)

Clear: Erica went to *her* mother's house with Marianne.

Pay particular attention to your use of the pronoun "this." Make sure that your readers can tell exactly what *this* refers to.

The house of Erica's "Auntie-Cedent."

Example:

Unclear: In the first part of the story, the narrator describes her reactions to an incident involving a drowned boy. *This* foreshadows what happens later in the story, when the narrator's own child is almost drowned. (It is unclear what "this" refers to.)

Clear: In the first part of the story, the narrator describes her reactions to an incident involving a drowned boy. *This unfortunate incident* foreshadows what happens later in the story, when the narrator's own child is almost drowned.

Who and Whom

Who and *whom* are called relative pronouns, and they refer to people. Use *who* the same way you would use *he* (for example), as the subject of a verb. Use *whom* the same way you would use *him* (for example), as the object of a verb or a preposition.

Examples:

My uncle, *who* is no longer with us, loved to juggle chain saws.

(It would be correct to say, "*He* is no longer with us," so use *who*. Notice that "uncle" is the subject of the verb "loved," and "who" is the subject of the verb "is.")

The uncle to *whom* I owe my juggling talent had a fondness for chain saws.

(It would be correct to say, "I owe my juggling talent to *him*," so use *whom*. Notice that "uncle" is the subject of the verb "had," "I" is the subject of the verb "owe," and "whom" is the object of the preposition "to.")

Indefinite Pronouns

An indefinite pronoun does not tell exactly what it refers to. Some indefinite pronouns are singular, some are plural, and some can be singular or plural depending on the situation.

Pronouns ending in *-one*, *-body*, or *-thing* (as well as the pronoun *one*) take a singular verb.

Examples:
Incorrect: Somebody among us *are* lying.
Correct: Somebody among us *is* lying.

Incorrect: Someone forgot *their* wig.
Correct: Someone forgot *his* wig.

The pronouns *some*, *none*, and *all* can be either singular or plural, depending on the sentence. In the examples, the words in square brackets show what the indefinite pronouns refer to.

Examples:
All [everything] *is* clear.
All [the pigs] *were* squealing in delight.
Some [books] *are* missing.
Some [of the paint] *is* flaking off.
None [of the money] *was* left.
None [of the coins] *were* left.

Personal Pronouns

The nominative form of a personal pronoun is used

- as a subject of a verb
- when it follows a form of the verb "to be"

Examples:
He gave it to Ted. ("He" is the subject that did the giving.)
It was *I* who rang the bell. ("I" follows "was.")

The objective form of a personal pronoun is used as the object of a verb or preposition.

Example: The committee gave the award to *me*. (The giving was done to me; "me" is the object of the preposition "to.")

Here is a list of personal pronouns.

Nominative	Objective
I	me
you	you
he, she, it	him, her, it
we	us
you	you
they	them

The sentences below show some of the more common mistakes writers make in choosing a pronoun form and how to correct these problems.

Incorrect: *Riswan and me* won the prize for best song.
Correct: *Riswan and I* won the prize for best song. ("Riswan and I" are the subject of the sentence.)

Incorrect: There are too many personal problems between *she and I*.
Correct: There are too many personal problems between *her and me*. (The people referred to by the pronouns are the object of the preposition "between.")

Apply It!

1. Look for errors of pronoun use in these sentences. Rewrite any that need correction.

   a) My mom and me like to go shopping together.

   b) Let's keep this a secret between you and me.

   c) Whom is coming with me?

   d) When Dad sat down with Grandpa, he drank his coffee.

   e) Each one of us have problems.

   f) After we have seen it, we'll pass it along.

2. Write six sentences using personal pronouns. Make some deliberate errors. Exchange your sentences with a partner to find and correct the errors.

Checklist

- Did I recognize problems between pronouns and antecedents?

- Did I recognize errors with "who" and "whom"?

- Did I make sure that indefinite pronouns had the right verb form?

- Did I recognize errors with forms of personal pronouns?

- Did I correct all the errors I could find?

Think About It: What are three rules of pronoun use that you just learned? What strategies will you use to remember them for your own writing?

Redundancy

Redundancy in writing means the use of unnecessary words. When writing, look for ways of cutting redundant words and stating ideas as simply as possible.

THE DEPARTMENT OF REDUNDANCY DEPARTMENT

Example:

Weak: In summary, I conclude that a female cow can produce more milk than a codfish can. ("Summary" and "conclude" express the same idea.)

Acceptable: I conclude that a cow can produce more milk than a codfish.

Here are a few common redundant expressions. When writing, use words from the right column to avoid redundancy.

Try It!

Start your own list or a class list of redundant phrases that you hear and read, and add to it over time.

Instead of...	Say...
repeat again	repeat
true fact	fact
false lie	lie; falsehood
have a preference for	prefer
take under consideration	consider
make an attempt	try
be in agreement	agree

Repetition

Try not to repeat the same word or phrase several times in a sentence or paragraph. Find another way to express what you want to say.

Weak: The light energy from the sun is absorbed by the leaves of the *plant*. The *plant's* leaves convert the light energy into chemical energy, which is stored in the *plant* as ATP. Meanwhile, the water taken up by the *plant's* roots reacts with the carbon dioxide in the plant to make glucose, a form of sugar the *plant* uses as food.

Acceptable: The light energy from the sun is absorbed by the leaves of the plant, *which* convert the light energy into chemical energy *and store it* as ATP. Meanwhile, the water taken up by *the roots* reacts with carbon dioxide to make glucose, a form of sugar used for food.

A thesaurus is a book that lists words in groups of synonyms and related ideas. When writing, if you find yourself repeating a word, use a thesaurus to find some synonyms to replace the repeated word.

Checklist for Redundancy and Repetition in Writing

- Have I checked my work for redundancy and removed all unnecessary words?
- Have I looked for repetition in my writing and tried to express repeated words or phrases in different ways?
- Have I used a thesaurus to find synonyms to avoid too much repetition?

Vocabulary and Writing

Revising and editing often involve improving word choices you made in your original draft. To make the best choices, you need to have a good vocabulary. How can you improve your vocabulary?

Denotations and Connotations

Know the levels of meaning words can have. The *denotation* of a word is its dictionary meaning. *Connotations* are the emotional connections that affect how people respond to a word. Think of a word's connotations when you make word choices in your writing.

Example:
Poor: The movie star was *skinny* and well dressed. (Here "skinny" has a negative connotation.)
Better: The movie star was slender and well dressed.

A thesaurus is an excellent resource if you are looking for synonyms, especially words with the connotations you want.

Prefixes, Suffixes, and Root Words

Understand the parts of words. Some words might have these parts:

prefix: the part of a word added to its beginning
root word: the base word from which the longer word was made
suffix: the part of a word added to its end

Example: indefinable
prefix: "in" means "not"
root word: "define" means "give the exact meaning"
suffix: "able" means "capable of"
Indefinable means not able to be given the exact meaning of.

Specialized Terms

When reading and writing material in special subject areas, you'll often find specialized terms associated with the subject.

When reading, you may need to find out what certain terms mean. When writing, you will need to spell them correctly. For both purposes, you can use

- a general dictionary
- a textbook glossary
- a general or specialized encyclopedia
- a specialized dictionary
- the Internet

Make sure any specialized terms you use in your writing are clearly explained for a general reading audience.

Apply It!	**Checklist**
1. In the following sentence, find a word with a different connotation to replace "perspiration." We worked all day in the hot sun and were covered with *perspiration*.	✔ Did I use a dictionary or a thesaurus to find other words for "perspiration"? ✔ Did I understand how the connotations were different?
2. Break the word *inextricable* into the prefix, root word, and suffix. Predict its meaning based on your knowledge of the word's parts. Check your prediction in a dictionary.	✔ Did I identify the prefix, root word, and suffix? ✔ Did I use the parts to predict the meaning of the word, and then check in the dictionary?
3. Find the meaning of these specialized terms and define them in your own words: junk bonds, glycolysis.	✔ Did I use the appropriate resources to find the meanings of the specialized terms?

Think About It: What can you do in your writing to make the best vocabulary choices for the audience?

Comparative and Superlative Adjectives and Adverbs

Most adjectives and adverbs have three forms: the positive, the comparative, and the superlative. Here are some examples.

Positive	Comparative	Superlative
soft	softer	softest
fast	faster	fastest
careful	more careful	most careful
bad	worse	worst
good	better	best

Use the *comparative* when you're comparing two things. Use the *superlative* when you're comparing more than two things.

Examples:
Which of the two brands of cereal do you like *better*?
Of the three brands of cereal, which do you like *best*?

Double Negatives

Never use two negatives in a sentence.

Examples:
Incorrect: *Don't* you *never* do that again!
Acceptable: *Don't* you *ever* do that again!
Acceptable: *Never* do that again!

As well, when you use a negative word such as barely, scarcely, or hardly, you actually create a positive.

Examples:
Incorrect: I am so excited I *can't hardly* think!
Acceptable: I am so excited I *can hardly* think!
Acceptable: I am so excited I *can't* think!

Apply It!

Rewrite the following sentences to correct any problems with comparative and superlative adjectives or adverbs, or with double negatives.

a) Of the two cars, the Porsche is fastest.

b) Melanie doesn't have to answer to nobody.

c) Though Wong and Miller are gifted speakers, Singh is the more qualified of the three candidates running for office.

d) I don't know no one who has been there before.

e) The oldest twin was born 10 minutes before her sister.

f) She wasn't barely bigger than the dog!

Checklist

 Did I recognize errors of the use of comparative and superlative adjectives and adverbs?

 Did I correct them?

 Did I find and correct examples of double negatives?

Think About It: How can using the strategy of working with a partner help you with rules such as these in your own writing?

Commonly Confused Words

It's easy to confuse some pairs of words, especially if they sound alike and/or look similar. The chart below shows a few commonly confused words.

Try It!

Start a class list of confusing words. Keep it posted for reference and add to it over time.

Words	Meaning	Examples
• accept • except	• verb meaning "receive" • preposition meaning "but"	• The team *accepts* the trophy. • Everyone *except* Raginder was at hockey practice.
• advice • advise	• noun meaning "suggestion" • verb meaning "offer a suggestion"	• Do you want my *advice*? • I *advise* you to stop smoking.
• affect • effect	• verb meaning "cause a change" • noun meaning "the result of a change"	• Nervousness *affected* my performance. • Nervousness had a great *effect* on my performance.

Words	Meaning	Examples
• climactic	• adjective meaning "a point of great importance"	• The capture of the thief was the *climactic* moment in the play.
• climatic	• adjective meaning "weather conditions"	• Fog is one of the most hazardous *climatic* conditions when driving.
• compliment	• noun meaning "praise"	• Thanks for the *compliment* about my hair.
• complement	• verb meaning "to go well with"	• The scarf *complements* her dress.
• emigrate	• verb meaning to "leave one's country"	• The Singhs *emigrated* from India.
• immigrate	• verb meaning "to come to a country other than one's native land as a permanent resident"	• The O'Briens *immigrated* to Canada from Ireland.
• eminent	• adjective meaning "distinguished"	• The *eminent* scientist won a prize for chemistry.
• imminent	• adjective meaning "about to happen"	• There has been so much conflict in the area that war is *imminent*.
• sight	• noun meaning "the ability to see with the eyes"	• He obtained glasses to improve his *sight*.
• site	• noun meaning "a place where something happened"	• They placed a monument at the *site* of his birth.
• cite	• verb meaning to "give an example or support an argument"	• When writing an essay about a poem, you should always *cite* evidence from the poem to support your ideas.

Apply It!

1. Rewrite the following sentences replacing the incorrect word.

   a) The Pattersons immigrated from England.

   b) He lost marks in the essay for not sighting evidence from the short story.

   c) The imminent politician was named as a senator.

   d) You should brake accept in icy conditions.

2. Write 10 sentences using the incorrect version of words from the chart, or using others you know. Exchange your sentences with a partner's and correct each other's.

Checklist

✓ Did I refer to the chart to spot incorrect words in the sentences?

✓ Did I find an incorrect word in each sentence?

✓ Did I use any words other than those in the chart to write my own "mistakes"?

✓ Did I find and fix the incorrect words in my partner's sentences?

Think About It: Describe how you could use a chart of commonly confused words as a strategy to help you choose and use the correct words in your writing.

Literary and Rhetorical Devices

Generally, use literary and rhetorical devices when you wish to make a strong point or create a special effect. The following are some common literary and rhetorical devices.

Similes

A simile compares one thing to another, using the word "like" or "as."

Example: From the sky, an area of clear-cut forest looks like a scar.

Metaphors

A metaphor describes a thing as something else in order to suggest a likeness.

Example: A steel snake was winding through the valley far below. (The steel snake refers to a train.)

A simile is like a smile.

Alliteration

Alliteration is using two or more words that begin with the same sound. Use alliteration to draw attention to an important word, image, or idea.

Example: Children need both *p*raise and *p*rotection.

Rhetorical Questions

A rhetorical question is asked to make the reader think or anticipate what is to come in a piece of writing. It is not expected that the reader will answer the question.

Example: Do we not understand the impact of pollution on our community?

(In an essay, you would then explain the impact of pollution on your community.)

Hyperbole

Hyperbole is an exaggerated statement that is not to be taken literally. It might be used to create dramatic or comic effect.

Example: If I have to wear braces, I'll never smile again.

Irony

Irony is a method of expression in which the intended meaning is the opposite of, or different from, what is expressed.

Example: [Referring to a small bungalow] This is the mansion we call "home."

Language to Avoid in Your Writing

Cliché

A cliché is an overused expression. Most clichés began as strong images and expressions, but because they have been used so often, they have lost their impact.

Examples:

add insult to injury	in the long run
narrow escape	cool as a cucumber
slowly but surely	easier said than done
this day and age	finishing touches

Jargon

Jargon refers to special terms or unnecessarily complicated language used to make writing sound important. Usually such language makes ideas and information difficult to understand.

Example:

Positive input into the infrastructure impacts systematically on the functional base of the firm in that it stimulates a concretization of meaningful objectives from a strategic standpoint.

Jargon should be replaced with *plain language*—language that is simple, direct, and easy to understand.

Euphemism

A euphemism is a word or phrase that names a thing in an indirect or mild way because the direct way is considered unpleasant or harsh. Use euphemisms when you want to soften the truth. Here are a few euphemisms with their plain language meanings.

Examples:

laid to rest = buried

developing nations = poor countries

pleasingly plump = overweight

pre-owned, reconditioned = used

passed over; passed on = died

Usually it is best to be direct in your writing and not use euphemisms.

Apply It!	Checklist
1. Write a simile to describe the blue of the sky on a sunny day.	✓ Did I use "like" or "as" in my simile?
2. Write a metaphor for a thunderstorm.	✓ Did I write a metaphor that calls the thunderstorm something else that it is like?
3. Write a sentence describing a river. Include an example of alliteration.	✓ Did my alliteration contain two or more words that start with the same sound?
4. Write a rhetorical question that could be used in one of your writing pieces.	✓ Did I write a rhetorical question that relates to something in one of my pieces of writing?
5. Write an example of hyperbole to express how you feel after a breakup with a boyfriend or girlfriend.	✓ Did I create an example of hyperbole that was either dramatic or comedic (or both)?
6. Look through print materials to find at least one example each of a cliché, jargon, and a euphemism.	✓ Did I find examples of clichés, jargon, and euphemisms in print materials?

Think About It: Which of these devices are familiar to you? Which will you need to work on? How will you do that?

Strategies for Fixing Writing Problems

Writing Groups

Share your draft with your writing group.

A good strategy for finding and fixing problems in your writing is to share the draft with a writing group and to ask members for feedback. Here are some guidelines for running a successful writing group.

Writing Group Guidelines

- Keep the size of the group to no more than five or six people.
- As a writer, don't be defensive about criticism of your work. Make sure you understand the criticisms raised. Ask questions to clarify comments.
- Use your own judgment when deciding whether to use a group member's suggestion in your revision. Remember, you are the writer.
- As a reader and writing-group critic, make sure your criticism is honest, constructive, and clear.

You can use a checklist like the one below to evaluate each group member's draft.

Writing Group Checklist

Organization:

- Are the paragraphs well structured and logically arranged?
- Is the topic introduced clearly? If it is an essay, is the thesis clearly stated?
- Does the conclusion sum up everything without having too much repetition? Does it mention all the main points of the piece of writing?

Record general comments about the structure.

Content:

- Is there enough information? If not, what is needed?
- Is there too much information? If so, what could be cut?
- Are lots of examples given and/or supporting evidence provided?
- Are any quotations suitable and correctly punctuated?
- Did the writer answer all your questions on the topic? If not, what questions remain unanswered?

Record general comments about the content.

Focus:

- What do you think the writer was trying to accomplish? Did the writer successfully accomplish his or her overall writing goal? Explain why or why not.

   Record general comments about the focus.

Style:

- Is the draft enjoyable to read?
- Does the writer use clear, accurate, and powerful words?
- Does the writer use transition phrases or words to link ideas?
- Is the tone appropriate for the writer's purpose and audience?

   Record general comments about the style.

Overall Impression:

List at least one positive feature and at least one area that needs improvement.

   Note that you could also use the checklist on your own to revise and edit your work before presenting it to the group. Then, the checklist could be used again in the writing groups to evaluate how well you achieved your revising and editing goals.

Troubleshooting: Finding and Fixing Problems in Your Writing

Interest

Topic Seems Dull

- Ask yourself whether your writing suits your audience and your purpose. Consider each paragraph in this light and cut anything that seems off topic.
- Change the tone: add more humour, enthusiasm, or personal anecdotes.
- Use comparisons with everyday experiences and things.

Writing Is Dull

- Break up some of your longer sentences into short, sharp statements to emphasize particular points.
- Use more precise (specific) nouns (e.g., Oldsmobile instead of car; beagle instead of dog).

Try It!

Use the writing group strategy and the checklist to evaluate and then improve a draft of your writing. Discuss with group members how you could improve the strategy, including the checklist, the next time you evaluate each other's work in a writing group.

- Replace forms of the verb "to be" in sentences with more precise or more active verbs.
- Use descriptions and metaphors, similes, and other figures of speech to appeal to your readers' senses (especially sight, hearing, smell, and touch). However, do not overuse figures of speech.
- Avoid clichés such as "sharp as a tack." Try to think of fresh images and phrases to replace tired ones.

Clarity

Writing Is Confusing

- Reorganize your paragraphs using an outline or diagram to show the arrangement of ideas.
- Use transition words to show connections between ideas in paragraphs and sentences.
- Look for run-on sentences and sentence fragments. Revise them to create complete sentences.
- Avoid using jargon or other words that may be unfamiliar to your audience.

Writing Lacks Focus

- Narrow your topic.
- Write a clear introduction, setting out what you intend to do.
- Link every paragraph to your introduction.

Language

Too Formal

- Write in the first person ("I").
- Use contractions, such as "can't" or "won't."
- Shorten some of your sentences, but keep a variety of lengths.

Too Informal

- Avoid using the first person ("I").
- Use formal language only, which means no slang expressions or contractions.
- Lengthen your sentences but keep some variety, and use shorter sentences to emphasize particular points.

Writing Sounds Choppy

- Combine sentences by joining subjects, objects, verbs, phrases, or clauses.
- Avoid repeating the same words or phrases. Try using a thesaurus to find synonyms (words that mean the same thing).

Length

Too Long

- Look at each paragraph and ask yourself if it is necessary to accomplish your purpose or to prove your thesis. If you can do without that paragraph, cut it.
- Look for simpler ways of saying things.

Too Short

- Broaden your topic to include more action, more ideas, more detail, or more arguments.
- Make sure you have supported each of your ideas thoroughly.

Try It!

Make yourself a poster like the one shown here. Keep it nearby when you are writing.

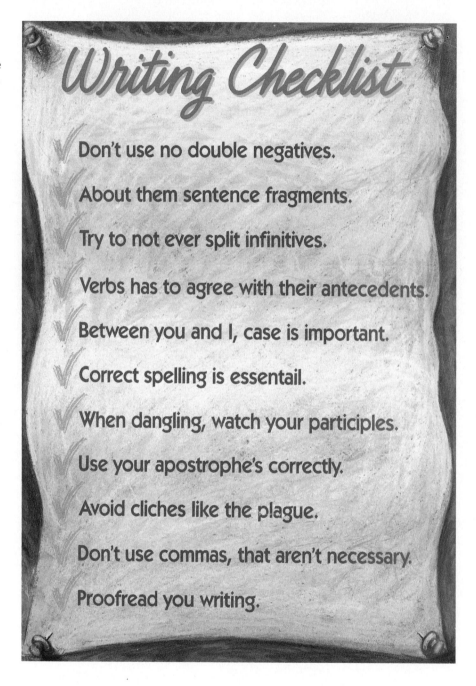

Writing Checklist

✔ Don't use no double negatives.

✔ About them sentence fragments.

✔ Try to not ever split infinitives.

✔ Verbs has to agree with their antecedents.

✔ Between you and I, case is important.

✔ Correct spelling is essentail.

✔ When dangling, watch your participles.

✔ Use your apostrophe's correctly.

✔ Avoid cliches like the plague.

✔ Don't use commas, that aren't necessary.

✔ Proofread you writing.

CHAPTER 5

Presenting Your Work

You might think with all the revising and editing you've done that your writing work is complete. Actually, there's still a lot of checking and correcting work to do.

"Presenting" in the writing process is where the pride in your work kicks in, as you try to make any writing assignment the best you possibly can.

In this chapter you will learn to

- proofread your final draft
- check that your final copy follows all the rules of good writing and looks appealing on the page
- do a final check to make doubly sure every last detail is correct

Contents

Presenting Written Work 112

Formatting 133

Adding Front and Back Matter 138

Learning Goals

- proofread to produce final drafts
- learn about and use correct rules of spelling
- learn about and use correct rules of punctuation
- learn about and use correct rules of capitalization
- create polished presentations using correct writing formats

Presenting Written Work

To best present your finished piece of writing, you need to

1. proofread the final draft

2. decide on a format and make sure your final copy follows all the rules of that format and looks good on the page

3. make a final check

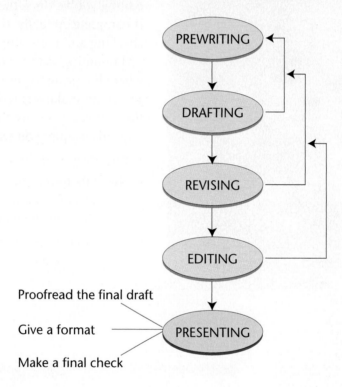

Proofread for Spelling, Capitalization, and Punctuation

To catch and correct errors in spelling, capitalization, and punctuation, you need to have a good set of proofreading strategies. Here are some strategies to use when you proofread your writing.

Proofreading Strategies

1. Use a computer spell checker before you print out a hard copy to work on. But remember that most spell checkers are programmed for American, not Canadian, spelling.

2. Proofread your work on hard copy. It's too easy to miss things on a computer screen.

3. Make corrections and changes in pencil. Use the editing symbols in Chapter 4 or create your own method.

4. Read as slowly as you can. Look at each word separately. Keep a dictionary handy.

5. Try proofreading your work backward, one sentence at a time. That way you'll be able to focus on the individual words rather than on the content of what you have written.

6. Ask a friend to proofread your work after you have finished proofreading it yourself.

7. Ask a friend to read your work out loud while you listen for problems.

Proofreading Tips

When you are proofreading your work, check that you have

- spelled everything correctly
  - Check your work against a list of common spelling mistakes.
  - Check your work against a list of commonly confused words. See Commonly Confused Words, pages 101 to 102.
- used correct punctuation. See Punctuation, pages 125 to 131.
- used abbreviations that are appropriate to the type of writing. See Abbreviations, pages 119 to 120.
- used a consistent style of numbering. See Numbers and Metric Units, pages 121 to 123.
- used capital letters in appropriate places. See Capital Letters, pages 123 to 125.

> ### Cross-Reference
>
> See Editing Marks, page 72.

Try It!

Enter a list of proofreading tips into your computer so you can refer to them whenever you need them.

- indented every new paragraph.
- used quotation marks around shorter quotations and indented quotations of longer than four lines. See Quotation Marks, pages 129 to 131.
- acknowledged all outside sources properly. See Giving Proper Credit to Sources, pages 177 to 182.
- identified titles of works using underlining, italics, or quotation marks, as necessary. See Quotation Marks, pages 129 to 131; and Italics and Underlining, page 132.

Apply It!	Checklist
1. Choose a piece of writing in your writing portfolio. Use the proofreading strategies and tips described in this section to improve the presentation of your piece of writing.	Did I try proofreading strategies and tips to help me improve the presentation of my piece of writing?
2. Photocopy a sample of your writing and give it to a partner to proofread. Proofread it yourself at the same time, but separately. Then compare the results.	Did I use a checklist to help me catch and fix as many writing problems as possible?
	Did my partner and I compare results?

Think About It: Make note of the proofreading strategies you used. Which ones would you use again? What proofreading strategies have you developed on your own?

Spelling

Many spelling rules have exceptions, or cases that break the rules. When in doubt, check in a good Canadian dictionary.

The following questions will lead you to some helpful spelling rules and patterns.

Six Common Spelling Questions Answered

1. How do I know if a word is spelled -*ie* or -*ei*?
Learn the rhyme below:

I before E
Except after C,
Or when sounded like A,
As in neighbour or weigh.
Except seize and seizure,
And also leisure,
Weird, height, and either,
and neither.

Examples
field, thief, believe, chief, friend
receive, ceiling, receipt, deceive
neighbour, freight, eight, sleigh

Be careful, as there are other words that break the rules, such as *science* and *protein*. The above rhyme can help you to remember the main rule and some of the common exceptions to it.

2. How do I know when to drop the final *-e* if I'm adding a suffix?

  a) Drop the final *-e* when the suffix (word ending) to be added begins with a vowel.

      race + -ing   =   racing
      love + -able   =   lovable

  Exception: Some words ending in *-ce* or *-ge*.

      province + -al   =   provincial
      courage + -ous   =   courageous

  b) Keep the final *-e* when the suffix to be added begins with a consonant.

      sincere + -ly   =   sincerely
      arrange + -ment =   arrangement

  Exception: *argument, ninth, truly*

3. When do I double the final consonant if I am adding a suffix?

  a) Never double the final consonant when the suffix to be added begins with a consonant.

      commit + -ment   =   commitment
      wet + -ness   =   wetness

  b) Usually double the final consonant when the suffix to be added begins with a vowel.

      commit + -ing   =   committing
      prefer + -ed   =   preferred

  Exception: If the accent is not on the last syllable, don't double the final consonant. *Hint:* A dictionary is a good tool for finding out where an accent falls in a word.

      benefit + -ed   =   benefited
      profit + -ing   =   profiting
      open + -ing   =   opening

  For words ending in a single vowel and *-l*, double the *-l* before a suffix that begins with a vowel.

      level + -ing   =   levelling
      travel + -er   =   traveller

Sceintist? Or scientist?

Try It!

Add your own hard-to-remember words to your computer's spell check dictionary.

4. When do I change the final -*y* to -*i* if I am adding a suffix?

   a) If the final -*y* follows a consonant, change the -*y* to -*i*.

   envy + -ous   =   envious
   baby + -s   =   babies

   Exception:

   pity + -ous   =   piteous

   b) If the final -*y* follows a vowel, keep the -*y*.

   play + -ed   =   played
   donkey + -s   =   donkeys

   Exception: Always keep the -*y* when adding -*ing*.

   try + -ing   =   trying

5. What do I do when I add the suffix -*ly* to a word ending in -*l* already?

   Make no change. Just add -*ly*.

   wonderful + -ly =   wonderfully
   casual + -ly   =   casually

6. When do I double the -*s* when adding *dis*- or *mis*- at the beginning of a word?

   Make no changes. Just add *dis*- or *mis*-.

   dis- + appear   =   disappear
   mis- + spell   =   misspell

   There are no exceptions!

Canadian Spelling

Canadian English spelling is influenced by British and American spellings. Differences between British and American spelling can be seen in the following groups of words.

1. Words ending in -*our*/-*or*

   British: neighbour, colour, labour, honour, flavour, humour
   American: neighbor, color, labor, honor, flavor, humor
   In Canadian English, the base word changes when a suffix is added.

   humour + -ous   =   humorous
   labour + -ous   =   laborious

2. Words ending in *-re/-er*
British: theatre, centre, fibre
American: theater, center, fiber
Note: In Canadian spelling, machines that measure end in "meter" (thermometer, water meter); units of measure use "metre" (metre, kilometre).

3. Words you just have to remember
British: aeroplane, catalogue, grey
American: airplane, catalog, gray

How can you tell this sign is in the United States?

Whenever you are in doubt, check a good Canadian English dictionary. The preferred spelling will be the first one listed in the dictionary entry.

Apply It!	**Checklist**

Apply It!

1. Use a Canadian dictionary to look up the preferred spelling of these words.

   kerb or curb   omelette or omelet
   mustache or moustache

2. Proofread the following passage. For each error you spot, correct it and name the spelling rule the word follows.

Checklist

✓ Did I choose the first listing in the dictionary as the preferred spelling?

✓ Did I check all the words in the passage for spelling errors?

✓ Did I find a spelling rule for each correction?

✓ Did I use a dictionary to check any word I was unsure how to spell?

His beleif was that he could enjoy his love of car raceing to a very old age. His attitude was the happyiest of anyone I've known. He just took life's problems very casualy. Nothing gave him disscomfort—not even almost crashing an aeroplane.

Think About It: Which three spelling rules give you the most difficulty? What can you do to remember them?

Hyphenated Words

The hyphen (-) is a sign used to join two words or a word and part of a word such as a prefix. This chart shows many of the rules for using hyphens.

Category	Rule	Examples
Numbers	• Hyphenate compound (more than one joined together) numbers between twenty-one and ninety-nine.	• twenty-one ninety-nine
	• Spelled-out fractions require a hyphen between numerator and denominator.	• one-half seven-eighths
	• When a number + a unit of measure come before a noun, put a hyphen between the number and the unit of measure.	• two-metre wall 1000-m race five-litre can
	• When writing a number + *year* + *old*, put a hyphen after the number and after year.	• eight-year-old girl a two-year-old
	• When spelling out time, put a hyphen between the hour and the minutes.	• one-thirty five-fifteen
Hyphenated Prefixes	• When placing a prefix before a proper name, separate the two with a hyphen.	• pro-American all-Canadian
	• When combining *half* + another word, put a hyphen after *half*.	• half-baked half-mast Exception: halfway
Family Relationships	• When writing *in-law*, put a hyphen after the relationship word and after *in*.	• sister-in-law brothers-in-law
Compound Modifiers Preceding the Word They Modify	• Hyphenate a combination of word + participle (word formed from a verb) when the compound comes before a noun.	• thirst-quenching drink Canadian-made piano time-saving device
	• Compound adjectives that come before a noun are hyphenated.	• well-known region best-dressed man
Clarifying Hyphens	• Hyphenate prefixes when confusion with other words is possible.	• Re-cover the chair after you've recovered from the accident.

Sometimes the dictionary can help you decide if a hyphen is needed.

Apply It!	**Checklist**
1. Rewrite the paragraph that follows, placing the missing hyphens in the correct place. 2. Compare your work with a partner. To explain why you added every hyphen, match each hyphen to a rule on the chart.	Did I check words I think might need hyphens against rules and examples on the chart? Did I check words I think might need hyphens against the dictionary?

> The Treetops Hotel is a well known tourist attraction in Kenya. This five metre high hotel is built in a tree, right beside an all important watering hole for animals. In the past, the well known patrons of the hotel have included the twenty six year old daughter of King George VI, Elizabeth, along with the King's son in law, Philip. Elizabeth received the news of her father's death and that she would become queen while staying at Treetops.

Think About It: Which hyphenated words did you miss in the activity? What will you do to remember the rules for next time? Write strategies for yourself.

Abbreviations

Generally, avoid using abbreviations in your formal written assignments. Here are a few guidelines about using abbreviations.

Avoid	**Acceptable**
e.g.	for example
i.e.	that is
Xmas	Christmas
etc.	and so on/and so forth
Sept. 14/93	14 September 1993
Fri., Sat.	Friday, Saturday
Eng., Hist.	English, History

Here are the five kinds of abbreviations that you can usually use in written work.

1. Before Proper Names

Abbreviate titles before proper names. Common abbreviations are

Mr., Mrs., Dr., Mme., M.

Note: "Ms." is a title, but is not an abbreviation.

2. After Proper Names

Abbreviate titles and professional degrees after proper names. Some of the most common abbreviations are

Jr., Sr., B.A., M.D., Ph.D., D.D.S.

Never use more than one abbreviation with the same meaning.
Never: Dr. N. Osborne, M.D.
Acceptable: Dr. N. Osborne
            N. Osborne, M.D.

3. Agencies and Organizations

Abbreviate names of government agencies and organizations when the abbreviations are more commonly used than the spelled-out names. Some examples are

R.C.M.P. or RCMP   NATO
S.P.C.A. or SPCA   UNICEF

More and more people are leaving out periods from abbreviations, especially abbreviations of organization names. If you are in doubt about whether to use periods, check in a dictionary.

4. "Saint"

Abbreviate *Saint* when it is part of a place name.

St. John's, Newfoundland
St. Thomas, Ontario

Exception: Saint John, New Brunswick

5. Other Cases

In certain kinds of papers and assignments, abbreviations of sums of money, time, and units of measurement are accepted.

• Money $41.75

• Time 9:30 a.m., 11:15 p.m.

• Measurement 16 km, 454 t, 6 mL

Do not use periods after metric symbols unless they come at the ends of sentences.

Apply It!

1. In a dictionary, look up the full name of any abbreviations appearing on this page that you do not know. Write out each in complete words.

2. Copy the paragraph below in your notebook. Underline all the abbreviations. Meet with a partner and discuss whether each abbreviation is acceptable in formal writing. Explain why.

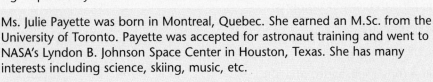

Ms. Julie Payette was born in Montreal, Quebec. She earned an M.Sc. from the University of Toronto. Payette was accepted for astronaut training and went to NASA's Lyndon B. Johnson Space Center in Houston, Texas. She has many interests including science, skiing, music, etc.

Checklist

 Did I use a dictionary to look up some abbreviations?

 Did I check the use of abbreviations against the rules given in this book?

Think About It: What are two things you just learned about abbreviations? Where will you use this knowledge?

Numbers and Metric Units

Numbers

In formal writing, numbers are usually spelled out. Here are three important rules for working with numbers in your writing.

1. Numbers Below 101

Numbers below 101 are usually spelled out. Compound numbers between twenty-one and ninety-nine are hyphenated.

   ninety-six kilometres
   sixteen players
   135 cars

Note: Round numbers over 101 are usually spelled out; for example, two hundred books, a thousand people.

2. Numerals

Use numerals in dates, street numbers, room numbers, sums of money, telephone numbers, temperature readings, page numbers, numbered sections and chapters in books, statistics, and with a.m. and p.m. to indicate time.

   11 February 1940 or 11/02/40   25 °C (not 25 degrees Celsius)
   6622 Elmwood Avenue   page 92, Chapter III

3. Beginning a Sentence

When a number begins a sentence, it should be spelled out.

   Two hundred and ninety-five children sang together.

Metric Units

This chart shows common metric units, what each unit measures, and the symbol for the unit.

Quantity	Unit	Symbol
mass (weight)	gram (one-thousandth of a kilogram)	g
	kilogram	kg
	tonne (one thousand kilograms)	t
volume and capacity	cubic centimetre	cm^3
	cubic metre	m^3
	millilitre (one-thousandth of a litre)	mL
	centilitre (one-hundredth of a litre)	cL
	litre	L
length	millimetre (one-thousandth of a metre)	mm
	centimetre (one-hundredth of a metre)	cm
	metre	m
	kilometre (one thousand metres)	km
area	hectare	ha
	square centimetre	cm^2
	square metre	m^2
speed	metres per second	m/s
	kilometres per hour	km/h
time	second	s
	minute	min
	hour	h
temperature	degree(s) Celsius	°C

Here are a few guidelines to keep in mind when making decisions about using metric units in your writing.

1. Avoid mixing numerals and the full names of metric symbols.
   Avoid: I bought 3 kilograms of meat.
   Acceptable: I bought 3 kg of meat.
   Acceptable: I bought three kilograms of meat.

2. Avoid using a period after a metric symbol unless the symbol is at the end of a sentence.
Avoid: There are over 11 000 ha. of wheat in Canada.
Acceptable: There are over 11 000 ha of wheat in Canada.

3. Use a hyphen between the numeral and the symbol when they are used to modify a noun.
Avoid: I went for a 5 km hike.
Acceptable: I went for a 5-km hike.

4. Use decimals rather than fractions in metric units.
Avoid: That fence is 1 2/3 m high.
Acceptable: That fence is 1.66 m high.

Apply It!	Checklist
Correct the following phrases or sentences if there are number or metric-unit mistakes in them.	✓ Did I check the rules about numbers and metric units as I made corrections?
a) one hundred and one Dalmatians	
b) 386 people were at the party.	
c) 32 degrees Celsius	
d) The high jumper cleared 2 1/3 m.	
e) He bought 50 centimetres of string.	
f) The 2 t. truck got stuck.	
g) They own a hundred and fifty ha ranch.	

Think About It: Write in your own words three rules that you learned in this section that will be most useful in the type of writing you do.

Capital Letters

Here are the key rules to remember when making decisions about which words need capital letters.

1. Major Rules
Capitalize the first word of a sentence, the pronoun "I", and proper nouns such as names.

Rule Category	Examples
a) first word in sentence and pronoun "I"	My mom says I need a hobby.
b) names of people and animals	Farley Mowat, Flipper

Capital Capitals

St. John's, NF
Charlottetown, PE
Halifax, NS
Fredericton, NB
Quebec City, QC
Toronto, ON
Winnipeg, MB
Regina, SK
Edmonton, AB
Victoria, BC
Whitehorse, YK
Yellowknife, NT
Iqaluit, NU

c) geographical locations	Vancouver, Niagara Falls
d) days, months, and holidays	Monday, July, New Year's Day
e) specific school courses	Canadian Geography 11
f) names of companies and organizations	Canadian Tire, Canadian Cancer Society
g) nationalities, races, and languages	Irish, Caucasian, French
h) religions	Islam, Christianity
i) buildings	CN Tower
j) parts of addresses	126 Mayfield Drive

2. Direct Quotations

Direct quotations are words quoted directly from what people say. Capitalize the first word.

> "Tomorrow morning, we'll have a short test on long division," announced Ms. Williams.

3. History References

Capitalize the names of historical events and documents.

> Second World War, Charter of Rights and Freedoms

4. Titles

Capitalize the first word and all important words in the titles of books, movies, plays, songs, articles, poems, and short stories.

> *Titanic, Who Has Seen the Wind?*

5. Parts of Letters

Capitalize the first word in the salutation (greeting) and closing of a letter.

> Dear Abby, Dear Ms. Takahara, Yours truly, Sincerely

6. Titles Before Names

Capitalize titles before the names of people.

> Rabbi Morris, Ambassador Rodriguez, Ms. Geertz
> Tell Doctor Piltz what is bothering you.

Note: Titles used alone are not capitalized.

> The doctor gave me a prescription.

7. Some Other Capital Letter Rules

Capitalize words such as *father*, *mother*, and *aunt* and *uncle* when they are part of a person's name or when they are used in place of a person's name.

> Tell me, Doctor, how long will my hand be in a cast?
> My brother went looking for Uncle Mario.

Cross-Reference

See Quotation Marks: Titles, page 131, and Italics and Underlining: Titles, page 132.

Do not capitalize *north*, *south*, *west*, *east*, or any combination of these directions, unless they are part of a proper name, such as *North York* or *South Dakota*. Do not capitalize the seasons: *spring, summer, fall, autumn, winter*.

Apply It!	Checklist
Write out the following letter, adding capitalization as necessary.	Did I refer to the rules for capital letters? Did I use capital letters correctly?

dear fionna,
i've just read the most amazing book on the war of 1812 called forgotten fight. My teacher, professor moore, kept raving about it. "read this book," He kept saying. The paperback is organized by seasons, starting with Spring and ending in Winter. You just have to buy it.

sincerely,
ennie

P.S. My Father is coming along well after his operation at vancouver general hospital.

Think About It: Brainstorm and record your own list of rules for capital letters. Check it against the rules given in this chapter. What can you do to remember the ones you missed?

Punctuation

Punctuation is the common marks and signs in writing that are used to separate words into sentences and into parts of sentences called clauses and phrases.

Period, Question Mark, Exclamation Mark

Period
The main purpose of the period is to end sentences, such as statements or commands.

> The golfer's final shot won the Canadian Open.
> Study the mathematics chapter for Monday's test.

> Periods are also often used in abbreviations.

Question Mark
Use the question mark to end a sentence that asks a question.

> Where can I get some grape gum?
> What is the meaning of life?

Exclamation Mark
Use the exclamation mark to show surprise or strong feeling.

> Take off!
> I can't believe you fed my fish to the cat!

Cross-Reference

See Abbreviations, pages 119 to 120.

"I can't believe you fed my fish to the cat!"

Apply It!	Checklist
Use your proofreading skills to find and then correct the following punctuation errors. It was the first time I'd been to a Blue Jays game The first baseman took the count to two strikes and three balls with the game tied in the last inning. Can you believe the excitement. On the next pitch he hit the ball about 125 m over the left-field fence for a home run. I jumped out of my seat and screamed, "We win."	✓ Did I use periods and questions marks correctly? ✓ Did I use exclamation marks only in appropriate places? ✓ Did I read the paragraph out loud to check how it sounds?

Think About It: Make a list or chart to show what you know about when to use the following: period; question mark; exclamation mark.

Comma

A comma signals the reader to pause, and it is used to make writing clearer. Here are some places to use commas.

1. Lists

Use a comma to separate the items in a series or list.

> The Six Nations Confederacy includes the Cayuga, Mohawk, Oneida, Onondaga, Seneca, and Tuscarora.
> The ball rolled down the driveway, between two parked cars, and onto the road.

The comma before the *and*, as in " ... Seneca, and Tuscarora" is a matter of choice. If you decide to use the comma before *and*, you must follow that style throughout your writing.

2. Introductory Words or Groups of Words

a) Use a comma after introductory words such as "No," "Well," "However," and so on.

> "Well, did you feed my fish?"
> "Yes, I fed the fish to the cat."

b) A phrase at the beginning of a sentence should be followed by a comma if it is long or if its meaning could be misunderstood.

> Without waking up, José got in the car and drove across town.
> Hanging up, the coat looked ragged and shapeless.

3. Words of Address

Use commas to set off words of address.

> "Dino, did you understand that part about multiplying exponents?"
> "I didn't understand it at all, Mr. Laroche."
> Dear Santa,

"Fish? What fish?"

4. Additional Information

Use a comma to mark off additional, but not essential, information about a noun.

The cat, a fluffy fellow with orange stripes, sat at my door.

Apply It!	Checklist
Copy these sentences into your notebook. Place commas in the correct places.	✓ Did I place commas according to the rules?
a) Raginder do you think we have a chance of winning?	✓ Did I check whether I can leave out any comma I now have?
b) We had a meeting that included the pitchers catchers infielders and outfielders.	✓ Did I read aloud sentences to hear how the commas made them sound?
c) No I don't plan on contesting the class election.	
d) The convict who had a long criminal record was caught.	

Think About It: List at least three things you learned about commas in this section.

Colon

The colon is most often used to introduce ideas and items. Here are some places to use colons in your writing.

1. Lists

Use a colon to introduce a list of items.

Bring these items: a pen, a pencil, a piece of paper.

2. Quotations

Use a colon to separate introductory words from a formal quotation that is a complete sentence.

A famous line is often quoted: "It was a dark and stormy night."

The part before the colon must be an independent clause. This means that it must have a subject and a verb, so it would be a complete sentence if it stood on its own.

3. Business Letters

Use a colon after the greeting of a business letter.

Dear Mrs. McDonnell:

4. Time

Use a colon to separate the numerals of hours and minutes.

The bus leaves at 3:10 p.m.

5. Subtitles

Use a colon to introduce a subtitle of a book or article or to introduce a section in one of these.

"New Zoos: Taking Down the Bars" (article)

Apostrophe

The apostrophe shows possession and replaces missing letters in contractions. Here are some guidelines.

1. Possession

a) *To show possession of singular nouns, add -'s.*

the school's book

Marco's speech

b) *To show possession of plural nouns not ending in -s, add -'s.*

the men's department

the mice's tails

c) *To show possession of plural nouns ending in -s, add only an apostrophe.*

the boys' books (more than one book, belonging to more than one boy)

the teachers' room (one room belonging to more than one teacher)

d) *Do not use an apostrophe or an -'s to show possession for the pronoun "who" or for personal pronouns.*

Here is a list of personal pronouns with their correct possessive forms.

Personal Pronoun	Possessive
I	my/mine
you	your/yours
he, she, it	his, her/hers, its
we	our/ours
you	your/yours
they	their/theirs
who	whose

However, do use an apostrophe and *-s* to show possession with these words.

one	one's
everybody	everybody's

Ali's room, Ali's scooter, Ali's radio, Ali's lamp.

2. Contractions

Use an apostrophe in a contraction to show where one or more letters have been dropped. Avoid using contractions in formal writing.

Here are some common contractions. The apostrophe replaces
the underlined letter or letters.

don't   do n<u>o</u>t
can't   can<u>no</u>t
should've should <u>ha</u>ve
it's   it <u>i</u>s
who's   who <u>i</u>s

Contractions are
everywhere.

Quotation Marks

Quotation marks (" ") separate a person's exact words from other
text. Here are some common uses of quotation marks.

1. Direct Speech

Direct speech is what someone actually says, word for word. Use
quotation marks to show the speaker's exact words, not in indirect
reports of what someone said.

Direct Speech: Mulder said, "My sister was taken away by
                     extraterrestrials!"
Indirect Speech: Mulder said that his sister was taken away by
                     extraterrestrials.

If a question is asked in the direct speech, put the question mark
inside the quotation marks.

Mulder said, "Do you think my sister was taken away by
extraterrestrials?"

If the entire sentence asks a question, put the question mark outside the quotation marks. You don't need to put a period inside the
quotation marks.

Did Mulder say, "My sister was taken away by extraterrestrials"?

2. Dialogue

Quotation marks also show the exact words of different speakers
in a conversation. The following are examples of dialogue in short
stories. They show some rules for using quotation marks and punc-
tuating dialogue.

**Use a new set of quotation marks when a new sentence of
dialogue is spoken.**

"I drive a motorcycle," growled Simon. "Let's go for a ride."

Use a comma when part of a sentence is broken up by a speaker tag (e.g., she said).

"My name, by the way," she added, "is Mary Brennan. I don't live here but I stop here often."

Start a new paragraph for each new speaker.

"So when will it be fixed?" asked Simon. "I have places I'm supposed to be."

"It'll be two, maybe three days," said the mechanic.

3. Quotations in Essays

Use quotation marks in your essays around words that come directly from another writer or speaker.

a) *Shorter Quotations in Essays*

Try to work shorter quotations into the body of the essay or report text. Here are some examples.

> In Michelle Macafee's article she claims, "The company soon plans to release a dictionary of about 2000 words and phrases."
>
> A good example of alliteration comes from Alice Major's poem, where the poem's speaker describes the thief as a "thug with thick fingers."

b) *Longer Quotations in Essays*

"Long" means more than four lines. Instead of using quotation marks, indent a longer quotation five spaces from both the left-hand and right-hand margins, and single space it.

> In "Creating a Visual Package," the author states:
>> The best advice for using graphics is: keep it simple. A graphic should be easy to read and should be helpful in conveying important information. Research shows that photographs and other graphic images are used by readers as entry points onto a printed page.

4. Quotation Within a Quotation

If the writer you are quoting has already included quoted material in a sentence, use regular quotation marks around the whole passage, and change the writer's quotation marks to single quotation marks around the "inside" quotation.

> Here is a quote from Jerry Buckley's article on David Suzuki. "There was never much question about the young David's future profession. 'Right from the beginning, it was nature,' Suzuki remembers."

5. Titles

Use quotation marks around the titles of magazine and newspaper articles, book chapters, poems, songs, short stories, and essays.

"Running for Health"   (magazine article)
Chapter 3, "Presenting Your Work" (book chapter)
"In Flanders Fields"   (poem title)
"O Canada"   (song title)
"The Knife Sharpener"   (short story)
"Everything It Carries Away"   (essay)

6. Words as Words

Use quotation marks to draw attention to certain words.

Some Canadians have a habit of ending every sentence with "eh."

Apply It!

Proofread and then write out the following sentences, adding colons, apostrophes, and quotation marks where necessary.

a) Dawns mother is one of those people for whom its impossible to pass up a chance to help people. She volunteers at a womens shelter from 2 30 to 4 30 everyday, and she helps coach a girls hockey team.

b) Ill come later he replied

But your grandfather wants to see you his mother explained.

Its not that far. Ill walk.

c) The latest issue of the magazine has a wonderful article Fighting Your Zits, a great short story titled Why I Love My Skateboard, and a moving poem called Ode to My Hot Rod.

Checklist

 Did I use colons correctly?

 Did I use apostrophes to show possession?

 Did I use apostrophes in contractions?

 Did I use quotation marks correctly?

Did I use the correct punctuation with the quotation marks?

Think About It: Write down an example of a word that needs an apostrophe and a rule about using quotation marks that you have trouble remembering. What can you do to help yourself remember?

Italics and Underlining

Italics and underlining are used in writing to show titles of works and to communicate emphasis. Use italic type if you write with a computer; use underlining if your writing assignment is handwritten.

1. Titles

Use italics or underlining for the titles of books, magazines, newspapers, plays, TV series, and movies, as well as the names of specific ships or planes.

Famous Lasting Words	(book)
Canadian Geographic	(magazine)
Calgary Herald	(newspaper)
Freaks	(play)
The Nature of Things	(TV series)
Mission Impossible	(movie)
H.M.S. Queen Elizabeth II	(ship)

2. Emphasis

Use italics or underlining to emphasize words in a sentence.

I most certainly do *not* want a surprise party on my birthday, even though I will be out until 8:00 p.m. that night, and will be leaving my key under the mat.

Apply It!	**Checklist**
Write out the paragraph below, using italics or underlining to show titles.	Did I check the uses of italics and underlining in this section?

One of the first places I looked in my research strategy was the Canadian Encyclopedia. For more current information, I might check a national newspaper like The Globe and Mail. If I want a little more background, I might read an article or two in Maclean's.

Think About It: In your own words, write a rule for using italics or underlining. Include examples.

Formatting

Formatting Your Final Draft

Your final tasks are to

1. lay out your pages correctly in an appealing way

2. add front matter and back matter

Layout

Layout is the very basic organization of the parts and look of each page. Here are some rules to follow. These rules apply whether you are writing your assignment on a computer or by hand.

Layout Rules

- Use regular (letter)-sized white paper: blank for writing done on word processors and lined if you are writing by hand.
- Leave a 3-cm margin all round any text on the page.
- Leave one line space between each line of writing (double-spaced).
- Indent each paragraph.
- Use one side of the paper only.
- Put a heading in the top right-hand corner of each page (except the first) with your name and page number. Your teacher may want you to include his or her name, the title, and the date, as well.

Cross-Reference

See Titles and Headings, page 135.

Try It!

If you are using a computer, you can put information such as the title, date, your name, and your teacher's name in a "header." The computer will then add that information to the top of every page.

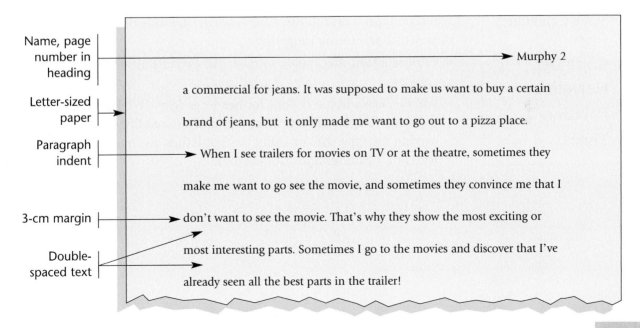

Name, page number in heading

Murphy 2

Letter-sized paper

a commercial for jeans. It was supposed to make us want to buy a certain

brand of jeans, but it only made me want to go out to a pizza place.

Paragraph indent

When I see trailers for movies on TV or at the theatre, sometimes they

make me want to go see the movie, and sometimes they convince me that I

3-cm margin

don't want to see the movie. That's why they show the most exciting or

Double-spaced text

most interesting parts. Sometimes I go to the movies and discover that I've

already seen all the best parts in the trailer!

Apply It!	Checklist
1. Take an assignment from your writing portfolio. Lay out a page of the assignment following the rules you just learned in this section. 2. Give your page to a partner for proofreading. He or she should check that you've followed each layout rule. Make any needed changes your partner points out. Keep the page in your writing portfolio as a personal style guide to help you lay out all your writing assignment pages.	Did I follow all the Layout Rules in my writing presentation? Did I ask someone to check it for me? Did I make suggested changes?

Think About It: Make some notes on how the new page layout is different from the one you used before.

Formatting on the Computer

A computer can help you create a very polished presentation. Most word-processing programs allow you to

- use different styles and sizes of fonts, or typefaces
- create titles and headings with boldface, italics, and underlining
- add visual touches—boxes, lists, visual aids—to help the reader understand information

Explore the different features of your program, but keep these guidelines in mind when it's time to make decisions.

Fonts

Fonts are typefaces. You can easily change the style of your fonts in most word-processing programs.

- Choose a font that is easy to read. Times or Palatino are good choices.
- You can use a different font for headings (e.g., Helvetica), and use the same font for all your headings and subheadings. Consider varying the type size, or using bold or italics, to show different levels of headings and subheadings.

> **Some Common Fonts**
>
> Courier
> **Helvetica**
> Palatino
> Times

Type Sizes

> **Some Commonly Used Type Sizes**
>
> 10 point 12 point 14 point 18 point 24 point

Try It!

Make a font and type size style sheet to help you remember what they look like. Keep it in your writing portfolio so you can check it whenever you are making these decisions for a presentation.

- Type size is measured in points. Use 11- or 12-point type for the body of the text. Try a larger type size for headings and subheadings. Set the title in even larger type, but don't go any larger than 24 points.

Titles and Headings

Titles and headings are an important part of the organization and look of your presentation. Here are some tips for making titles and headings useful for your reading audience.

1. If the title is on a separate title page, centre it horizontally (across), and use a larger type size—perhaps 14 or 18 points. See the sample title page on page 139.

2. Here are some ways you can make the various levels of headings and subheadings look different.

- Leave space between the heading and the text that follows (the more space you leave, the more important the heading appears).
- Vary the type sizes (the larger the type size, the more important the heading).
- Capitalize all the letters in important headings and only the first letter of each word in subheadings.
- Use boldface, italics, or underlining.

3. As much as possible, keep the wording of your headings and subheadings similar. For example, if one of your headings is "Preparing the Paints," don't make the next one "Begin to Paint." Instead, it should read "Beginning to Paint."

Format to communicate your ideas clearly.

Boxes, Lists, and Visual Aids

Visual features can help you to communicate ideas clearly to your reader.

Boxes

Putting an outline border around a group of words is a good way to draw attention to them. However, don't use boxes or outlines when you are writing essays. The important points should come clearly from the way you write and structure your arguments, rather than from the page layout.

As part of a magazine article about dogs used in police work, this information appeared in a box:

Further Information

For more information on canine policing, visit Sergeant Fackrell's Web site or that of Toronto Police Services.

- http://webhome.idirect.com/~herc/
- www.torontopolice.on.ca

Lists

A list is a series of connected or related items. Here are some guidelines to follow.

1. Use a colon or a period in the sentence or sentence part before the list, but try to use the same punctuation each time.

2. If each item in the list is a sentence fragment or a single word, you may begin each item with a lowercase letter. If the listed items are complete sentences, begin them with capital letters.

3. Use the same end punctuation throughout your list. Some acceptable ways include the following:

   - End each item with a period (especially if the item is a full sentence).

   - Put no punctuation at the end of each item.

   - Use semicolons or commas at the end of list items. However, for the second-to-last item, follow the semicolon or comma with the word *and* or *or*. At the end of the last item, use a period.
     Three of the most popular activities are
     – walking,
     – running, and
     – swimming.

4. Use numbers for items that need to be presented in a certain order (for example, a set of instructions such as a recipe). For other types of lists, you can use markers such as bullets (•) or letters (a, b, c).
   When studying English, you need to master

   - reading
   - writing
   - speaking
   - listening

Visual Aids

Visuals aids such as illustrations, figures, and tables can be a big help when writing reports. They communicate ideas and information simply and clearly. Here are some examples.

Figures

Figures include maps, graphs, illustrations, tables, and diagrams.

Graphs

A graph is a type of figure. Graphs are useful when you need to present numerical information in a way that is easy for the reader and viewer to understand. Some common graphs are circle (or pie) graphs, line graphs, and bar graphs.

Cross-Reference

See Visual Aids, pages 30 to 32 and pages 238 to 240.

Apply It!

1. Choose a format (box, list, or other visual aid) to present each of the following sets of information:

   a) To make this dish, you need chicken pieces, curry powder, a frying pan, and butter.

   b) Chicken Curry Dish

   Heat butter in a large frying pan. Mix in curry powder and cook. Add chicken and stir.

2. Format the text below with attention to fonts, type size, title, and subheadings.

Checklist

✔ Did I choose appropriate formats of visual aids?

✔ Did I follow the rules of the formats I chose?

✔ Did I use no more than two fonts?

✔ Did I keep the type sizes consistent?

✔ Did I clearly show the differences between title and subheadings?

Advertising

We are surrounded by advertising everywhere we go, almost every minute of the day. It assaults our senses so constantly that it's a wonder any of us pay any attention to it at all. Yet it is a booming business, involving billions of dollars. Companies have to be ready to make use of every medium they can, and strive for creativity at every step. As the potential consumers, we are bombarded with advertising from a variety of sources.

TV**How many different commercials did you watch last night? How many products do you remember? If you had any idea how much each commercial cost, you would be astounded. And how effective are they?**

Radio Many of us listen to the radio but don't really hear the advertising. Sometimes a particular jingle will stay with us. But, when that happens, it's usually so annoying, we vow not to buy the product or service anyway.

BILLBOARDS

Think About It: Note two or three ways that proper formatting helps the reader.

Adding Front and Back Matter

Not every type of writing you do will need front and back matter. For example, a short story will likely not need back matter. Check with your teacher about what to include.

Front Matter

Title Page

For a short piece of writing, you can put your title at the top of the first page. For most longer pieces, add a separate title page. Check with your teacher to see which is required.

Guidelines for a Good Title Page

- Capitalize all the important words in a title. Usually, you don't have to capitalize smaller words such as *a*, *the*, *to*, *for*, or *in* unless they are the first word in the title.

- Don't put a period at the end of the title.

- Don't underline the title. However, you may want to use boldface type in a larger point size if you are writing on a computer.

Here are three examples of how to present your title.

Sample 1: Title for a short essay

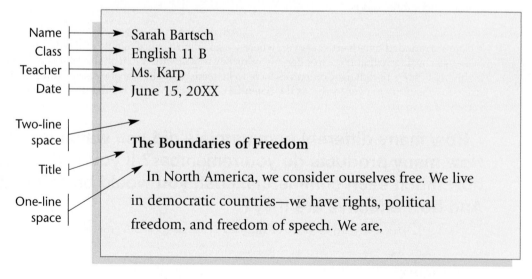

Name	Sarah Bartsch
Class	English 11 B
Teacher	Ms. Karp
Date	June 15, 20XX

Two-line space

The Boundaries of Freedom

Title

One-line space

    In North America, we consider ourselves free. We live in democratic countries—we have rights, political freedom, and freedom of speech. We are,

Sample 2: A separate title page for a longer essay or research paper.

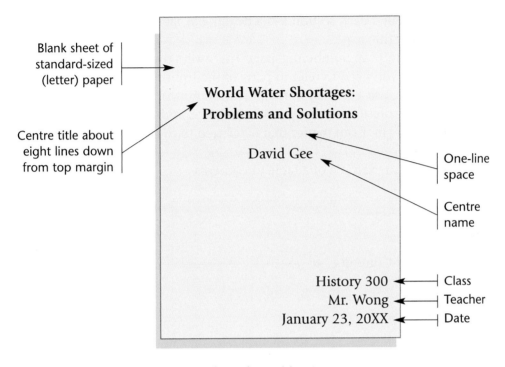

Blank sheet of standard-sized (letter) paper

World Water Shortages: Problems and Solutions

Centre title about eight lines down from top margin

David Gee

One-line space

Centre name

History 300 — Class
Mr. Wong — Teacher
January 23, 20XX — Date

Sample 3: A separate title page for a formal business report

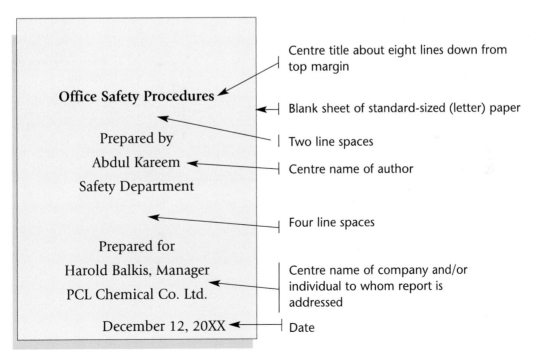

Office Safety Procedures

Centre title about eight lines down from top margin

Blank sheet of standard-sized (letter) paper

Prepared by

Two line spaces

Abdul Kareem

Centre name of author

Safety Department

Four line spaces

Prepared for

Harold Balkis, Manager
PCL Chemical Co. Ltd.

Centre name of company and/or individual to whom report is addressed

December 12, 20XX — Date

Table of Contents

Include a table of contents only if your piece of writing has several sections and each section has a heading. A table of contents goes right after the title page.

In your page numbering, page 1 is always the first page of the text itself. If you need to refer to parts of the front matter in your table of contents, use a Roman numeral (for example i, ii, iii, iv, and so on).

Never place a number on the title page, and only use Roman numerals on front matter that is referred to in the table of contents.

Here is an example of a table of contents.

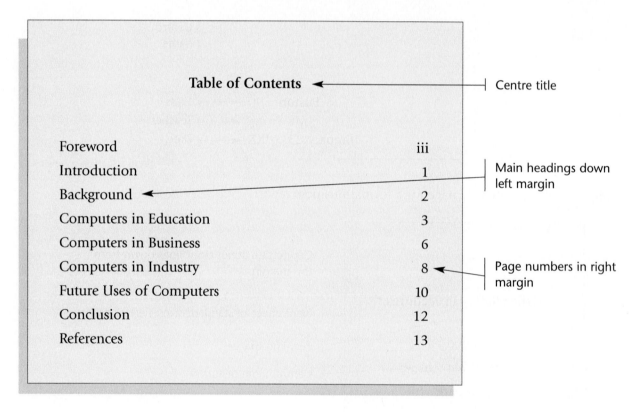

Table of Contents ← Centre title

Foreword	iii
Introduction	1
Background	2
Computers in Education	3
Computers in Business	6
Computers in Industry	8
Future Uses of Computers	10
Conclusion	12
References	13

Main headings down left margin

Page numbers in right margin

Apply It!	Checklist

Apply It!

1. Select the most appropriate title-page format (if you think a title page is needed) to show your report title ("The Effects of Housing Developments on Local Wildlife"), your name, class (Environmental Studies 11), teacher (Mr. Manjit), and date, using the best layout, fonts, and type sizes.

2. Look through your favourite magazines to find an article that has a title and several subheadings. Make a table of contents for the article following the format in the sample.

Checklist

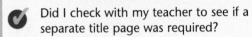 Did I check with my teacher to see if a separate title page was required?

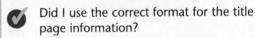 Did I use the correct format for the title page information?

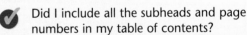 Did I include all the subheads and page numbers in my table of contents?

Think About It: What are three things you have learned about adding front matter?

Back Matter

Works Cited List and/or Bibliography

If you have used any outside sources in researching and preparing your essay, it is very important that you acknowledge, or credit, them in the text of your writing assignment and in a list at the end of the paper. This list is called a bibliography. The proper formats for works-cited lists and bibliographies are covered in Chapter 7.

Cross-Reference

See Giving Proper Credit to Sources, pages 177 to 182.

Appendices

Appendices contain information that is either too detailed or too long to include in the body of your paper, such as

– supporting documents

– long tables

– other background information

If you include appendices at the back of your report, follow these rules:

• Create a page for a table of contents. Give it the heading "Appendices."

• Label the first appendix "Appendix A," the second "Appendix B," and so on. Include a descriptive title, if you want (e.g., Appendix A: Survey Results).

• In your report, refer to each appendix title where it belongs.

• List each appendix in your table of contents.

APPENDICES
Table of Contents

Appendix A: Survey Results   12

Appendix B: Map of Canada   14

Appendix C: Provinces and Territories   16

Formatting Checklist

Before handing in any piece of writing, check to make sure you've done the following.

Have I:

- Printed my work on clean white paper?
- Double-spaced between each line?
- Left a 3-cm margin all round?
- Included a title, either at the top of the first page or on a separate title page?
- Included a header at the top of each page after the first page?
- Numbered each page of text?
- Made sure that all the elements of the work are in place, including (if required) a table of contents, a list of references or a bibliography, and any appendices if they are needed?
- Used the same format for all headings and lists within my writing assignment?
- Made sure I have followed all the appropriate rules, guidelines, and tips mentioned in this chapter?

CHAPTER 6

Writing Essays

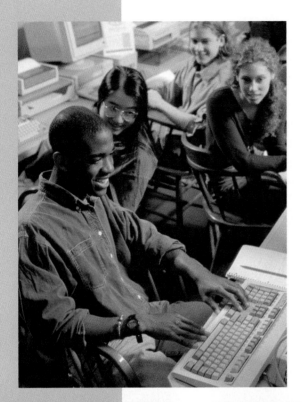

Many students think that essays are difficult to write. However, an essay is really just a series of paragraphs. Each paragraph logically develops a topic and expresses your viewpoint on that topic. Whenever you introduce a new idea, you start a new paragraph. Writing an essay gives you an opportunity to express your insights and opinions on a topic.

Writing essays develops your writing skills and your ability to present your own ideas and arguments. This chapter will show you the rules of writing effective essays and provide you with three essay models: literary, persuasive, and research essays.

As you read the chapter and apply skills, ask yourself: How can I use the information in this chapter to develop my essay-writing skills?

Contents

Applying the Writing Process   144

The Three Parts of an Essay   145

Structuring Your Essay   149

Model Essays   150

Learning Goals

- know and apply the writing process when writing an essay
- understand the parts of an essay
- analyze different forms of essays, including literary, persuasive, and research essays
- write an essay

Applying the Writing Process

Stage	Activity	Tips and Techniques	Where to Look
Prewriting	Find and limit your topic.	Limit your topic so that your essay won't be too long.	• Find and Limit Your Topic, page 56
	Define your purpose and audience.	The keywords in this chapter will help you clarify the purpose of your essay.	• Define Your Purpose and Your Audience, page 57 • Keywords in Essay Topics, page 149
	Gather your thoughts.	Except in the case of a research essay, essays generally are based on your ideas.	• Model Essay #1: Literary Essay, page 150 • Model Essay #2: Persuasive Essay, page 154
Drafting	Organize your ideas.	For longer essays, use an outline or tree diagram.	• Prepare an Outline, page 60 • Tree Diagram, page 147
	Write a draft.	Include a thesis statement in your introduction and ensure that each paragraph relates to it.	• The Three Parts of an Essay, page 145 • Creating Reader Expectation, page 145
Revising	Revise for organization, content, and focus.		• Revising, pages 66 to 68
Editing	Edit paragraphs, sentences, and words.		• Editing, pages 69 to 74
Presenting	Proofread for spelling, punctuation, and grammar.		• Presenting Written Work, pages 113 to 132
	Format the final draft.	Depending on the essay type, add elements such as a title page, table of contents, and appendices.	• Formatting, pages 133 to 137 • Adding Front and Back Matter, pages 138 to 142

The Three Parts of an Essay

The Introduction

The introduction of an essay has two main goals:

1. to generate interest

2. to tell the reader what to expect

Generating Interest

To create interest, your introduction must catch the reader's attention. Try starting your essay with one of the following approaches:

- an anecdote
- a shocking statistic
- a question
- a challenge
- one person's experience
- a quotation
- a joke
- a description

Creating Reader Expectation

Every essay has a thesis. A *thesis* is just another word for a main idea or argument. The first paragraph (or sometimes the first two) describes your thesis. It introduces your topic in general terms. Somewhere in your introduction, you must also include a clear statement of your position. This is your *thesis statement*. Most often, it is the last sentence in your introduction. Everything you write in your essay should relate back to it.

Here are some points to remember when you write a thesis statement.

- Avoid facts or statistics. The sentence "Toronto Blue Jay Carlos Delgado makes over $17 million a year" is not a good thesis statement because it's a fact—it cannot be argued. A better thesis statement would be "The salaries paid to sports figures are way too high." Then you can go on to justify your argument with facts.

- Don't make broad generalizations. They are hard to defend. The broader the statement, the harder it is to support it. If you say "Cloning is wrong," you must cover *all* aspects of cloning. There *may* be times when cloning is useful. Be more specific about when you believe cloning is wrong.

  Here are some effective thesis statements for an essay on cloning.

- Cloning opens brand new frontiers in biotechnology. (Essay will argue that cloning is good.)

> **Try It!**
>
> Before you begin writing an essay, write a sentence expressing your purpose, audience, and thesis. Keep this statement posted on your computer or by your desk so you can refer to it when you are writing.

Immoral? Dolly, the first cloned mammal.

- Cloning technology raises ethical issues that must be resolved now. (Essay will examine three issues.)
- Cloning of human embryos is immoral and must be made illegal. (Essay will argue that human cloning should be stopped.)

Notice that each of these statements presents a position and provides a purpose for the essay.

Here is a sample introduction to an essay about cloning, with the thesis statement at the end.

In October 1993, a scientist announced that he had completed an unusual experiment. Dr. Jerry Hall had cloned 17 human embryos into 48. Essentially, he had created multiple human beings that were exactly alike. Though this experiment was undoubtedly significant, it also had horrifying implications. When we examine the implications of cloning, we will see that it should be made illegal.

Apply It!

1. Choose one of the following topics. Write at least two thesis sentences for the topic. Each statement should express a different position.

   - daycare
   - capital punishment
   - medical testing on animals
   - video games

2. After you have written your thesis statements, choose one and write an introduction to an essay.

Checklist

✓ Did I write two clear thesis statements for the topic?

✓ Did I choose one thesis statement on which to base an introduction?

✓ Did I write an introduction that will capture the reader's interest?

✓ Did I introduce my topic clearly?

✓ Did I present my position clearly?

Think About It: Look carefully at each point on the checklist and think about your introduction and thesis. Did you apply what you have learned? What would you change to improve them?

The Body

Have you ever argued with a friend? You might hear yourself saying, "First of all," "Second," or "Finally." You are making a series of logical points that support your thesis. This logical approach is the basic structure of an essay. Once you have introduced your thesis, you can then present a point-by-point explanation in the body. Each idea, or point, is presented in its own paragraph. In a long essay, it could take many paragraphs to explain each of your supporting points.

A "tree diagram" lets you see the logical development of your argument.

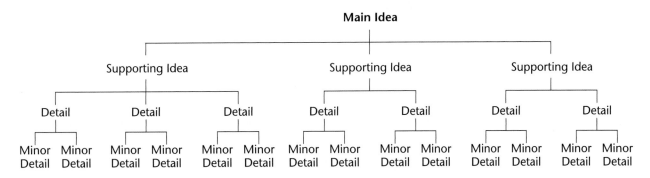

A tree diagram lets you see if you have developed your argument effectively, point by point. In some types of essays, you may want to place the most important idea first. In other cases, it may come last. It depends on your purpose for writing. By creating an outline, you can clearly see how you have ordered the different points and decide if this is the best order for your purpose.

Here is a sample outline for the body of the cloning essay and the topic it covers.

Thesis statement: When we examine the implications of cloning, we will see that it should be made illegal.

1. Cloning gives humans the ability to play God and to decide what shape humanity takes.

2. Clones might be seen as less than human and they could be exploited.

3. Cloning creates the possibility for a trade in human beings.

Cross-Reference

See Prepare an Outline, page 60.

Apply It!

Write down three points that support the thesis that you created earlier for the introduction. Use these points, along with the thesis statement, to create an outline or tree diagram for your essay.

Checklist

✓ Do my supporting points refer directly to my thesis statement?

✓ Do the supporting points support my thesis?

✓ Have I placed my supporting points in a logical order?

Think About It: How did using an outline or tree diagram help you organize your points? Was it an effective tool? Why or why not? What would you do differently the next time?

The Conclusion

The conclusion for your essay should be one or two paragraphs long. It should restate your main points and show once again how they support your thesis. This is not the time to introduce new facts, ideas, or arguments!

Here are some ideas to help you write an effective conclusion to your essay. Start by asking yourself what you want your readers to take away with them. Do you want them to share in your conclusions? Do you want them to take some kind of action? Try some of the following:

- Show how all your main ideas point to your thesis.
- Refer to a story or anecdote you mentioned in the introduction.
- Suggest a solution.
- Look to the future.
- Anticipate (and counter) any negative reactions to your ideas.
- Ask your readers to take some kind of action.

Here is the conclusion for the essay on cloning.

Would clones be "real people"?

> The possibility of producing a human clone is no longer science fiction. This new reality raises moral issues that need to be weighed carefully. Cloning lets us create a human being that could function as a "drone" or a source of "spare parts." Do we want to harvest the organs and limbs of some people to help others? Should other people get to be "perfect"? Are we willing to risk this becoming a reality? The answer should be a firm "no." Let's make cloning illegal before it is too late.

Apply It!

Write the conclusion for the essay that you have been developing over the past two sections. Avoid using the same wording in both your introduction and conclusion. Although they should say essentially the same thing, try to word your conclusion differently.

Checklist

 Does my conclusion show how the points in my essay body support my thesis?

 Have I provided the reader with something to think about?

 Have I brought my topic to a close?

Think About It: Which of the ideas suggested for writing an effective conclusion did you try? How did the example help you write your own conclusion? How will you approach it differently the next time?

Structuring Your Essay

The purpose of your essay is often dictated by the topic assigned. The order in which you present your ideas usually depends on the purpose of your essay. The assigned topic may also contain certain keywords. Look for these because they will help you approach the topic.

Keywords in Essay Topics

Analyze	Break down an issue into parts and show how the parts relate to one another.
Argue	Make a statement or express an opinion and support it with evidence.
Contrast	Bring out the points of difference.
Compare	Bring out the points of similarity and difference.
Criticize	Approve or disapprove of an opinion, and support your reasons with evidence.
Debate	Consider, discuss, or argue the affirmative or negative sides of a proposition.
Define	Explain the meaning of a word or concept.
Describe	Give an account of; tell about; give a word picture of the topic.
Discuss	Examine and analyze, and offer reasons pro and con.
Evaluate	Display the advantages and disadvantages of the statement with evidence.
Explain	Make the meaning of a topic clear; tell how to do something.
Review	Give an explanatory or critical account of a book, movie, and so on.

Read newspaper articles for examples of professional writing.

Model Essays

The following essays differ according to each writer's purpose. When you receive your assignment, turn to these samples and model your writing after the essay that is closest to the type you have to write.

Model Essay #1: Literary Essay (Using Comparison and Contrast Method of Development)

Essay Question: In *Fish House Secrets*, Kathy Stinson uses two main characters to tell the story. Compare and contrast Chad and Jill as characters and decide whether they are more similar or different.

A literary essay examines different elements of a literary work in a serious way. You are looking at the construction and meaning of a piece of literature. The elements you need to look at closely are

- plot
- theme
- tone
- style
- subtext
- character development

How you will study these elements (one or more of them) will depend on the wording of the essay question. In our example, the keywords in the assignment are *compare and contrast*.

The compare and contrast essay can be challenging to write. Going back and forth between the two things that are being compared is sometimes confusing for both the writer and the reader. There are two strategies that will help you deal with this difficulty.

- **The Block Method:** Deals separately with the two objects of comparison. In our example, you would deal with one character first and then the other character.

- **The Point-by-Point Method:** The elements of the two objects of comparison are treated at the same time, point by point. In our example, you compare and contrast the two characters (Chad and Jill) and what each represents.

Here are some other guidelines that will help you write this type of essay.

- Decide on your emphasis. Is your teacher asking you to compare one book that you have been studying in class with another that you have also been studying? If so, you want to emphasize both books. Or are you comparing one familiar work with another that is unfamiliar? In that case, you are probably meant to use the second work to find out more about the first.

- Compare similar things. For example, don't compare a theme with a character.
- Start with common ground (compare), and then show the differences (contrast).
- Create a chart to help you define the similarities and differences of the subjects you are comparing.

	Similarities	Differences
First point of comparison	Main characters	• Chad comes from a well-off home. • Jill comes from a poor home.
Second point of comparison	Both struggle with their fathers.	• Chad's father is overprotective. • Jill's father is a gambler.
Third point of comparison	Both are artists.	• Chad wants to be a painter. • Jill wants to be a dancer.

Jill dreams of being a dancer.

Chad dreams of being a painter.

The following is a sample literary essay responding to our question. When you read it, think about whether the writer is using a block or point-by-point structure.

Mr. Ponto

English 11B

January 12, 20XX

A Comparison of Characters in *Fish House Secrets*

Fish House Secrets by Kathy Stinson is a story told by two teenagers: a runaway girl from Halifax and a boy from Toronto. On the surface these characters seem quite different. However, on closer examination, these characters share many important personal qualities. Chad and Jill are actually more alike than different.

The story opens as Jill has just run away from home and Chad has just arrived with his father at Dutchman's Bay, Nova Scotia. While Chad comes from a well-off home, his life has been marked by tragedy. The previous fall, his mother died in a car accident en route to pick him up from a football game. By contrast, Jill's parents are both alive, but her family is poor. Her father gambles and her mother waitresses to support the family. When Jill spots Chad walking on the beach with his father, she thinks: "Must be nice to have a father like that" (Stinson 22).

Yet beneath the surface, Chad and Jill are struggling with the same issue. They are trying to find a new way to relate to their parents—not as children, but as adults. Chad wishes his father would not be so meddlesome and overprotective: "I'm fifteen years old. I don't need to be taken care of" (Stinson 10). Jill wishes her mother would recognize how her husband is hurting the family and leave him: "I don't know why Ma doesn't just dump him, but she says marriage is forever, for better or worse. Well, worse is sure what things have got" (Stinson 26).

When Chad and Jill meet, they seem to be a study in contrasts. Kathy Stinson places the fair-haired Chad at the top of a ladder, looking down at Jill. She places the dark-haired Jill at the base of the ladder looking up at Chad. Symbolically, there is one rung missing from the ladder, making it difficult for either teen to approach the other.

On the beach one day, Jill seems more spontaneous than Chad. She dances on the sand and goes swimming. Chad can only watch. However, it is in this setting that Kathy Stinson reveals the biggest similarity between Chad and Jill—they are both artists. Chad realizes this when he watches Jill dance:

> It's a fabulous thing what she's doing, like she's forgotten where she is, like there's some force inside her giving energy to her movement. The way it used to feel for me when my painting was going well. Seagull on air. Air on water. Water on rock. The music of the sea filling my head, like it's filling hers now (Stinson 75).

During this scene on the beach, Jill reveals to Chad that her father stole the money her mother had put aside for her dance lessons. Similarly, Chad believes his father disapproves of his painting. In some way, both characters view their fathers as standing in the way of their dreams. By the end of the novel, both characters realize that they need to resolve this issue.

Chad and Jill may be different superficially, but Kathy Stinson reveals that they are alike in many important ways—struggling with being a teenager, struggling to understand their fathers, and longing for the life of an artist.

Works Cited

Stinson, Kathy. *Fish House Secrets*. Saskatoon: Thistledown, 1992.

Apply It!

After reading the literary essay, work with a partner.

1. Identify the thesis statement of this literary essay.

2. Discuss how effective the writer was in proving the thesis. Was the comparison and contrast method an effective way to prove the thesis? Why or why not?

3. Rate the effectiveness of the conclusion on a scale of 1 to 5, defining the levels as you choose. Identify any weaknesses you see in the conclusion.

Checklist

Did the literary essay

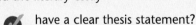 have a clear thesis statement?

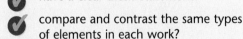 compare and contrast the same types of elements in each work?

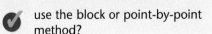 use the block or point-by-point method?

prove the thesis in the essay body and then restate it in the conclusion?

Think About It: How do you think that reading a literary essay and discussing elements of it will help you understand how to write effective essays? What did you find most helpful?

Model Essay #2: Persuasive Essay

Essay Question: Write an essay arguing for or against this statement: People need to take responsibility for their own safety during extreme weather conditions.

The keyword here is *argue*. When you argue for or against something, you are trying to persuade readers to agree with your position, to change their opinion, or to motivate them to do something. Your opinion is right up front.

Your success will depend on how well you support your opinion. The more solid facts you can present, the stronger your argument will be. Pay particular attention to your readers and what is likely to convince *them*. Don't be afraid to include opposing arguments. If you are able to counter them effectively, they will strengthen your case.

Make sure your arguments are

- clear
- logical
- well supported
- free of exaggeration

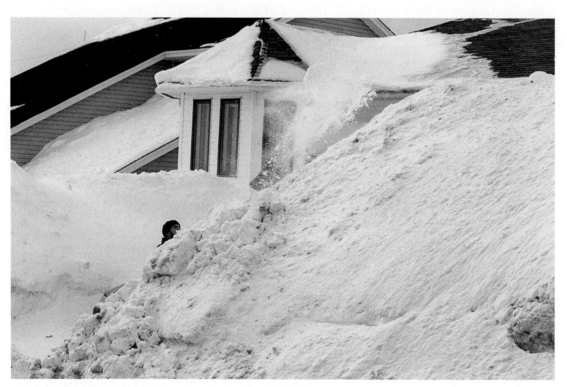

Newfoundland had record amounts of snow in early 2001.

Ms. Tamara
English 11D
January 30, 2001

Hey People, It's Snowing Out There!

The snow has been falling in Newfoundland for months. However, the snow itself is not the biggest problem. A more serious issue is the danger the snow presents. Failing to understand this danger can result in accidents, which could be avoided.

Cars are skidding along the roads, posing a threat to pedestrians. There are snow banks everywhere, and they extend almost as far into the street as they do into the sky. They obscure the vision of pedestrians and drivers, and they make edging out from a driveway a nerve-wracking experience.

For walkers, the situation is even worse. With each snowfall, the streets become narrower. In many places around St. John's, pedestrians have no sidewalks and nowhere to go when cars push them to the side—short of diving into a snow bank.

Many kids are also behaving in a reckless manner. They are trying out their snowboarding moves on homemade ramps and jumps, and many injuries are occurring as a result.

Children are not the only people who are taking unnecessary risks. The Heart and Stroke Foundation is also warning the adults to be careful when they shovel snow. They say that the cold weather combined with the strain of shovelling can raise blood pressure and increase the risk of heart attack and stroke.

As a result of these problems, everyone should slow down and stay alert. Drivers have to reduce their speed and give people space, while pedestrians have to keep a watchful eye out for cars. The walkers can help themselves by buying a lightweight reflective vest, similar to those worn by city workers. The kids have to play in safe areas and save the fancy snowboarding moves for another time. The adults have to ask themselves if they are truly fit enough to shovel all that snow.

With all this snow, it stands to reason that people cannot operate as they usually do. Everyone needs to take responsibility and think about the consequences of their actions.

Apply It!	Checklist
1. In groups of four, read "Hey People, It's Snowing Out There!" Identify: • the thesis statement • each supporting argument • the conclusion Discuss whether you were persuaded by the arguments in the essay. 2. As a group • identify an opposing argument • write a clear thesis statement from this argument • create an outline for the body of the essay (three paragraphs) • write the introduction and the three paragraphs of the body (one per group member) • do any needed research to find facts to support the arguments • bring together your finished paragraphs and revise and edit them • together, write an effective conclusion	✓ Did we identify the main parts of the sample essay? When we worked together to write the essay: ✓ Did we clearly identify each person's responsibility before starting? ✓ Did we include a clear thesis statement that opposed the sample essay? ✓ Did we write an introduction that grabbed the readers' attention? ✓ Did we combine our written pieces to make a good essay? ✓ Did we use facts to back up our arguments? ✓ Did we write a strong conclusion?

Think About It: What worked well about writing an essay in a group? What did not work well? How could the process have been improved? How would you change the essay if you were writing it by yourself?

Model Essay #3: Research Essay

Essay Question: In an essay, research the cultural reasons behind foot-binding in China.

In a research essay, most of your information is drawn from other sources. You contribute facts and ideas, you interpret them, and you organize them. In other words, you are using other people's ideas and information to support your own conclusions. How you present the information and how well you support your conclusions will distinguish a well-written research essay from a simple factual report.

Cross-Reference

For more on researching, see Chapter 7.

Writing a research essay involves the same process as any other writing project, with a few additions.

Here is an overview of how to write a research essay.

Stage	Activity	Tips and Techniques	Where to Look
Prewriting	Find and limit your topic.	Prepare a bibliography to focus your topic.	• Narrowing Down Research Resources, pages 170 to 171
	Define your purpose and audience.	Be clear about why you are writing and for whom you are writing.	• Define Your Purpose and Your Audience, page 57
	Gather your thoughts.	Write down everything you know about the topic, then write down questions you have. Use your questions to guide your research.	• Using Questions to Focus Research, page 172
		Answer the questions by reading and taking notes on the sources listed in your bibliography. To avoid plagiarism, record what was said, who said it, and where. Add new questions, and answer them as you research the topic.	• Taking Notes on Cards, page 174 • How to Avoid Plagiarism, pages 181 to 182
Drafting	Organize your ideas.	Make an outline or tree diagram based on your questions. Include only information that is relevant to your topic. Let the outline reflect your opinion on the topic.	• Organize Your Thoughts, page 59 • Tree Diagram, page 147
	Write a first draft.	As you write, avoid presenting other people's words or ideas as your own. Always include citations to indicate where you got your information.	• How to Avoid Plagiarism, pages 181 to 182 • Giving Proper Credit to Sources, pages 177 to 182
Revising	Revise for focus, content, and structure.		• Revising, pages 66 to 68
Editing	Edit paragraphs, sentences, and words.	Do not change the words in a direct quotation.	• Editing, pages 69 to 74 • Quotations in Essays, page 130
Presenting	Proofread and format the final draft.	Make sure you have acknowledged all your sources correctly.	• Giving Proper Credit to Sources, pages 177 to 182
	Present your research essay.	Choose any necessary visual aids you may want to include.	• Visual Aids, pages 30 to 32 and 238 to 240
		Add any elements that apply to your essay (e.g., title page, Table of Contents, and so on).	• Front and Back Matter, pages 138 to 142

The cartoon below illustrates a crucial step that you should not miss when writing a research essay. What is it?

Now, let's look closely at the sample essay.

Mr. Robbs

Social Studies 11A

March 13, 20XX

Foot-Binding: A Means of Control

"Cool!" "Neat!" "Beautiful!" Several women exclaimed enthusiastically at the newly opened shoe museum the other day. The object of such high praises was the Golden Lotus—a *three-inch* pair of shoes that was worn by Chinese women for hundreds of years. By binding their feet tightly from an early age, women shaped their feet to fit the Golden Lotus. If the women at the museum had known the history of foot-binding, they would have been less enthusiastic. This long, painful, and crippling process was a means of controlling the actions and movement of Chinese women.

Foot-binding started around 920 A.D. when Emperor Li Yu ordered his favourite concubine "to bind her feet with silk bands and dance on a golden lotus platform encrusted with pearls and gems" (Davin 28). This led other women of the royal court to bind their feet thinking them to be dainty, elegant, and favoured by the emperor. As in most societies, the practices of the elite were soon mimicked by the society.

As the practice spread, bound feet became a necessity if a woman hoped to marry well. Even if these hopes failed, bound feet were a symbol of status and beauty. For example, the Hans did not want their women to be mistaken for the Hakka women who did not bind their feet because they toiled in the fields (Davin 28). As well, in Chinese culture, chastity was held in extremely high regard. Since a woman's feet were bound, her movements were limited and she could never stray far from the family nor "stray after marriage" (Jaschok 97).

Many young girls waited fearfully to have their feet bound. One girl related: "At the age of seven, I began binding. I had witnessed the pain of my cousins, and … was … very much frightened" (Levy 225). After she had her feet bound, she experienced extreme pain, swelling, and deterioration of the flesh. She described it as follows:

> Relatives and friends praised them, little realizing the cisterns of tears and
> blood which they had caused. My husband was delighted with them…. I
> envy the modern woman…. The lot of the natural-footed woman and
> mine is like that of heaven and hell (Levy 226).

Today, many of the elderly Chinese women who had their feet bound still need to be carried because they have lost their ability to walk. Foot-binding continues to control these women. This is certainly not "cool," "neat," or "beautiful."

Works Cited

Choi, Evelyn. "Women Hobbled." *Cultural Review* February 2000: 40+.

Davin, Delia. "The Custom of the Country." *Times Literary Supplement* 24 April 1992: 28.

Goody, Jack. *The Oriental, the Ancient, and the Primitive*. Cambridge: Cambridge University Press, 1990.

Jaschok, Maria. *Concubines and Bondservants*. London: Oxford University Press, 1988.

Levy, Howard L. *Chinese Footbinding: The History of a Curious Erotic Custom*. New York: Walton Books, 1966.

Apply It!

Choose one of the following topics to write an essay. Decide which type of essay would best suit the topic.

1. Compare and contrast two characters or themes from a piece of literature that you have read.

2. Compare and contrast two literary works that you have studied.

3. Argue for or against advertising in schools.

4. Analyze the effects of the Internet on society.

5. Discuss the causes of the depletion of the ozone layer.

Now follow the writing process as outlined on page 144 and on page 157. You may work on your own or with a partner to revise and edit your essay. (Note: You may choose a topic of your choice. Consult with your teacher before you start to write.)

Checklist

- ✓ Did I write an introduction with a clear thesis statement?
- ✓ Did I use one paragraph for each of my ideas?
- ✓ Did I relate each paragraph back to the thesis?
- ✓ Did I use facts to support my arguments?
- ✓ Did I properly acknowledge sources when necessary in my research essay?
- ✓ Did I end my essay with something for readers to think about?

Think About It: How did you decide which kind of essay to write? What steps did you take before you started writing? How did this help you write your essay? What will you do differently in your next essay?

CHAPTER 7

Researching

You've just been assigned a challenging research task and you don't know where to start. What are you going to do? The first step is to form a good research plan, because that's really what good researching is—making and following an effective plan.

Researching is important in many of your school subjects, and it is a valuable skill in many careers. This chapter provides an overview of the research process and explains some of the time-saving strategies that are key to good researching.

Contents

Making a Research Plan 162

Using the Library 163

Using Questions to Focus Research 172

Giving Proper Credit to Sources 177

Learning Goals

- make a research plan to collect needed information within a schedule
- find quickly and use resources that provide the best information
- form good research questions to guide and focus the information search
- decide from a number of resources which ones provide the most useful and reliable information
- take helpful research notes
- organize research information from a number of sources clearly
- give honest, complete, and accurate credit to all information sources

Making a Research Plan

A research plan will put YOU in control. The student who made the research plan below had a final deadline of February 21 to complete her research. She identified the important tasks and then gave herself completion dates for these tasks so she could meet her February 21 deadline. She had trouble finding a book she needed, so she was late making her February 9 "mini-deadline." She made notes in the "Comments" section on how she might make up the time.

Research Tasks	Planned Completion Date	Actual Completion Date	Comments
Assignment received	February 2		
Locate and collect information in the library	February 9	February 11	Could not get book right away. Must plan for reading time.
Choose the best sources of information	February 12		
Take notes	February 14		
Organize information	February 16		
Acknowledge all sources used	February 18		
Due date	February 21		

Apply It!

1. Follow the format in the chart above to create your own schedule for a research assignment. Work backward from the due date to set reasonable "mini-deadlines" for each task. Try to figure out what each task involves so that your mini-deadlines will be more realistic.

2. Use the research plan and schedule for an assignment in one of your school subjects.

Checklist

✓ Did I list all the important tasks in my research process?

✓ Did I start backward from my due date and set reasonable "mini-deadlines" for each task?

✓ Did I keep track of how well I was meeting my research deadline goals?

✓ Did I make notes in the "Comments" column of how I could make up time so I'd still be able to meet my final deadline?

Think About It: What did you like about using a schedule like this? What worked for you? How could you change this strategy to improve it?

Using the Library

Always begin your research with a trip to the library. Depending on where you live, you might have a school library, a community library and, if you live in or near a bigger city, a research library. Libraries usually have the following valuable resources:

- books
- the Internet
- newspapers
- CD-ROMs
- magazines
- librarians

Your librarian. A valuable resource!

Locating Books

Using a Library Catalogue

Books are a great starting point for any research process. Let's say your assignment is to find biographical information about the Canadian author W.O. Mitchell, who wrote *Who Has Seen the Wind?* How do you find books about W.O. Mitchell's life?

Libraries list all their books in a catalogue, and most of these catalogues are now on computer systems. Having the catalogue entries on computer allows you to search for books in different ways. The main ways to search for a book are by subject, title, or author. You may also be able to search with only a few words in the title (keywords).

Since you want information about W.O. Mitchell, it's probably wise to choose "subject" on the computer search menu. Then enter "Mitchell, W.O." as the subject on which you'd like to find books. However, if you knew the title of a biography on Mitchell, you'd locate that book faster by choosing "title" from the search menu.

Once you've located the catalogue entry, write down the book's title, author, and call number. The call number tells you where to find the book in the library.

W.O. Mitchell. What do the *W* and *O* stand for?

Reference Resources

You might need background information that gives facts about your research topic in fairly short summaries. Where can you find this type of information? Try the reference section—it's usually located in a special area of the library. It contains specialized encyclopedias, manuals, and so on.

Try It!

Your greatest resource in a library is the reference librarian. Reference librarians enjoy answering questions and helping people to find what they need. Ask them for help!

Here is a list of the common kinds of reference books you'll find in a library's reference section.

Types of Reference	Purpose
Dictionaries	• Usually contain information about words. Look for a dictionary of Canadian English. There are also dictionaries of foreign phrases and even slang. • Biographical dictionaries provide brief, factual summaries about people's lives.
General encyclopedias	• A great place to start if you want a short summary on a certain topic.
Yearbooks and almanacs	• Provide up-to-date information on many general topics. • Yearbooks are arranged by subjects and list events that happened in a year. • Almanacs are yearly calendars of different kinds of statistical information.
Atlases	• Contain maps and often many other types of useful, geography-related information.
Books of quotations	• Provide quotations on various topics made by notable people throughout history. The quotations might be organized by topic or by person.

Here is a list of specialized dictionaries, encyclopedias, and handbooks for many subject areas.

1. Science and Technology References

These references can help you to understand important science and technology terms. Many are written for general readers, so they can also help you figure out difficult scientific ideas, sometimes with helpful diagrams, charts, and pictures. Interesting information about scientists and inventors is often provided.

2. Literature, Mythology, and Drama References

A literature reference can help you to find information about a novel, short story, poem, or author. A mythology reference can help you to research myths and mythological characters. A drama reference can answer questions about playwrights, plays, and the history of theatre.

3. History References

These summarize the major periods in history, including the important people and events.

Where can I find information about the Beatles?

4. Music and Art References

These give information on famous composers and artists. Information on modern and historic figures is provided.

Apply It!	Checklist
1. Visit your local library and find at least one reference in each of the four categories listed above. Record the title and call number in your notebook for future reference.	✔ Did I locate a reference book in all four categories?
2. Make a list of the reference resources you would check to find biographical information about W.O. Mitchell. When your list is complete, meet with a partner to compare and discuss your lists. What new ideas did you learn from sharing research ideas with your partner?	✔ Did I record the title and call number for each reference book selected? ✔ Did I compile a list of reference sources for getting biographical information on W.O. Mitchell? ✔ Did I meet with a partner to discuss my list and share ideas?

Think About It: How will you use this knowledge about reference materials? List three reference books you know you will use in the future.

Magazines and Newspapers

Magazine articles and newspapers provide more up-to-date information than can be obtained in most books. In addition, magazine articles and newspapers are the best sources of expert opinion on a topic.

Magazines, and some newspapers, are called periodicals and can be found in the periodicals section of the library. Ask your librarian where the section is located.

The Periodical Shelves

You will find current issues of magazines and newspapers on display or stacked on periodicals shelves. Ask your librarian where back issues are stored. Some may be stored on microfilm, which the librarian can show you how to use.

Periodical Indexes

How do you find articles on your topic? Use a periodical index. This reference tool lists articles by subject, author, and title. For example, if your topic is police dogs, look for "police dogs" in the index.

Periodical index books are usually located in the library's reference section. Some may be available on CD-ROM or on the Internet. Ask your librarian.

Be a top dog researcher.

Apply It!	Checklist
1. Visit your local library and try to locate an article (a) using a printed periodical index; (b) using an online periodical index; (c) using microfilm if it is available at the library. List the advantages and disadvantages of each method. Which method is the quickest? 2. Create a chart to record the periodicals in your library that could help you research any of your school subjects. List the periodical title, range of years for issues stored in your library, whether it is stored on microfilm, and other notes that may be useful for locating the information when you need it.	Did I try two or three strategies to find the information? Did I decide which strategy was quickest? Did I create a chart of helpful periodicals? Did I include the title and information on how each is stored and for how long?

Think About It: Name at least three things you learned about using the periodicals section of the library for research.

Special Library Resources

Many libraries have special resources. Ask the librarian which ones are available at your library. Here are just a few possibilities.

Databases

A database is a collection of information on a particular subject. Libraries might subscribe to different online databases. Some databases give just the title, author, and publication where you can find an article or other information. Other databases give this information and a summary of the article contents, or even the complete article.

Audio-Visual Materials

Most libraries have videos that you can borrow. Some also have compact discs, cassettes, films, and multimedia kits. Sometimes these resources are listed in a separate catalogue; other times they are included in the main library catalogue.

Resources from Other Libraries

If the book you want is not at your branch, it can be ordered from another library. This service is called an *interlibrary loan*. Your book may take a while to arrive, which will affect your research planning schedule, so ask for the book early in your researching process.

Apply It!	Checklist
1. Ask your librarian about any databases to which your library subscribes. Are there any free ones?	✅ Did I ask the librarian to see if there are any databases at the library that will help me find information on my research topic?
2. Check out at least two databases and make notes on what information is available. For example, is just the title of the resource given, a summary, or full text? Make note of any databases that might be useful to you in other research assignments.	✅ Did I make useful notes on the databases I examined?
3. List the types of audio-visual resources available in your library. Place a checkmark beside the ones you would use for research assignments.	✅ Did I check whether there are any audio-visual materials in the library that could be helpful in my research?

Think About It: Make note of skills needed to find information using computer databases and audio-visual equipment. Which skills do you have? Which ones do you need? How could you obtain these skills?

Sources Outside the Library

Don't forget that you can also locate information outside the library. Here are a few resources you should consider when making research choices.

1. Computer Networks

The Internet can link you to all sorts of useful information. The following are some of the ways this technology can help you to collect research information.

• **Electronic mail**

Use e-mail to talk to experts through their computers and ask questions too. For instance, you could write to a local politician to ask his or her opinion on a particular issue or to request information about an issue. Or join an e-mail list and take part in group conversations on a research topic.

• **Information retrieval**

Some information is available to the public in computer files on the Internet. Information in these files could be about businesses, government programs, major court decisions, and so on.

• **Bulletin boards**

If you are searching for information or ideas that are not commonly found in a library, try posting a question on an Internet bulletin board that deals with your research topic. You will almost certainly

Get online.

Try It!

Always look for the best and fastest way to locate information. Sometimes it can take much longer to find something on the Internet than to look it up in a book.

Cross-Reference

See Evaluating Research Information, page 173.

receive several answers. However, be very careful about using information from these sources—this kind of information must always be fact-checked since you don't know the source.

2. People in Your Community

People in your community are an excellent source of first-hand information. Interviews are useful when you are writing newspaper articles and some types of essays.

Establish a plan for your interview:

- Decide whom to interview, and then call the person to set up a time.

- Prepare a list of questions that will invite various responses, not just "yes" or "no."

- Arrive on time and be friendly and courteous. Ask permission to tape the interview.

- Ask questions one at a time. Listen carefully and take brief notes. If a response is interesting or surprising, ask the person to provide more details. If you would like to use a quotation, make sure you write each word exactly. Read the statement back to the person and ask permission to use it as a direct quotation.

- Manage your time carefully. If you have 30 minutes and 10 questions, do not spend 15 minutes on the first two questions. Ask the important questions first.

- Thank the person for his or her time. Follow up with a thank-you letter.

Get it on tape.

- Review your notes. Expand on what you have written while the interview is fresh in your mind. Record your thoughts and impressions. Draw conclusions.

- If you must phone the person to clarify a point, do so as soon as possible. Phone only once.

You will have to check any facts you learn from the person you are interviewing with reliable sources such as good books or articles.

3. Radio and Television

Check viewing guides for television or radio programs on the topic you are researching. Write down all the details (name of the show, name of the producer, date, time, and so on) so you can give proper credit to this media source in any research report or presentation.

4. Government Departments

The federal government has a toll-free number, 1–800–622–6232 (1-800-OCANADA), which you can use to find out about federal programs and services. If the person taking your call does not know the answer, he or she will tell you how to contact someone who does.

For some research you may need statistical information such as data and charts. A good source is Statistics Canada, the government department that collects statistics about Canada and Canadians. Statistics Canada can be reached toll free at 1-800-263-1136 or online at <www.statcan.ca>.

5. Community Agencies

Your local Chamber of Commerce can give you information about your community in areas such as business, tourism, and population. Other local business and public service organizations could also offer information on issues affecting your community. For example, if you are researching food banks, consider interviewing the local food bank director.

Contact your local food bank.

Apply It!	**Checklist**
1. Use the 1-800-622-6232 phone number to obtain information on the Web site for a government program.	✓ Did I locate a government Web site that interests me by calling 1-800-622-6232?
2. Take notes on information available on the Web site. Record the full Web site address. Share with a small group the types of information you found. Explain how the site would be useful for student researchers.	✓ Did I take notes on the Web site and prepare a brief oral report on my findings?
	✓ Did I show how the site would be useful to other researchers?

Think About It: What is the best way for you to find accurate information quickly? Discuss your response with a partner.

Good to the last drop?

Cross-Reference

For more information on clustering, see page 56; for bibliographies, see pages 179 to 180.

Narrowing Down Research Resources

Now you're ready to find the best information on your research topic. As with all stages in the research process, you need a strategy. Let's say your teacher assigns you the following topic: *Research an issue related to making sure community water supplies are safe.*

Strategy for Finding and Choosing Research Information

1. Start by making a cluster around the keyword "water." Clustering will help you identify useful search words that you can use to locate information in your library research.

2. Use the library's computer catalogue to do a general subject search under "water." If too many books are listed under that heading, narrow your subject by using some of the keywords from your cluster. For example, you might try entering "water safety" or "water quality." At this stage, you will want to gather several books related to your topic.

3. Use a list or 7 cm x 13 cm cards (one for each book or resource) to record complete information about the sources you locate. Copy complete information about the resource because you will need to use it later when you make a bibliography for your report or presentation. Record the book's call number for future reference. A completed resource list entry or card is shown here.

de Villiers, Marq   Call No. 333.91 DeV

Water

Toronto: Stoddart, 1999

A resource card.

4. Now locate each resource from the library stacks, using your information. Spend a few minutes carefully reviewing each resource. In your review, decide if the information will be useful in your research. Here are a few tips and questions to help you decide.

   • Check the table of contents, date of publication, and index. Do the table of contents and index include information on your research topic? Does the date of publication tell you the information is up to date?

- Scan sections within the book that look useful and decide which sections you could use.

- Note on your list or cards whether the information is general or detailed, or accompanied by charts, graphs, maps, or other illustrations.

Now you are ready to narrow down your research resources. Review your list, or go through your cards and choose the resources that include the best information that is most related to your topic. You might rank resources from most useful to least useful. Which ones are "must reads" and provide useful information that is closely related to your research topic? Which resources are less useful and might be set aside?

Try It!

Do not throw away any resource cards. They could be useful later if you have to fill in information gaps or check facts.

Apply It!

1. Follow the strategy described in this section for one of your research assignments. Narrow your research resources down to the five best ones. Record complete information about any resource so you can easily find it again if you need to, and you can accurately describe the resource in a bibliography entry.

2. Rank your resource cards or list of resources from most related to your research topic to least related. Explain to a partner why you ranked the resources as you did.

Checklist

- Did I follow each step in the strategy?
- Did I record complete information about all the resources I used in my research?
- Did I rank the resources from most related to least related?

Think About It: How did listing your resources or using cards help you to organize your research task?

Using Questions to Focus Research

"I have the resources. Now what do I do?"

You've got your resources—now how do you pinpoint the information you need within these resources? The solution is to ask good questions about your topic, based on what you already know about it, and what you want to find out.

1. Focusing
Organize your questions in a three-column chart such as the one below.

Topic	What I Know	What I Don't Know
Safety in our community water supply	Our drinking water needs to be tested.	• Who does the testing? • What kinds of tests are done? • How is testing done? • Where is testing done?
	If water isn't tested carefully, problems can appear in the water that can cause people to become ill and even die.	• What problems can develop in drinking water? • How are people affected? • How can the problems be fixed?

2. Focusing Further
You can then further focus your search for information. Create another chart like the one above, except make information from the second column your topic in the first column.

Topic	What I Know	What I Don't Know
Testing our community water	Someone in our town looks after water testing.	What knowledge and training does that person need?

By using this questioning strategy, you can clearly focus on the research information you need.

Apply It!	**Checklist**
1. Create "focusing" and "focusing further" charts for a research topic that interests you, or for a research assignment you are currently working on.	Did I make "focusing" and then "focusing further" charts to guide my research?
2. Exchange your completed charts with a partner. Edit each other's questions to see if you can make them more clearly focused.	Did I form good research questions in my charts?

Think About It: On a scale of one to five, with one being the highest, how would you rate your ability to form good research questions? How could you improve your personal rating?

Evaluating Research Information

You've found information to answer your research questions. Now, how do you decide which resources provide the best information? A crucial step in the researching process is evaluating information. It is especially important now that the Internet is so widely used.

Almost anyone can publish ideas and information on the Internet. For example, on a challenging topic such as community water supply safety, you might find information published recently by a leading world expert, or untrue information published years ago by someone who knows little about the subject. Here are some questions to help you to judge research information.

- **Relevance:** Does the information relate to your research topic and questions?

- **Currency:** Is the information up to date? For print materials, look at the date of publication. For Web sites, look for dates telling when the site was last updated.

- **Accuracy:** Is the information true? The best way to verify accuracy is to check information against facts presented in other sources.

- **Reliability:** Can you trust the supplier of the information? What is the author's education? What other books or articles has he or she written? Make sure the author is an expert in the field. What organization is behind the Web site? What are the organization's objectives?

- **Objectivity:** What is the author's purpose for writing? If someone is trying to sell you a product, he or she will present only the information that will persuade you to buy. Make sure you choose information from authors who present both sides of issues fairly.

Try It!

Always protect your personal privacy when you request information on the Internet.

"Trust me!"

Apply It!	**Checklist**
1. Evaluate the information in one book and one Web site. Summarize your conclusions.	Did I evaluate each resource for relevance, currency, accuracy, reliability, and objectivity?
2. Meet as a class to share your resource evaluations. Compile class members' evaluations in a booklet or database so it becomes a class researching reference.	

Think About It: How can you keep track of resources you know to be reliable and those that aren't? How would this be useful?

Taking Notes

You've found research resources on your topic and carefully evaluated them. Now, how do you record information that you gather from these resources? Here are two note-taking strategies.

Strategy 1: Taking Notes on Cards

This strategy works well if you are using many resources in your research. Two advantages of recording notes on cards are that you can group information into categories to help you see patterns, and you can arrange the cards in different ways. The ability to place cards in different arrangements will help you create a good organizational outline. Here's how to take notes using cards.

1. Read the parts of the resource related to your research topic.

Stewart, John Cary   Pollution

<u>Drinking Water Hazards</u>

Pesticides help us grow things, but
they cause long-term problems that
could affect drinking water.   p. 146

A note-taking card.

2. Write the author's name and the resource title (in a shortened form) in the upper left corner of each card you make.

3. Put one piece of information or quotation on each card. Include the page number where you found the information.

4. Record notes in your own words, rather than just copying information. When you write information in your own words, it makes you think more about what you're reading.

5. If you find a passage that you think would make a good quotation, copy it down exactly, and place quotation marks around the writer's exact words.

6. Leave the top right corner blank. Or, write a few keywords in pencil to remind you how the information relates to one of your research questions.

7. You can also make idea cards as you read. Idea cards can contain your own observations and thoughts about what you've read.

Strategy 2: Taking Notes in Chart Form

If you are using only a few resources in your research, you could set up a chart to collect and organize your notes. In the left column, write headings that come from your research questions. Across the top row, put the title of each resource you are using in your research. Here's the start of a note-taking chart in which three books were used.

	Don't Drink the Water	Good to the Last Drop	Testing the Waters
Problems with drinking water	• bacteria (p. 75) • pesticides (p. 9)	• pollution (p. 109)	• human error (p. 222)
Solutions to drinking water problems	• bottled water (p. 242)	• water purifiers (p. 307)	• standards (p. 512)

Apply It!

Use cards or a chart to take notes from several resources for a research assignment you are working on. If you are not working on one right now, choose a topic that interests you.

Checklist

 Did I choose the best note-taking strategy for the number of resources I am using in my research?

 Did I follow each step in the note-taking strategy I selected?

 Did I record all information completely and accurately?

Think About It: Which note-taking strategy will you use most often? Why?

Organizing Information

To organize your information, spread the cards on a table and group them into categories. Eventually subtopics will become clear. For example, in the sample topic: *Research an issue related to making sure community water supplies are safe*, cards might be clustered in these categories:

- testing for problems
- what the problems are
- how to solve the problems

Within these large groupings of cards, you can start identifying smaller groups. Then it's easy to create an outline like the one below.

Testing the waters.

Topic: Making Sure Community Water Supplies Are Safe

I. Testing to Find Problems in Community Water Supplies
    A. Types of Laboratories
    B. Kinds of Testing
    C. Test Methods
II. Problems That Can Harm a Community's Water Supply
    A. Biological Problems
    B. Chemical Problems
       1. Pesticides
       2. Industry Pollution
III. Solutions to the Problems
    A. Regulations and Penalties
    B. Changing People's Behaviours

Apply It!

A problem-solution format suits the water-supply safety topic. Think of an issue in your school that has problems and solutions, such as bullying, littering, or encouraging school pride. Jot down ideas about the problems and solutions on the topic. Organize your notes into an outline. If you have a computer and word-processing program, use them to create the formatted outline.

Checklist

 Did I look for ways to form both large and small topic groups?

 Did I organize topics in an order that makes sense?

 Did I follow the general outline format in the example provided?

Think About It: What are some pros and cons for you of grouping cards to organize information?

Giving Proper Credit to Sources

It is very important that you give honest and complete credit to any sources you've used for ideas or information. You can acknowledge your sources in three ways:

1. by acknowledging sources within the text of your research report

2. by providing footnotes at the bottom of pages in your report

3. by including a complete bibliography at the end of your report

Note that if you use (1) or (2), you must also acknowledge your sources in a complete bibliography.

Did you remember to credit your sources?

The Style of Your Acknowledgments

There are different ways of correctly acknowledging the research sources you use; for example, there can be differences in the way you organize and punctuate acknowledgments. The style used in these pages follows models given in the *MLA Style Manual*. (MLA stands for the Modern Languages Association.) Another popular style guide is *The Chicago Manual of Style*.

Acknowledging Sources in the Text of Your Research Report

You need to acknowledge your sources in these cases:

- when you are using someone else's idea, including when you are paraphrasing
- when you are quoting someone directly
- when a reader might question the accuracy of the information, such as statistics

You do not need to give an acknowledgment when you are expressing your own ideas or when the information is well known, such as for the dates of famous events.

Acknowledgments for Information in Books

An acknowledgment in the text of your report should include only as much information as the reader needs. He or she can look up the full information in your bibliography at the end of the paper. In the case of most books or articles, the information needed is the author's name and the page number:

> **Try It!**
>
> "Style" involves making language and formatting choices. Ask your teacher which style he or she prefers; for example, the MLA style.

> "Only about 1 percent of the water in the Great Lakes is replaced every year through the natural water cycle" (de Villiers 277).

If you give the author's name in the phrase leading up to the quotation, you don't need to include that information in the brackets; for example:

> According to Marq de Villiers, "Only about 1 percent of the water in the Great Lakes is replaced every year through the natural water cycle" (277).

Acknowledgments for Information on Web Sites

To acknowledge information from a particular part of a Web site, identify the paragraph in which the information appears:

> "We have lodgings for up to 12 dogs at a time in our indoor/outdoor runs" (Fackrell, par. 9).

Ask your teacher which style he or she would like you to use.

Acknowledging Sources Using Footnotes

Footnotes appear at the bottom of your research paper page. You can collect all your footnotes and write them in a numbered list at the end of your paper. This list is called *endnotes*. When signalling a reader about a footnote, the only mark you need to place in the body of the text is a superscript number:

> "Misuse of pesticides by homeowners is also a problem. Many people assume that when applying a pesticide, more is better."[1]

According to the *MLA Style Manual*, this is how a footnote should be set up at the bottom of a page:

> [1]John Cary Stewart, *Drinking Water Hazards* (Hiram: Envirographics, 1990), 153.

Apply It!	Checklist
Practise making in-text citations for text from resources that you are using in a current research assignment.	✓ Did I check with my teacher about the in-text citation style he or she prefers? ✓ Did I include all the necessary information in each in-text citation? ✓ Did I punctuate each in-text citation correctly? ✓ Did I proofread my in-text citations carefully?

Think About It: What do you find most difficult about acknowledging sources? How can you make it easier?

Bibliography and Works Cited

A *bibliography* includes all the reference works you read in your research, whether or not you mention them in your report.

A *list of works cited* includes *just* the resources you mentioned in your research paper.

For both the bibliography and list of works cited, the format and punctuation of entries are the same. The only difference is that in a list of works cited, all entries are double-spaced. Here is a sample entry for a book that could appear in a bibliography or list of works cited.

Crank, F. *Cooking with Bugs: The New Cuisine for Nature Lovers*. Toronto: Anthill Press, 1999.

Guidelines for Bibliography and Works Cited Entries

- Start the first line of each entry at the left margin. If the entry runs more than one line, indent all lines after the first.
- Put the author's LAST name first. Include all of the authors if there is more than one.
- Arrange the list alphabetically by author. For sources with no author, use the title of the book ("The," "An," or "A" don't count).
- Next, include the title, the place of publication, the publisher's name, and the date it was published. You will find all this information on the copyright page of the book.

Here are some sample entries for a bibliography. To make them correct for a list of works you would only need to double-space the entries.

Book with One Author
Aaronson, Sylvia. *A History of Cash Registers*. Toronto: Moneytalks Press, 1995.

Magazine Article
Backhouse, Frances. "To Do and Dare: Women on the Chilkoot Trail." *Beautiful British Columbia* Spring 1998: 18–24.

Newspaper Article
Smiley, Jane. "A Dickensian Life." *The Toronto Star* 24 December 2000: B1.

Web Site
The Early Modern English Dictionaries Database. Ed. Ian Lancashire. April 1996. U of Toronto. 15 October 1999 <http://www.chass.utoronto.ca/english/emed/emedd.html>.

CD-ROM
DISCovering Authors, Canadian Edition. Vers. 1.0. Biographical database. On CD-ROM. IBM. Detroit: Gale Research, 1994.

Movies and Videos
The Big Snit. Dir. Richard Condie. National Film Board of Canada, 1985.

Try It!

Remember, this is the style of the *MLA Style Manual* and other styles can differ. Ask your teacher which style he or she prefers.

Apply It!

Choose a research topic. Find as many of the above resources as possible (book with one author, magazine article, newspaper article, Web site, CD-ROM, movie or video).

Checklist

☑ Did I ask my teacher about his or her preferred style for entries in bibliographies or lists of works?

☑ Did I include all the information? Is the information in the correct format and punctuated correctly?

☑ Did I arrange entries in my bibliography or list of works in alphabetical order by author?

☑ Did I carefully proofread all my entries?

Think About It: Why do you think it is important to credit works cited? If you were a published author, how might you feel about it?

Plagiarism

Plagiarism is using someone else's words or ideas as if they were your own. It is cheating, and it is illegal. Your teacher will give a plagiarized assignment a zero.

How to Avoid Plagiarism

1. Put any direct quotations within quotation marks and acknowledge the source.

2. Reword and rephrase borrowed material (you must still cite the source).

3. Acknowledge a source for any phrases or ideas that are not completely your own.

An example of original source material:

> Many people, concerned about the safety of their water, run out and buy a water filter, attach it to their faucet, and sit back erroneously thinking that their faucet is now free of all possible contamination. An advertisement may list all the tremendous things a new device can do but you may not have the water quality problems they so artistically outline.
>
> —From *Drinking Water Hazards* by John Cary Stewart, page 207.

A plagiarized version:

> A lot of people who are worried about drinking water safety purchase a water filter, hook it up to their tap, and wrongly think their drinking water is completely safe. Many advertisements make claims about great things their water filters can do. However, a person's drinking water may not have the water quality problems they so artistically outline.

If you check the plagiarized version against the original, you will find that much of the last sentence has been copied without giving credit to the correct source.

How could you use the important information in the original version and not plagiarize? There are two main ways to do it. Either place quotations marks around direct quotations, or paraphrase the author's words. With both strategies you must acknowledge the sources of the information.

Avoid plagiarism by using quotation marks:

A lot of people who are worried about drinking water safety purchase a water filter, hook it up to their tap, and wrongly think their drinking water is completely safe. Many advertisements make claims about great things their water filters can do. According to environmental chemist John Cary Stewart, however, a person's drinking water "may not have the water quality problems they so artistically outline" (207).

Avoid plagiarism by paraphrasing (using your own words):

A lot of people who are worried about drinking water safety buy a water filter, hook it up to their tap, and figure their drinking water has been made safe. Many advertisements make claims about great things their water filters can do. However, a person's drinking water may not have the problems the water filter advertisements say they will fix (Stewart 207).

Apply It!

Read the text below. Identify where the plagiarism occurs and fix the problem.

Original Source

While the commonplace teenage stereotype may suggest a high-tech, fashion-and-money obsessed cyber-teen, thousands of young Canadians are going to youth workshops, participating in environmental cleanups, joining music and drama groups, and working hard at school.

—From "Designer Teens" by Ian Haysom, page 4.

Plagiarized Version

A frequent stereotype of teens is that they are high-tech individuals who are fashion and money obsessed. In truth, thousands of young Canadians are going to youth workshops, participating in environmental cleanups, joining music and drama groups, and working hard at school.

Checklist

 Did I use quotation marks for direct quotations?

 Did I paraphrase where possible?

 Did I use in-text citations as necessary, even for paraphrases?

Think About It: Use your own words to write a definition of "plagiarism."

CHAPTER 8

Business and Technical Writing

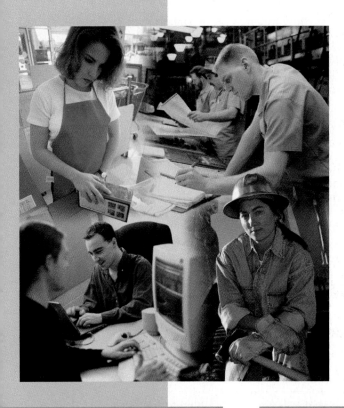

At some point in our lives, we all have to communicate in writing with a business or government office. The advice in this chapter will help you write effective business letters, memos, e-mails, letters of application, résumés, and follow-up letters. It also provides guidelines for attending a job interview, samples of a variety of reports, and tips on presenting technical information to a non-technical audience.

Contents

Applying the Writing
  Process   184

Preparing to
  Communicate for
  Business Purposes   185

Communicating in the
  Business Setting   187

Communicating to Get
  a Job   200

Reports   211

Communicating
  Technical Information   223

Learning Goals

- know and apply the writing process to business communication
- understand and write business letters, memos, and e-mail messages
- understand and write effective letters of application, résumés, and follow-up letters
- apply the rules of effective job interviewing
- understand the parts of various types of reports (informal, formal, and scientific)
- understand and apply some of the rules for presenting technical information

Applying the Writing Process

Stage	Activity	Tips and Techniques	Where to Look
Prewriting	Find and limit your topic.	In business writing, your topic is usually predetermined by the situation.	• Find and Limit Your Topic, page 56
	Define your purpose and audience.	Know who your audience is, how much they know about your topic, and what you want them to know about it. Consider any secondary readers, who may need extra information.	• Define Your Purpose and Your Audience, page 57 • The Business Audience, page 185
	Gather your thoughts.	Use a list or cluster diagram to record all the information you have about your topic or idea.	• Clustering, page 56
Drafting	Organize your thoughts.	Put the most important information up front. The rest of the writing fills in the details.	• Organize Your Thoughts, page 59
	Choose a form.	Decide whether your message is best conveyed by a letter, memo, fax, e-mail, or report.	• Communicating in the Business Setting, page 187
	Write a first draft.	Tell your audience what they need to know. Leave out unnecessary details.	• The Structure of Business Writing pages 185 to 186
Revising	Revise for focus, structure, and content.	The more you revise, the better your work will be.	• Revising, pages 66 to 68
Editing	Edit paragraphs, sentences, and words.	Use sentences and words that will quickly get your message across and result in prompt action (e.g., verbs and the active voice).	• Editing, pages 69 to 74 • Active and Passive Voice, pages 93 to 94
Presenting	Proofread for spelling, punctuation, and grammar.	Be conscientious. Errors will affect how others view your work.	• Presenting Written Work, pages 113 to 132
	Format the final draft.	Know which format goes with which business form.	• Business Letters, pages 187 to 195 • Other Types of Business Writing, pages 196 to 199

Preparing to Communicate for Business Purposes

The Business Audience

Your audience for business or technical communication is likely to be extremely busy. Always get right to the point. Decide what information is most important and make sure that it clearly stands out. Remember that different audiences with different needs will probably read your document. For this reason, you should

- quickly and clearly outline your purpose
- present facts clearly, concisely, and in an easily understood format
- provide background information where necessary
- state the bottom line (costs, schedules, revenues)
- outline any processes and strategies related to your topic

Busy people are always on the run.

The Structure of Business Writing

The Beginning

Your first paragraph should say what you most want your reader to know. One way to make sure you come right to the point is to begin with the words "I want to tell you that…." Later, you can cross out these words and use what is left as your introduction.

> (I want to tell you that …) The furnace at 75 Wooster Road, Unit 45, exploded on Monday. There was extensive damage to the basement, but there were no personal injuries to the occupants. We need to replace the furnace and repair the damage to the structure as soon as possible.

The Body

The body of your writing fills in the necessary background and details. Make sure your audience has all the information needed to act.

The End

How you end a business document depends on your purpose in writing. Your ending may

- summarize the contents of the document
- recommend a course of action
- make a specific request
- present qualifications

Apply It!

Read the proposal on pages 219 to 222 and identify its audience and each part of its structure: beginning, body, and end. Has the writer structured the proposal to suit the needs of a diverse audience? Explain.

Checklist

Use the following Checklist whenever you prepare any kind of business communication.

- ✓ Did I clearly establish who will read my document?
- ✓ Did I quickly and clearly state my purpose in the first paragraph?
- ✓ Did I provide enough background information and details?
- ✓ Did I end my document appropriately?

Think About It: In your notebook, briefly write about anything new that you have just learned about preparing a business communication.

A recommended course of action.

Communicating in the Business Setting

Business Letters

When writing business letters, pay close attention to both content and format.

The Content of a Business Letter

When writing your letter

- know your purpose and audience
- keep your language formal, clear, and concise
- pay careful attention to grammar, spelling, and punctuation
- address your letter to a specific person whenever possible
- let the reader know in the first paragraph exactly why you are writing
- keep the tone of the letter formal and polite, without being flattering or apologetic
- make it clear what action you expect as a result of the letter
- thank the recipient in advance for taking the desired action
- use one of the following closings:

  Yours very truly,

  Yours sincerely,

  Yours faithfully,

  Yours respectfully,

The Format of a Business Letter

Here are some format details for business letters.

- Use standard 21.5 cm x 28.0 cm ($8\frac{1}{2}$" x 11") white paper.
- Whenever possible, use a computer. If you must write by hand, be neat!
- Include an "inside address" (the address of the person or organization to whom you are writing the letter).

- If your letter takes up more than one page
  - write "continues" in the bottom right corner of each page (except the last)
  - at the top left corner of each page (except the first), write the name of the person or company the letter is addressed to, the page number, and the date

CATHY

A Letter Requesting Information

- Address the letter to a specific person.
- Come to the point right away in the first paragraph.
- Use a formal and polite tone.
- Clearly describe what you are requesting.
- Include a sentence of "thank you in advance" in the last paragraph.

Purpose: To find out more about my ancestors from the archives of the Canadian Jewish Congress

Audience: Director of Archives at the Congress, Ms. Janice Rosen

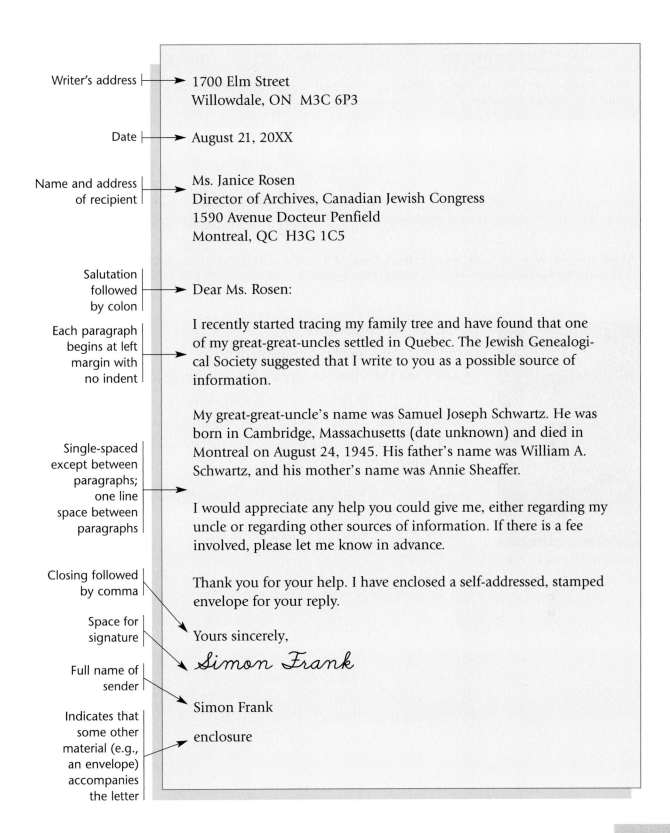

Writer's address → 1700 Elm Street
Willowdale, ON M3C 6P3

Date → August 21, 20XX

Name and address of recipient → Ms. Janice Rosen
Director of Archives, Canadian Jewish Congress
1590 Avenue Docteur Penfield
Montreal, QC H3G 1C5

Salutation followed by colon → Dear Ms. Rosen:

Each paragraph begins at left margin with no indent → I recently started tracing my family tree and have found that one of my great-great-uncles settled in Quebec. The Jewish Genealogical Society suggested that I write to you as a possible source of information.

Single-spaced except between paragraphs; one line space between paragraphs → My great-great-uncle's name was Samuel Joseph Schwartz. He was born in Cambridge, Massachusetts (date unknown) and died in Montreal on August 24, 1945. His father's name was William A. Schwartz, and his mother's name was Annie Sheaffer.

I would appreciate any help you could give me, either regarding my uncle or regarding other sources of information. If there is a fee involved, please let me know in advance.

Closing followed by comma → Thank you for your help. I have enclosed a self-addressed, stamped envelope for your reply.

Space for signature → Yours sincerely,

Simon Frank

Full name of sender → Simon Frank

Indicates that some other material (e.g., an envelope) accompanies the letter → enclosure

Apply It!	**Checklist**

Write a letter to a college you are interested in attending, requesting information about admission requirements, course offerings, and anything else you want to know. Work with a partner to revise and edit your first draft.

✓ Did I address my letter to a specific person?

✓ Did I come to the point quickly?

✓ Did I use a tone that is formal and polite?

✓ Did I clearly describe what I am requesting?

✓ Did I thank the person?

Think About It: What have you learned about writing a letter requesting information? What tips would you add to the list for next time?

Dissatisfied? Write a letter of complaint.

A Letter of Complaint

- Address your complaint to the right person.
- Use a tone of respect to explain the situation objectively.
- Use any relevant facts to support your claim.
- Outline what actions you expect in response to your complaint.
- Politely ask for a response, including the actions you can expect and when they can be expected.

Purpose: To exchange a sweater that was different from the one that was ordered

Audience: Sales manager of Jerseys Are Us

2203 Elizabeth Drive
Gander, NF A1V 2H8

November 20, 20XX

Mr. Tim Harding
Jerseys Are Us
Rue Sainte Catherine
Montreal, QC H3H 5T6

Dear Mr. Harding:

I am returning the hockey sweater you sent me on November 16 for an exchange or refund. Not only does it have the wrong team logo, but, as you can see, it fell apart after only one wearing.

On November 1, I ordered a Montreal Canadiens hockey sweater for my son through your Fall and Winter catalogue (item no. 402 067 32Y A, p. 247). The sweater that arrived two weeks later was a Toronto Maple Leafs sweater. Although my son was very disappointed, I was willing to overlook the mistake and keep the sweater.

Unfortunately, my son wore the jersey once to play hockey, and the next day the material had disintegrated almost completely. We have never had any problems with the sweaters we have purchased from your company in the past, so I am sure this is an isolated case.

Please replace the sweater that I am sending in this package. I have enclosed the bill I received from you. I would appreciate it if you would send a Montreal Canadiens sweater as quickly as possible. If you do not have any in stock, please refund my money since we are not interested in receiving another Maple Leafs sweater.

Thank you for your swift attention to this matter. My son looks forward to receiving his new sweater.

Yours truly,

Marie Carrier

Marie Carrier

Apply It!	Checklist
At a recent concert that you attended, you found that a large pillar blocked your view of the stage. With a partner, write a letter of complaint to the management of the stadium or the ticket agency. Work with a partner to revise and edit your letter.	✓ Did I state the reason for my complaint along with all the related facts? ✓ Did I use an objective—not emotional—tone? ✓ Did I use effective and appropriate language? ✓ Did I outline my expectations? ✓ Did I provide a time frame for receiving a response?

Think About It: What did you find most difficult about writing a letter of complaint? How can you make it easier next time?

A Letter to the Editor or to a Member of Parliament

Write your member of Parliament.

If you disagree with something that is happening in your community, or would like to express your opinion about a political issue, you may want to write to your local newspaper or to your member of Parliament.

• Be clear about why you are writing.

• If you are responding to a news article, cite the headline, newspaper, date, and page number. If you are writing to a member of Parliament or other official, make sure that you are writing to the appropriate representative (municipal, provincial, or federal), and describe the situation you are referring to.

• State your views firmly, but politely, and back them up with reasons, facts, and logical arguments. You may make an emotional appeal as well, but don't let emotions take the place of hard facts.

• If it is appropriate, suggest possible solutions or actions that you think your reader(s) should take.

• Make a copy of the letter and keep it for reference.

Purpose: To express my views regarding the no-skateboarding bylaw passed by City Council

Audience: The general public and members of City Council

7 Simpson St.
Milborne, SK S4P 5T3

May 8, 20XX

Editor
Milborne Sentinel
14 Main Street
Milborne, SK S8R 2P8

Dear Sir or Madam:

I am writing to express my disagreement with the decision of city council to outlaw skateboarding in Saint Patrick's Square (see "City council bans skateboards," *Sentinel*, May 7, 2001, p. A4).

This decision is unfair to young people. Wouldn't city councillors rather see us engaged in a healthy and entertaining sport than hanging around in malls or wandering the streets with nothing to do? There are not many places for young people to spend their time downtown. Take away our skateboarding, and there will be even fewer.

If safety is the councillors' main concern, why not simply pass a bylaw that skateboarders must wear proper protective gear? No one I know would object to that, since we all wear pads and helmets anyway.

Or is the real purpose of the bylaw to get young people out of the square altogether?

I urge the councillors to reconsider their decision and the public to let their support for skateboarding be known.

Yours truly,

Philippa Lao

Philippa Lao

Apply It!	**Checklist**
Write a letter to the editor of your local newspaper expressing your view on an issue that concerns you. Revise and edit your letter before submitting it to your teacher.	Did I state my reason for writing in the first paragraph?
	Did I include useful and relevant background information?
	Did I use facts to support my position?
	Did I use a respectful but firm tone?
	Did I end my letter with a clear request for any action I want my reader to take?

Think About It: Did you find the advice on writing a letter to the editor or to a member of Parliament helpful? What would you do differently the next time?

Sending Your Letter

Envelopes and Folding

- Use a standard white business-size envelope measuring 24 cm x 10.5 cm ($9\frac{1}{2}$" x $4\frac{1}{8}$").
- Fold business letters in thirds.
- Remember to include any extra material. (Note the number of "enclosures" at the bottom of your letter.)
- Print or type the complete address of the person you are writing to in the centre of the envelope.
- Include your return address in the top left corner of the envelope.
- Check the envelope before mailing your letter. Is the address complete and correct (including the postal code)?

Letter

21.5 cm x 28.0 cm
($8\frac{1}{2}$" x 11")
White paper

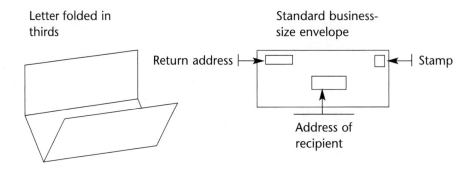

Letter folded in thirds

Standard business-size envelope

Return address

Stamp

Address of recipient

Faxing

When sending a letter or document by fax, include the following information on a separate cover sheet:

- the name of the person you are writing to, his or her title, the company's name, and the fax number of the receiver

- your name and address. If you are writing on behalf of a company, include your title. If your company's name is on the letterhead, you do not need to include it here.

- your phone number

- the total number of pages in the transmission, including the cover sheet

- the date

Here is an example of a fax cover letter:

Fax Transmission

To: Joseph Coughlin, Manager
Sweetie Pie Restaurant
Fax: (519) 555-7777

From: Oded Tavaler, Owner
Tavaler Sweets
12400 – 104 Avenue
Edmonton, AB T2R 2A8
Phone: (780) 482-2222
Fax: (780) 482-2223

Pages including this one: 2

May 30, 20XX

Comment: The accompanying letter is confidential and to be read only by the recipient named above.

Try It!

If you have access to a computer with a word-processing program, look for a built-in template for a fax cover sheet and see what information it provides.

Other Types of Business Writing

Memos

Memos are one form of communication between members of the same business or organization. They are also used as a formal record of what occurs in the business. Although a memo may be sent on paper, e-mail is becoming more common.

When you write memos, identify your audience and your purpose. Memos usually begin with the following headings:

To:

From:

Subject:

Date:

You may want to "copy" a memo to people who are not addressed directly in the letter, but who should receive a copy for reference or information. Include these names on a separate line before the subject, under the heading "cc" (for "carbon copy" or "courtesy copy").

You will sometimes see "Re" used instead of "Subject." It is an abbreviation for the word *regarding*, which means *about* or *concerning*.

Here are some other points to remember:

- Be accurate. Memos provide a written record of your actions, so it is important that all information is correct. Check dates and schedules, and choose your words carefully to avoid sending unclear messages.

- Be brief. Don't include unnecessary information.

- If more than one person will receive the memo, list the recipients in the order of the rank they hold in the company, from highest to lowest. For example, if the memo is addressed to your manager, your co-worker, and the vice-president, list the vice-president first, your manager second, and your co-worker third.

- Cover only one subject per memo. If you have two issues to discuss, write two memos.

- In the final paragraph, explain exactly what action (if any) you expect the recipient to take.

- If you are sending a paper memo, sign or initial it either at the bottom of the page, or next to your typed name at the top. You don't need to include a salutation or a closing.

Purpose: To remind and inform members about the trip to the Tapp Gallery

Audience: Members of the photography club

MEMO

To: All Photography Club Members
From: Sandra Hong, Photography Club President
cc: Ms. DiGravio, Principal
            Mr. Heffernan, Art Teacher
Subject: Tapp Gallery Field Trip
Date: November 10, 20XX

As we discussed at our last meeting, Ms. DiGravio has given us permission to attend the photography exhibit at the Tapp Gallery on Friday, November 18. Mr. Heffernan will be coming with us. Since the gallery closes at 4:00 p.m., we will be leaving the school early, at 2:30 p.m., in order to get there in time. Remember to bring bus fare, and meet in the main lobby at 2:30 p.m. sharp.

If you want to come, please fill out the form below and have it signed by your parent or guardian. Then return it to me by next Thursday noon. Hope to see you all there!

Sandra Hong

I authorize my son/daughter _____ to leave school at 2:30 p.m. on Friday, November 18, 20XX, in order to attend the photography exhibit at the Tapp Gallery.

_____
Signature of parent or guardian

E-Mail

Here are some things to keep in mind when writing e-mail messages.

- Use e-mail for short, simple communications. If your reader has to scroll down the screen, your message is too long.

- Be concise and come to the point right away. Reading on-screen is hard on the eyes.

- Think before you send a message. Once it leaves your computer, intentionally or not, it has gone.

- Don't write an e-mail message while you are upset. Calm down before you begin writing.

- Don't write anything that you would not want someone else to read. E-mails are about as private as a postcard, so treat them as such. Also, erasing a message doesn't mean that it has gone; e-mails can sit on the company server for years.

- Use correct language, grammar, spelling, and punctuation. Remember that your reader will judge your writing even if you think of e-mail as an informal way to communicate.

Purpose: To explain why you are delaying the launch of the e-commerce Web site

Audience: Your manager and team menbers

"Ten-down—only 48 more e-mails to read!"

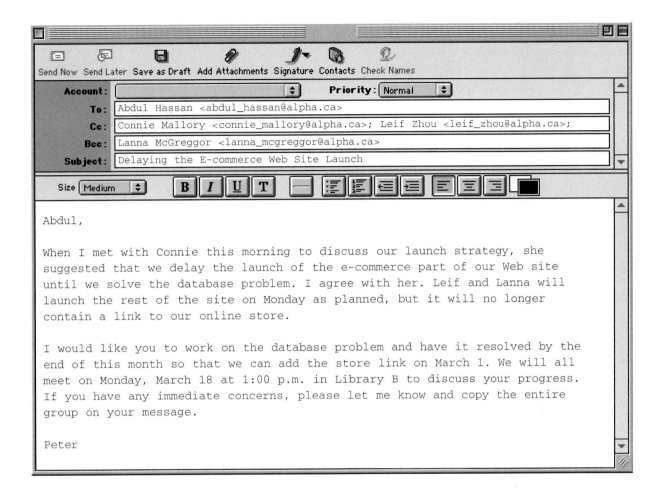

Account: [   ] **Priority:** [Normal]
To: Abdul Hassan <abdul_hassan@alpha.ca>
Cc: Connie Mallory <connie_mallory@alpha.ca>; Leif Zhou <leif_zhou@alpha.ca>;
Bcc: Lanna McGreggor <lanna_mcgreggor@alpha.ca>
Subject: Delaying the E-commerce Web Site Launch

Abdul,

When I met with Connie this morning to discuss our launch strategy, she suggested that we delay the launch of the e-commerce part of our Web site until we solve the database problem. I agree with her. Leif and Lanna will launch the rest of the site on Monday as planned, but it will no longer contain a link to our online store.

I would like you to work on the database problem and have it resolved by the end of this month so that we can add the store link on March 1. We will all meet on Monday, March 18 at 1:00 p.m. in Library B to discuss your progress. If you have any immediate concerns, please let me know and copy the entire group on your message.

Peter

Apply It!

With a partner, brainstorm situations at work that might require you to write a memo or e-mail. Choose one of these situations, think about the purpose and audience, and work together to write either a (paper) memo or an e-mail message.

Checklist

- ✓ Did we copy the message to all the appropriate people?
- ✓ Did we use a descriptive subject line?
- ✓ Did we cover only one subject?
- ✓ Did we use concise language?
- ✓ Did we use correct language, grammar, spelling, and punctuation?

Think About It: What would you add to the Checklist for writing memos and e-mail messages to make it more complete and more helpful?

Communicating to Get a Job

When you apply for a job, it is extremely important to make a good impression. Once you have identified a job that you wish to apply for,

1. write a letter of application
2. prepare a résumé tailored to the position you are applying for
3. attend an interview
4. write a follow-up letter thanking the person for his or her time and consideration

The Letter of Application

A letter of application is often called a cover letter. It is a one-page letter that always accompanies a résumé, even if you've already spoken to the person.

The following example is a suggested format. Notice that each paragraph has a specific function. Be sure to pay attention to the details of the format as well as spelling, grammar, and punctuation.

Purpose: To apply and be favourably considered for a job advertised in the newspaper

Audience: Ms. Vera Shimano, Human Resources Director

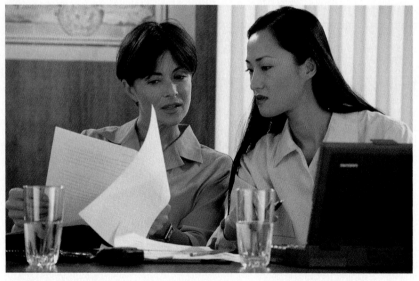

A letter of application helps prospective employers decide whether to read your résumé.

The first paragraph identifies the purpose of the letter and the specific job you are applying for.

These paragraphs call attention to your qualifications, highlighting areas that apply to the specific job, and mention that a résumé (and any other supplementary information) is enclosed.

The last paragraph expresses enthusiasm for the job and the company and a desire to be granted an interview.

May 2, 2001

Ms. Vera Shimano
Human Resources Director,
Rent-a-Clown Enterprises
27 Robson Street, Suite 17
Vancouver, BC V5C 2B8

Dear Ms. Shimano:

I am writing to apply for the position of clown at Rent-a-Clown enterprises, as advertised in the *Vancouver Sun* on April 29.

Last year, I took part in a workshop on clowning and street theatre given at our school. This experience gave me a strong interest in clowning, which I am eager to pursue. Since September, I have been a volunteer at the Children's Hospital, entertaining sick children once a week as KoKo the Clown.

For the last three years, I have been actively involved in the drama club at Cartwright High School, from which I will graduate in June of this year. Last year, I was president of the club. As well as performing in every major play the club has staged in the last three years, I have worked on lighting, makeup, props, and other aspects of production. I especially enjoyed acting in our year-end comedy revue. My one-person mime skit won the prize for best performance of the evening.

My résumé, which is enclosed, shows that I have spent the last two summers working as a camp counsellor at Camp Oranoak. This experience taught me leadership skills, including how to keep young children interested and entertained. In addition, I know how to perform magic tricks and can make animals out of balloons.

I would very much like to meet with you to learn more about the position at Rent-a-Clown and to discuss my qualifications. I will call you next week to find out when it would be convenient for us to get together.

Yours sincerely,

Maya Lefkowitz

Maya Lefkowitz (alias KoKo the Clown)

enclosure

Unless you have been told specifically not to phone, end your letter by promising to make a follow-up call. If you just say, "I look forward to hearing from you," you may have a long wait!

Apply It!	Checklist
Prepare a letter of application for one of the following jobs, or for a job you found listed in your local newspaper:	✓ Did I clearly identify the job I am seeking?
1. a summer job as a camp counsellor	✓ Did I describe any of my skills that are particularly well suited to the job?
2. a part-time job working as a receptionist in an office	✓ Did I refer to my résumé that I would be including?
3. a summer job working for a painting company	✓ Did I clearly show that I am interested in and enthusiastic about the job?
4. a summer job planting trees	
5. a part-time job working at a fast-food restaurant	
6. a summer job cleaning cages at the zoo	

Think About It: How did you use the sample letter of application shown in this section when you wrote your own letter? What other help would you need next time?

The Résumé

A résumé provides an overview of your qualifications for a job. Most employers will want to see one before they hire you. Ideally, this is a one-page document, but use two pages if the information looks cramped. (Make sure your name and phone number appear on each page.) Your résumé should cover the following areas, which are usually presented in the order shown:

Personal Data

Try It!

Consider spending a little extra to have your résumé and letter of application laser-printed on high-quality paper. Choose conservative colours of paper, like white, off-white, cream, or grey.

DO include your

- name
- address
- phone number
- e-mail address if you have one

DO NOT include

- date of birth
- marital status
- race
- religion
- photograph
- social insurance number
- any information that does not relate directly to your ability to do the job

Education

- Include the name of the school you attend and the years that you have been there.
- Show a list of any courses, seminars, or workshops you are taking or have taken that relate directly to the kind of job you are seeking.
- Call attention to any awards you have received or any outstanding scholastic achievements.

Work Experience

- Include any full-time, part-time, or summer jobs you have had.
- Include any volunteer work you have done.

Activities and Interests

Use this section to tell your potential employers about your hidden talents and to show that you are responsible, a team player, and a well-rounded person.

- Include any important skills you have not mentioned elsewhere.
- Outline any special activities you have participated in.
- List any hobbies or interests that reflect well on you.

References

Choose two or three people who know you well enough to speak knowledgeably and fairly about you. Do not include relatives unless you have worked for them. Always ask permission before including someone's name as a reference. Here is a list of references that you might use:

- former employers
- teachers
- school staff
- neighbours
- friends' parents

Your teacher can be a reference.

Instead of listing names, you may simply state, "References available upon request," and bring the references with you on a separate sheet of paper when you go to the interview.

Purpose: To show your qualifications for a job

Audience: Ms. Vera Shimano, Human Resources Director

Maya Lefkowitz
15 Scargill Avenue, Vancouver, BC V2A 2T7
Phone: (604) 555–2223   mayal@infomania.ca

EDUCATION

September 1999–Present	Cartwright High School, Vancouver, BC – will graduate in June of this year – have maintained a B average overall – earned As in drama past three years
June 2000	Workshop: Be a Clown!

WORK EXPERIENCE

September 2000–Present	Volunteer Clown, Vancouver Children's Hospital – Entertaining sick children once a week
September 1999–May 2000 September 2000–Present	Sales Assistant, Darrah's Florists – serve customers, create flower arrangements, take phone orders
June–August 1999 June–August 2000	Camp Counsellor, Camp Oranoak, Carswell, BC – supervised children aged 7 to 9 in a variety of activities – organized, acted in, and directed the "Oranoak Revue," a talent show for campers and counsellors – was promoted from Junior Counsellor to Senior Counsellor

OTHER SKILLS AND INTERESTS

September 1999–Present	Member of Cartwright High Drama Club – acting President for part of this time
May 1998	Completed Red Cross First Aid Course.

REFERENCES	Ms. Pauline Jessamyn, Director, Camp Oranoak, 17 Doxton Crescent, Vancouver, BC V6T 9B9 (604) 555-3333
	Mr. Frederick Warner, Volunteer Coordinator, Vancouver Children's Hospital, Vancouver, BC V5H 3F4 (604) 555-6766

Apply It!	Checklist
Create a résumé that will accompany the letter of application you wrote in the last section. Tailor it to the position you are applying for.	✓ Did I state my contact information on every page (if my résumé is longer than one page)? ✓ Did I outline any education that applies to the job? ✓ Did I clearly outline my work experience, including volunteer work? ✓ Did I include my interests and hobbies that show that I would be a good employee? ✓ Did I include a References section?

Think About It: Reflect on the rules that you followed to create your résumé. Which ones do you think are most important? Why?

The Job Interview

A job interview is an opportunity for the employer to find out more about you, and for you to find out more about the job and the employer. You both have a purpose: the employer wants to find a good employee, and you want to find a job that you will enjoy doing. Be prepared to both answer and ask questions.

Think of a job interview as a chance to show off in a professional way.

Preparing to Answer Questions

The table that follows lists some typical questions that you might be asked, along with some tips on how to respond.

Question	Suggested Response
What do you feel you have to offer this company? or, Tell me about yourself.	Questions like these give you a chance to summarize your qualifications for the job. You might discuss your experience, your education, and your personality traits. Make sure your responses relate to the job.
Why are you applying for this position?	Make sure you relate them all directly to the position and company in question.
Do you prefer working with other people or by yourself?	Think about which style of working is likely to be emphasized in the job you are applying for. (*Hint:* Most jobs require both styles to some degree.) Answer honestly, but make it clear that you are able and willing to work both cooperatively and independently.
How do you respond to criticism?	Make it clear that you welcome constructive criticism. If possible, have ready an example of how you have used criticism to improve your performance at school or in another position. Make sure the example emphasizes the positive result rather than any less-than-perfect action that brought on the criticism.
What about your future educational plans?	Be honest, but leave the door open to future studies.
Are you willing to work overtime when necessary?	If you really won't be willing to work overtime and the job demands it, you will probably not last long anyway. On the other hand, consider how much the job means to you. It might be worth a few extra evenings. A good compromise is to say something like "within reason."
What are your major strengths and weaknesses?	Name your weakness first, and try to make it sound as if it is almost a strength! For example, you might say, "I think sometimes I'm too much of a perfectionist," or, "Until last year, I might have said I was afraid of public speaking, but I've been working hard at it, and I think I've made great strides." Finish your answer with a description of what you think your best asset is in relation to the job.
What aspect of yourself would you like to improve?	If possible, think of an aspect of yourself that you are already in the process of improving. For example, "I am very interested in improving my computer skills, and I will be starting a computer programming course in the fall," or, "For the past three months, I have been doing volunteer work with younger children, which has already helped me improve my leadership skills."

Answering Questions Effectively

Here are some hints for answering questions in an interview.

- Listen carefully to each question and answer it thoughtfully, directly, and concisely.

- Speak clearly and use appropriate language when answering. Do not use slang and *never* use foul language, even if the interviewer does.

- Make eye contact.

Remember to make eye contact.

- Always answer honestly.

- Although you should always be honest about your qualifications, answer in a way that emphasizes your strong points. An interview is no time to be modest!

- Know when to be quiet. Some of the best interviews occur when the interviewer does all the talking. This shows that you are willing to listen and learn.

Asking Good Questions

This is a part of interviewing that many people don't do well. You not only have a right to ask questions, but interviewers want to know that you have thought about the job.

- Ask questions about the job and the company. Ask what the company's mission is. What role do the executives see the company playing in the community? How do they view the employer-employee relationship? What role do they think your job plays in achieving their mission?

- Be enthusiastic and appear interested.

- Don't ask questions about wages until the time is right. Waiting until you know more about the job shows the employer that you are interested in the job, not just the money. Also, if the employer has decided to offer you the job, you are in a better position to discuss wages.

Try It!

To deal with pre-interview jitters, role-play an interview with a friend or family member.

Dress appropriately for the interview.

Making a Good Impression

Here are some tips for making a good impression at an interview.

- Dress neatly and appropriately for the job. For example, wear a suit for an office job. You can dress less formally for a construction job.

- Be on time. Make sure you know exactly how to get to the place of the interview and how long it will take to get there.

- Be courteous and respectful, but not too modest or shy. You are trying to "sell" yourself, so be confident in your ability to do the job.

- Avoid saying anything negative about previous employers, schools, and so on. Focus on the positive whenever possible.

- Thank the person for his or her time. If you are interested in the job, say so. Ask when he or she will be making the final decision and ask if there is anything further that you can do to help them with the decision.

GRANTLAND®

WHAT'S UP?

YOU'RE 10 MINUTES LATE!

HEY, MOMMA, THAT'S OKAY. I WAS 15 MINUTES EARLY FOR MY LAST INTERVIEW.

Apply It!	Checklist
With a partner, write a script for a job interview that resulted from your letter of application and résumé. Take turns role-playing the interviewer and the job applicant. Be prepared to present your role-play to the class.	✓ Did we prepare a list of possible questions and responses? ✓ Did we mention my skills that relate to the job? ✓ Did we include questions that I want to ask of the interviewer? ✓ Did I think about how I should dress for the interview? ✓ Did we make eye contact during the interview? ✓ Did we remember to say "thank you" at the end?

Think About It: Make notes on what you found difficult about preparing for and performing the job interview role-play. How can you make the real thing go better?

The Follow-Up Letter

Always write a follow-up letter of thanks immediately after any job interview. A good follow-up letter

- shows courtesy, persistence, and initiative; it exhibits professionalism—something that employers look for in potential employees
- keeps your name in front of the employer
- lets you sell your strengths one last time

Purpose: To follow up on my job interview

Audience: Ms. Vera Shimano, Human Resources Director

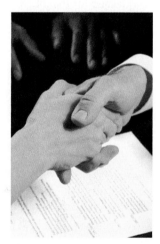

Thank the interviewer with a follow-up letter.

Paragraph 1 thanks the interviewer for granting you the interview and mentions the job in question specifically.

Paragraph 2 notes something specific you learned in the interview and tells why this piece of information was interesting and exciting to you. Use this paragraph to remind the interviewer that you are well-qualified for the job.

Paragraph 3 restates your enthusiasm for the job and the company.

May 12, 2001

Ms. Vera Shimano
Human Resources Director
Rent-a-Clown Enterprises
27 Robson Street, Suite 17
Vancouver, BC V5C 2B8

Dear Ms. Shimano:

Thank you for taking the time to discuss the summer position at Rent-a-Clown yesterday. It was both entertaining and enlightening to learn about the challenges and rewards of working as a children's entertainer.

I was particularly interested to hear that you provide ongoing workshops for your clowns. As I mentioned during the interview, I am always interested in learning new clowning skills, and I love working with young children.

I know that I could be an asset to your firm and would like the opportunity to prove it to you. Again, thank you for considering my application. I look forward to hearing from you and possibly working with you in the near future.

Yours sincerely,

Maya Lefkowitz

Maya Lefkowitz (alias KoKo the Clown)

Apply It!

Write a follow-up letter for the interview that you had with your classmate. "Send" it to your partner so that he or she can give you feedback.

Checklist

 Did I refer to the job I applied for?

 Did I mention something that I learned at the interview?

 Did I restate my interest in the job?

 Did I thank the person for his or her time and consideration?

Think About It: In your own words, list rules for writing a follow-up letter. What would you do differently next time?

Reports

A report is prepared for a specific purpose and aimed at a specific audience. Here are some things to keep in mind when writing a report in a business setting.

- Be clear about your purpose—are you trying to inform, analyze, or persuade?

- Know who your audience is.

- Collect all the necessary information. You may
  - check company files and publications, including corporate Web sites.
  - interview employees, suppliers, technicians, and so on.
  - make personal observations. These can be used in informal reports. Back them up, however, with at least one other source for more formal reports.
  - do library research. Not all reports require this, but you may find useful information in recent business articles and periodicals.

- Order the material logically. This *usually* means putting the most important information up front. However, if a different order makes sense, such as by time or feature, feel free to use it.

- Present important ideas and conclusions first, and then use the body of the report to fill in the supporting details. In longer or more technical reports, the actual supporting data may be included at the end in appendices. This data may also be inserted into the body of the report in tables and charts.

- Always write in a formal style.

- Be as objective as possible. Let the facts speak for themselves, present both sides of an issue, give options, and avoid exaggerations and emotional appeals.

- Unless your report is very short and informal, use headings to identify its various parts. Here are some tips for creating effective headings.
  - Begin with the heading "Introduction."
  - End information reports with a "Summary" section.
  - End evaluations or proposals with either a "Conclusions" or "Recommendations" section.

Cross-Reference

See Chapter 7 for information on researching.

Cross-Reference

For examples of formal and informal writing, see page 63.

– Use descriptive headings for the body discussion. For example, instead of "Background," a report evaluating the usefulness of CD-ROM technology might have headings such as "How CD-ROM Technology Works" or "Current Uses of CD-ROM Technology."

Cross-Reference

See pages 177 to 178 for more on in-text citations.

- Always acknowledge your sources. Use the in-text citation method outlined in Chapter 7. Not only is this a legal requirement, but it also shows the reader that you have done some research.

- Informal reports are sometimes presented as memos or letters. To decide how to present your report, check other reports in the company files. Ask your manager or supervisor where to find them.

Progress Reports

Progress reports are often used in businesses to let managers know if a particular project is on schedule and on budget.

Here are the main parts of a progress report.

1. The introduction highlights the most important information found in the body of the report. It should

Try It!

Charts can be useful for summarizing schedule changes. Try writing specific tasks or phases to be completed down the left-hand column, followed by columns headed Scheduled Completion Date, and Actual Completion Date.

   - identify the project
   - summarize what has been completed
   - describe the present situation
   - summarize the work remaining
   - highlight any problems
   - state whether the project is on schedule and on budget

2. The body of the report should begin with an overview of the work that has already been completed. The amount of detail you include will depend on how much your reader knows or needs to know. Even when your audience is involved in the project and is familiar with what has happened, you should include a brief summary to remind them.

3. Next, describe the present situation—what is being done and by whom—as well as report any delays or problems and how they are being dealt with. End the section by stating when you expect the present phase to be completed.

Try It!

You will find guidelines for making and placing figures and charts in papers and reports on pages 30 to 32 and pages 238 to 240.

4. In the next section, outline the work still to be done. Anticipate any problems that might arise, and predict when you think the project will be completed.

5. A summary is optional in a progress report. If you wish, end with a brief overview of the situation as it stands, and a look at what lies ahead.

Charbridge Construction
RR 3, Carforth, AB T6R 1V3
Phone: (403) 555–3333
Fax: (403) 555–1111

To: James Charbridge, President
From: Bob Shaftoe, Supervisor
Subject: Construction Project, 18 Joseph Avenue
Date: July 24, 20XX
No. of Pages: 2 (including this one)

Introduction
This is the update that you requested regarding the project at 18 Joseph Avenue. The discovery of a lack of foundation in part of the existing house has required changes in the plan and construction. This has resulted in increased cost, which will be the responsibility of the client. We will also have to move the completion date ahead to November 15, which is a delay of two weeks.

Background
The project at 18 Joseph Avenue involves building an addition onto an existing home, which is approximately 120 years old. The owner of the property, Mr. Miles Matsumoto, had been acting as general contractor until about two weeks ago, when excavation revealed significant design and construction problems. At that point, Charbridge Construction was called in to take over. The project is now being completed under my supervision.

Work Completed
The excavation for a new foundation is complete. It was during the excavation that it was discovered that there was no frost wall underneath the summer kitchen (see Appendix A, attached). Concrete had been poured around the base of the walls in a good imitation of a foundation wall. At this point, we were contracted to manage the project.

Work Underway

After we were called in, I went to examine the excavation myself, along with Mr. Matsumoto. We decided that the summer kitchen should be demolished and entirely rebuilt, requiring substantial changes to the existing plans. New plans are presently being drawn up. Mr. Matsumoto has agreed to cover the additional costs for these changes. The new plans mean the following changes need to be made:

- The creation of new frost walls to support the side wall of the new kitchen addition (there will be a crawl space).
- The creation of a concrete bench to support the foundation of the main house.
- The second floor joists will be cantilevered over the new kitchen. Truss joists will be used to meet span requirements.

Work Remaining

We expect the new plans tomorrow (July 25). Work on the foundation will resume Saturday and by Tuesday, framing will begin. I anticipate no further major delays, but the original schedule will have to be revised by approximately two weeks, giving a completion date of November 15, 20XX.

Summary

Although the lack of a foundation was a major setback, the rest of the construction on Joseph Avenue should be fairly routine. Once the new plans have been approved, the construction schedule will resume its normal course. It is even possible that we could make up some of the time lost, if the weather holds during framing.

Apply It!

Write an informal progress report for a project you are currently working on for one of your classes.

Checklist

 Did I include an introduction?

 Did I provide an overview of the work that has already been completed?

 Did I describe the work that is under way?

 Did I outline the work that still needs to be done?

 Did I choose to include a summary?

Think About It: What do you think are the three most important things you learned about writing a report?

Evaluative Reports

An evaluative report does more than provide information: it analyzes the information and makes recommendations. An evaluative report might be used to help purchasing decisions or to resolve a procedural problem in the workplace.

Here are the parts of an evaluative report.

1. In the introduction
   - describe what the report is about
   - identify who asked for it
   - briefly outline your conclusions and recommendations

2. Begin the body of the report by filling in the background: present the problem or situation that led to the report being written, along with any other necessary information.

3. Describe your findings: what methods you used to investigate the issue and what you found out. For example, if you based your results on a survey, you might explain how many people you polled, what questions you asked, and how you chose your subjects. Try to use descriptive headings in this section to help your readers find important information.

4. In the "Conclusions" section, analyze the results.

5. Finally, in the "Recommendations" section, explain specific actions the company can take to act on the conclusions. Use an objective tone and back up your recommendations with logical, rational arguments that are based on the facts.

Analyze and make recommendations.

File Code: F21
Date: 20XX 02 14
Memo To: T.D. Laskin
             Director of Education
From: G.C. Petrovsky
             Superintendent of Operations
             R.D. Adler
             Supervisor of Transportation
Re: Cost-Benefit Analysis of Board Bus Fleet

Introduction

As requested by the members of the Board of Education, we have examined the issue of whether or not to continue to run the Board of Education's bus fleet. We conclude that the fleet remains the most cost effective and efficient way to meet the Board's transportation needs.

Background

In July, 20XX, the Ministry of Education announced it would no longer provide Boards with capital funding for replacement vehicles, effective July 1, 20XX. The Ministry also stated that the daily budget operating the Board buses would be similar to the amounts provided for contract operators. As a result of these changes, a decision was made to determine if it makes financial sense for the Board to continue to operate its own bus fleet, or whether it should turn its transportation services over to a private operator.

Cost-Benefit Analysis

In investigating this issue, we relied heavily on a cost-benefit analysis of the Board bus fleet (see Appendix A). The figures are taken from actual or projected costs of running the fleet over the last two years and in the near future. In all three cases, the Board's net operating costs are substantially lower than those of the contract operators. Also, the unrecognized operating costs, for which the Board receives no grants, are substantially lower for the Board buses than they are for the contract operators.

Additional Benefits of a Board Fleet

In addition to the cost advantage of maintaining a Board fleet, some other benefits to this arrangement should be noted:

- A cost-efficient Board-operated fleet is a necessary tool in negotiations with contract bus operators in that the Board has the advantage of "having a pulse on the situation."
- The Board is more sensitive to the daily costs and problems concerning the operation of a school bus fleet and is less likely to be taken advantage of by an operator.
- The Board fleet sets high standards for driver safety and vehicle maintenance. Operators must practise the same standards.
- The Board buses provide an opportunity for transportation staff to evaluate the effectiveness of features designed to enhance student safety and/or overall efficiency. The following list gives examples of bus features the Board fleet has tested:
  - Cross-over arms
  - Vista "snub-nosed" buses
  - 78-passenger buses
  - Video camera on buses
  - Back-up alarms
  - Reflective tape
  - In-line diesel engine
  - Disc brakes
  - Larger tail-lights
- The Board fleet ensures that schools receive the best possible field trip rates.

Recommendations

Given these findings, we recommend that the Board continue to operate its fleet of school buses. We further recommend that a similar cost-benefit analysis be conducted every three years or after any significant change in the Ministry's transportation grants.

Apply It!	Checklist
With a partner, think about a problem that faces your school or community. You may need to do some research to find out more about the problem and possible solutions. Write an evaluative report outlining the problem and offering a recommendation.	☑ Did I use the introduction to describe what the report is about and who asked for it, and to outline my conclusions and recommendations? ☑ Did I provide the necessary background information? ☑ Did I describe the research findings? ☑ Did I analyze the results in the "Conclusions" section? ☑ Did I suggest specific actions in the "Recommendations" section?

Think About It: Compare your evaluative report with the report you wrote in the previous section. How did you make them different?

Proposals

Show them your solution.

A proposal is a report in which you describe a need or problem, suggest a solution, and try to persuade the reader to agree to your solution. Proposals can be hundreds of pages long or one paragraph.

Here are some guidelines and tips to help you organize an informal proposal.

1. Use facts to make your argument for you, and avoid appeals to theories or emotions.

2. In the introduction, provide highlights from the body of the report. Briefly describe the problem or need and the proposed solution. Include the total cost of the proposal and the completion date, if applicable.

3. Begin the body of the proposal with background information: describe the problem in more detail and suggest ways of evaluating possible solutions.

4. Next, describe your proposal. Include relevant details such as how long it will take to put in place, how the work will proceed, and a breakdown of costs.

5. Use your proposal to describe what's needed for solving the problem, and to show how your suggestions fulfill each need.

6. To show that your proposal is the best, you could present other solutions, and analyze each one according to the needs you have presented.

7. Describe the qualifications and experience you or your company has in the field.

8. You could end with a summary of the benefits to be derived from your proposal. Be enthusiastic, but maintain a formal tone.

Request for Funding

To: Friends of the Environment Foundation
From: The Ontario Public Interest Research Group, Guelph

Introduction
We are requesting funding in order to improve a very popular interactive display, designed to educate the public about "green" environmental practices in the home. The estimated total cost of the project is $7596.72. After receiving a donation of some display panels, we still need $4596.72. Construction of the display would begin in April (or earlier if a part-time coordinator is hired) and be completed by the end of May.

Background
In 1989, OPIRG-Guelph developed an extremely popular educational display called the Urban House of Horrors. The display is a mock-up of a house with real fixtures (bath, toilet, stove, and so on). Individuals walk into the display as they would rooms of their own home and are presented with information, in a variety of forms, that provides practical and simple alternatives to common household activities that are bad for the environment. There are flaps to lift, quizzes and puzzles to solve, and buzzer boards to press. Literature is provided for individuals to take home with them.

During the summer, we conducted a door-to-door survey in Guelph. Over 8000 households were visited and over 1500 environmental surveys were collected. This project provided us with important background research on what people need to make their lives more environmentally friendly. We learned that people were very eager to make a difference, but still lacked friendly ways of getting information to make the necessary changes in their lifestyle.

Proposal

We are seeking funds to improve our version of the Urban House of Horrors. The concept is fully developed, but we want to make it more professional looking and lightweight, so that it can be easily moved and set up. We would like to make a new model that would stand up to a lot of use.

Rationale

The number of environmental disasters and problems can be overwhelming for most people. It is often difficult to see how individuals can have an impact on problems as large as global warming. The importance of the Urban House of Horrors display is that it shows how individuals can make significant contributions to their local and global environment.

The Urban House of Horrors is an interactive display that has proved popular with both adults and children of all ages. The display is fun, and yet manages to convey an enormous amount of information. The positive feedback that we have received about the display is evidence of the fact that it is an extremely accessible way of presenting information. We have received many requests to exhibit our display both within and outside Guelph, but because of its unwieldy size, we have not often been able to fulfill these requests.

Uses of the Display

The display will first be shown at the Guelph Spring Festival Block Party on May 23, with an expected attendance of between 3000 and 4000 people from Guelph. The display will then go into a mall (Stone Road Mall, The Eaton Centre, or Willow West Mall) as part of National Environment Week (June 1 to 7) activities in Guelph. The display will be used at numerous community events, particularly during the summer.

During the fall and winter, we would like to book the display into schools. We have talked to several area teachers involved in environmental education, and they are extremely excited about setting up the display in their schools. We would concentrate on school bookings in Guelph initially, and slowly extend our range into adjacent municipalities.

Costs

Project coordinator	2560.00	(1)
Benefits	286.72	(2)
Display panels	3000.00	
Materials and supplies	1000.00	(3)
Printing and promotion	750.00	(4)
Total expenses	7596.72	
In-kind contribution	3000.00	(5)
Request from Friends of the Environment Foundation	4596.72	

Budget Notes

1) The project coordinator's position will be full time for a period of 8 weeks at $8.00/hour (or alternatively a half-time position for 16 weeks). The coordinator will be responsible for developing the display, coordinating volunteers, and organizing the staffing and set-up of the display at the Block Party.
2) Benefits include Unemployment Insurance, Canada Pension Plan, Employer's Health Tax, and vacation pay (4%).
3) Materials and supplies (e.g., cardboard, Bristol board, laminating) to rebuild components of the display.
4) Printing of educational materials and promotion of the display.
5) We have received a contribution of modular display panels and travelling cases.

Staffing

We are a volunteer organization. We have two permanent staff and a variable number of grant staff. We have a volunteer board of students and community members and numerous volunteers working on a wide variety of issues. This kind of project will draw on the ideas and advice of many of these people, and the project coordinator will be responsible for coordinating volunteer contributions to the project. At least one of the permanent staff will be involved in supervising the project. Depending on the various granting agencies, we may also have grant staff to assist with various aspects of the display. Certainly, we will have numerous people to draw on to staff the display at the Block Party and during Environment Week.

Schedule
We would like to begin the project in April (or February if we have someone part time for 16 weeks) and finish at the end of May for the Guelph Spring Festival Block Party.

Credentials
We have enclosed a copy of our last progress report that describes our organization and the type of projects that we work on.

Apply It!

Work with the same partner you had for writing the evaluative report to rewrite your report as a proposal. Consider how you will sell your idea, and explain why your solution would be better than anyone else's.

Checklist

✓ Did I use the introduction to highlight key information from the body?

✓ Did I provide background information?

✓ Did I clearly state the needs and/or problem?

✓ Did I describe the proposal in terms of the needs, including the costs?

✓ Did I choose to restate the benefits in the summary?

Think About It: Which parts of writing a proposal did you find easiest? Which parts were hardest to write? What will you do next time to make it easier?

Checklist for Writing Reports

Use the following general checklist when you write any report—formal or informal.

✓ Did I keep my purpose and audience in mind?

✓ Did I choose the most appropriate format for my message?

✓ Did I include information that is appropriate to my audience and purpose?

✓ Did I place the most important information at the beginning?

✓ Did I write formally and objectively?

✓ Did I use headings to break up the text and to guide my reader?

Communicating Technical Information

Techno transfer is a term that describes the process of presenting technical information to a non-expert audience.

Understanding Technical Information

Let's first look at how you can approach technical information when you find it. Once you experience some of the difficulties, you'll be better able to help your audience.

When approaching technical material:

- Read with a purpose.
- Begin by looking at any headings and subheadings, and thinking about or listing what you already know about or associate with them.
- Look at any graphics before reading the material. This will help you create images in your mind when you do read the material.
- Look for a glossary of terms. If there is one, skim through it quickly before you read, then refer to it whenever you come to an unfamiliar term.
- Decide whether what you are reading is describing a process, procedure, or thing (e.g., a piece of machinery).
- List questions or terms you do not understand. If you still do not know the answers after reading through the entire document, do some research or ask someone knowledgeable to explain it to you.

Presenting Technical Information

How would you describe how to tie a shoelace to someone who grew up with Velcro? Suddenly, a simple process with which you are very familiar becomes a complex, multi-step procedure. Here are some ways to help you address an audience that is unfamiliar with your subject matter.

- Use visual aids, such as labelled illustrations, charts, flow charts, and graphs to make information easier to understand.
- Use clear and informative headings and subheadings in written material. Your readers will use the headings to help them get an overview of the subject matter.

Cross-Reference

Many of these tips apply to reading and listening in any situation. For more details on effective reading and listening strategies, see Chapters 1 and 10.

- Use analogies and comparisons. Relating unfamiliar concepts or processes to ones that your audience is familiar with can make the material easier to understand and remember.

Cross-Reference

For active and passive voices, see pages 93 to 94; for Parallelism, see pages 87 to 88.

- Use the active voice: it suggests that action should be taken.
- Link parallel ideas, steps, or objects using parallel constructions.
- Use language that your audience is familiar with. Avoid jargon and abbreviations. If you must use an uncommon term, define it in the text and/or in a glossary.

Apply It!

Choose a simple process that you are familiar with (such as the "tying a shoelace" example, setting a car clock, setting a VCR to record on timer). Prepare a presentation that would explain the process to an audience with little or no knowledge of the topic.

Checklist

- ✓ Did I write clearly and in logical steps?
- ✓ Did I use headings and subheadings?
- ✓ Did I use appropriate visual aids?
- ✓ Did I use analogies and comparisons?
- ✓ Did I provide a glossary (optional)?

Think About It: What did you learn about presenting even "simple" technical information? How will this help you with your next presentation?

Defining Terms

When you are explaining technical information to a non-technical audience, it is particularly important to define your terms clearly. Here are some steps to follow in creating useful definitions.

1. Start by explaining what general class of things or ideas the term belongs to.

A ptarmigan is a member of the grouse family.
A camshaft is a long shaft.
A radius is a line segment.
An optical scanner is a piece of computer hardware.

2. Then describe the features of the term that make it different from others in the same general class.

> A ptarmigan is the only member of the grouse family that has snow-white winter feathers.
>
> The camshaft is a long shaft with knobs, or cams, protruding from it at intervals.
>
> A radius is a line segment that joins the centre of a circle to a point on the circumference.
>
> An optical scanner is a piece of hardware that allows a computer to read printed material.

3. If necessary, add more information about the term that is relevant to your audience and purpose. Think of who, when, where, what, and how questions that your audience might need or want answered. For example:

> What does it look like? (Describe and/or include a graphic of the item.)
> What parts does it have?
> What is it similar to?
> What is its significance?
> What features does it have?
> What is an example?
> Where does it come from?
> When is it used?
> Who made/discovered it?
> How is it used?
> How does it work?

Unclear technical information causes frustration.

    Diagrams, photographs, or other graphic representations can be helpful when you are defining parts of machinery or equipment.

Apply It!	Checklist
Choose two or three terms used in one of your hobbies that someone unfamiliar with your hobby wouldn't know. Define these terms and give them to someone who is unfamiliar with them. Use visuals if necessary. Then listen while that person explains your terms to a third person.	Did I describe the items or ideas as accurately and completely as I knew how? Did I provide examples or comparisons? Did I use graphics or visuals if necessary or appropriate? Did I give definitions that could be explained to a third person?

Explaining a Process or Procedure

Writing Instructions

Here are some tips to help you write instructions explaining how to use or to do something.

1. Begin by listing all the tools and materials needed to complete the task.

2. Define all the terms (names of parts, for example) that you will be referring to in your instructions. One way to do this is with a labelled illustration like the one below.

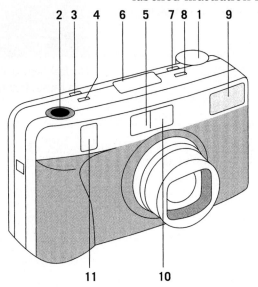

1. Zooming lever
2. Shutter release button
3. Drive button
4. Infinity-landscape button
5. Autofocus window
6. LCD panel
7. Mode button
8. Red-eye reduction flash button
9. Built-in flash
10. Viewfinder window
11. Light sensor window

3. Number each step.

4. Do not include too much information in each step.

Confusing: Form a loop with the string in your left hand, making sure that you have 2–3 cm of string left dangling. Pinch the base of the loop between your left thumb and index finger, and circle the right string counterclockwise around the base of the loop. This new loop is called the encircling loop.

Better:
1. Form a loop with the string in your left hand, making sure that you have 2–3 cm of string left dangling. This loop is called the left loop.
2. Pinch the base of the left loop between your left thumb and index finger.
3. Circle the right string counterclockwise around the base of the loop. This new loop is called the encircling loop.

Try It!

Perform the actions as you write to remind yourself of the steps involved.

One way to avoid repeating long tedious phrases is to give names to particular parts of the process. In the previous example, note how the author names the different loops (left loop, encircling loop) to make it easier to distinguish them in later instructions.

5. Try to start each sentence with a verb. Avoid the passive voice and the phrase "you should."

Cross-Reference

Passive voice is explained on pages 93 to 94.

Weak: A right loop is then formed by passing a piece of the right lace under the encircling loop to the right of the left loop.

Weak: You should form a loop near the end of the right-hand lace, and pass it underneath the encircling loop to the right of the left loop. This new loop is called the right loop.

Better: Form a loop near the end of the right-hand lace and pass it underneath the encircling loop to the right of the left loop. This new loop is called the right loop.

6. Keep your terminology as simple and consistent as possible. While repeating words and phrases many times is not usually desirable, it is better to repeat the same word than to confuse your reader with too many synonyms.

Looks easy doesn't it?

Weak: Hold the top of the right hand bow between the right thumb and index finger, and the left loop between the left thumb and index finger. Pull both sides outward gently, until the encircling loop tightens. Do not allow the ends of the laces to pass through the middle loop.

Better: Hold the top of the right loop between the right thumb and forefinger and the top of the left loop between the left thumb and index finger. Pull both loops outward gently, until the encircling loop tightens. Do not allow the ends of the laces to pass through the encircling loop.

Try It!

When possible, carry a portion of the demonstration into the centre of the audience to involve them in the presentation.

Cross-Reference

See Giving an Effective Presentation, page 257.

7. Often, a graphic, or series of graphics, is the best way to convey instructions. Imagine how much simpler it would be to explain how to tie a shoelace if you could use diagrams as well as words.

Demonstrating a Process to an Audience

Think of a demonstration as an illustrated talk or an "instruction performance." Here are some tips on how to do a demonstration.

- Begin by explaining the overall purpose of the demonstration.
- Show the audience each of the articles you will use in the demonstration and identify them.
- At each step of the demonstration, make certain that everyone in the audience has a chance to see exactly what you are doing.
- Practise in advance so you can talk naturally while you are demonstrating.

Apply It!

Choose a procedure that interests you. Either write a set of instructions or prepare a demonstration for an audience. Give your instructions to a partner to follow, or present your demonstration to a small group.

Checklist

- Did I list all the tools and materials?
- Did I define technical or unfamiliar words?
- Did I break down the process into manageable steps?
- Did I use graphics (instructions)?
- Did I show and explain each article to the audience (demonstration)?
- Did I follow my own instructions as a test (instructions)?
- Did I practise my presentation in advance?

Think About It: What surprised you about writing instructions or demonstrating a procedure for other people? What's the most important thing you learned?

CHAPTER 9

Representation Strategies

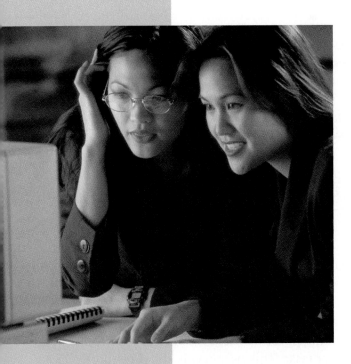

Visual images express ideas, experiences, and feelings. As viewers, we remember what we see. Think about your own experiences. When you remember events that affected you, do you see a picture or do you hear someone speaking? Most people see a picture.

In this chapter, you will stand on the "other side" of the picture by learning the strategies for creative design. You will learn about the design process and how to use it to create photographs, posters, visual aids, brochures, videos, and Web sites. These products are called representations.

Contents

The Design Process:
  An Overview   230

Photographs   233

Posters   235

Visual Aids   238

Brochures   241

Videos   244

Web Sites   248

Learning Goals

- create a variety of representations that express ideas clearly and effectively
- plan, design, revise, and publish representations to fulfill a purpose and to create the desired effect in specific audiences
- explain how design and production choices and solutions suit the representation situation
- use computer technology to serve your purpose
- seek others' responses to clarify and rework ideas
- assess the usefulness of various planning and production strategies

The Design Process: An Overview

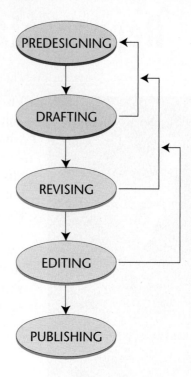

Creating a representation takes skill and involves many activities. As with writing, your representations will be more effective if you break down the process into smaller tasks. This overview is about getting started. So for now, focus on the process, not the product.

Predesigning/Planning

1. Decide on your purpose.

- What is your main goal? Now is the time to lose any needless details. Include only what you need to get your message across. Everything else will distract your audience.

2. Identify your audience.

- Use appropriate language and design elements that will appeal to your audience.

3. Think about the conditions under which your audience will view this material.

- How much time will people actually spend viewing your brochure, poster, Web site, or video? Knowing this will help you decide how much detail to include.

4. Draw up a rough plan and some sketches to organize your thoughts.

- Include a clear statement about your purpose and audience in your plan. Though the plan may change as you move along, your purpose and audience should drive all your decisions.

Troubleshooting: Finding Your Creative Process

Use your own experience with media to guide your creative efforts. What catches your eye? What features make information clearer for you? You are unique in the way you look at images, so use this information to guide your own creative process.

When creating a plan and designing your image, try using different methods to record and track your ideas. Try a group brainstorming session. Use a tree diagram or clustering to keep track of your ideas.

Cross-Reference

See pages 56 and 147 for notes on brainstorming, tree diagrams, and clustering.

Drafting/Designing

1. Draft some rough sketches of your representation. Don't stop at your first idea; make as many rough sketches as possible.

2. Look for models of visual media that appeal to you. Think about how the elements are organized and arranged.

3. When you create an image that you feel good about, make sure that all the elements in your project work together. Have you used a layout that is attractive and eye-catching? Is each element where it should be? Is your main idea clear?

Try It!

If you are using computer software, find out exactly what it can do to help create your visual product. Professional templates are usually a good starting point.

Revising and Editing

These are important stages so don't be tempted to skip them.

1. Review your project step by step. Have you covered everything you wanted to cover? Did you achieve your purpose? Did you keep your audience in mind?

2. Ask someone to look at your work and give you feedback.

Publishing/Production

Once you have finished all your design and revision stages, take another look at the whole representation, and then prepare the final product.

Apply It!	Checklist
The design process applies to every medium. Imagine that you are part of a design team that has been asked to overhaul the school yearbook. Everyone in the school hates the old design, which is boring, outdated, and disorganized. There is often too much text on a page. The design lacks visual appeal. As a team, do the following: • Discuss the purpose of a new yearbook design. • Describe the audience. Who are they? When and where will they look at the newly designed yearbook? • Brainstorm ideas for a new design. • Figure out how to get feedback on the new design. • Develop a plan of action for drawing up some rough sketches.	✓ Did we decide on a purpose for our new design? ✓ Did we identify the audience and their situation? ✓ Did we brainstorm our own ideas, taking into account what we find attractive and readable? ✓ Did we figure out how to get feedback on our ideas? ✓ Did we draw up an action plan for a number of rough sketches and drafts?

Think About It: Did any part of the planning process not work very well? Would you do anything differently next time?

Photographs

Photos are used in many ways:

- to provide a personal record of people and events
- to add drama to news reports
- to demonstrate a product or a process for business purposes in advertisements, training materials, and technical manuals

Your photos will be more effective when you apply some basic rules of composition.

How to Create a Photograph

1. Know the purpose of your photograph.
   - Does it tell a story?
   - Does it make a social comment?
   - Does it sell a product?
   - Does it capture the character or activities of a person?
   - Does it illustrate a process?
2. Remember your audience and their situation as they view your work.
   - Your photo must grab your audience's interest immediately.
   - If your audience does not have time to view your work in the detail that you expect, they will not receive the complete message.
3. Be clear about the focus of your photo. A focal point can be created by
   - ensuring that the most important elements of your photo are in sharp focus
   - avoiding distracting backgrounds
   - showing your subject in close-up
   - using colour, contrast, balance, movement, shape, and line to direct the viewer's eye to the subject
4. Use lighting to add impact to your photos. Lighting adds emphasis and drama to pictures. Bright light creates a feeling of clarity (you see people and things clearly) and soft or subdued lighting creates a feeling of subtlety (you feel that the scene has different meanings or overtones).

What is the purpose of taking photos?

Cross-Reference

For more on photographs, and how to view them, see pages 33 to 35.

Try It!

One of the most powerful lines in creating focus is the "line of sight." In other words, your viewer will tend to look where people in your photo are looking. Try creating a "line of sight" in your next photo.

Don't forget your camera! Photo opportunities are everywhere.

Troubleshooting: What Should I Photograph?

New photographers sometimes have difficulty deciding what they should photograph. In fact, photo opportunities are everywhere. Keep your camera handy and your eyes open.

Apply It!

1. Write a paragraph describing how you could use photos to help you communicate for one of the following:

   • a report of an accident that happened at work (for your supervisor and your company's insurance company)

   • a science report for a school course

   • an article for a school magazine on a sporting event

   • an advertisement for one of your favourite products or for a business that you would like to start up

2. With a small group, create a photo essay entitled "A Day in the Life of Our School." Start by brainstorming possible content and organization for your essay. Divide up the tasks, take your photos, and then meet to choose the ones you will use and to plan the layout for your photo essay.

Checklist

✔ Did I know my purpose and audience for the situation I chose?

✔ Did I describe how photos could be used as a communication tool in that situation?

✔ Did I brainstorm the content and organization for the photo essay?

✔ Did I perform my task?

✔ Did I take the photos assigned to me?

✔ Did I meet with the team to select the photos and plan the layout for the photo essay?

Think About It: How might you have used the techniques in this section to improve photos you've taken in the past? What is one thing you'll be sure to do when you take your next photo?

Posters

As you read in Chapter 2, a poster has very little time to capture the attention of its audience—it must get its message across quickly. It also tries to convince you of something. How do you create an attractive, persuasive poster?

Cross-Reference

For more on posters, and how to view them, see pages 36 to 38.

How to Create a Poster

1. Make sure the focus is clearly on your main message.

   • What is your purpose? Are you trying to persuade or inform? Think about your purpose and make sure that your poster includes these details. Remove anything else.

2. Think about what is important to your intended audience.

   • What will catch your audience's attention? What do they care most about? These types of questions will help you decide on the images and words that you should use.

3. Think about where your poster will be seen.

   • Will your poster be on a moving object, such as the side of a bus? Or will your poster be posted in a place where your audience can look at it closely? These questions will help you decide how much text to use and how large the font should be.

4. Plan the words you will use.

   • What effect do you want to create? Strategies that are sometimes used are words that shock, amuse, or cause confusion. Each of these strategies can get the audience to take a second, more careful look at your poster.

5. Decide how you will balance visuals and words.

   • How do your images and words work together? Where should they be placed to create the most effective presentation? Create a number of small, rough sketches so that you can see how the whole thing will work together.

6. Proofread, proofread, and then proofread again!

   • Remember to check your poster for spelling and grammar. Always ask someone else to review your text for errors and to ensure that you achieve the response that you are looking for.

Your library, your home? Hey, it's a student's second home. You can find everything you need here. Research a project. Study for a test. Borrow movies and CDs. Go on the Internet.

The library. Your home away from home.

Your Library, Your Home?

Hey, it's a student's second home.
You can find everything you need here.

- Research a project
- Study for a test
- Borrow movies and CDs
- Go on the Internet

The library. Your home away from home.

Find one near you at 1-800-111-1111

What makes a poster successful? Which of these two posters do you prefer? Why?

Troubleshooting: Some Design Tips

Keep your design as simple as possible.

- Don't use too many different sizes, styles, and types of fonts or you will end up with a confusing mix of words and effects.
- If you are using a coloured background for your text, make sure that your words show up well on that background.

Apply It!

1. In a small group, imagine that your school has decided to put on a concert featuring a number of local bands. The money raised from the concert will go to UNICEF. Your group will be responsible for creating a poster for the event.

   a) Review the design process (pages 230 to 232) and create a rough sketch of a poster.

   b) Discuss your design decisions. In a report, explain how your use of visuals and text suits your purpose and audience.

   c) Discuss your design in terms of where you think the poster will be posted.

   d) Create your poster.

   e) Present it to the class and discuss any production problems that you might have faced and how you overcame them.

Checklist

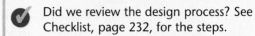 Did we review the design process? See Checklist, page 232, for the steps.

Did we produce a rough sketch of the poster?

Did we offer reasons for our decisions?

Did we consider where and how the poster will be displayed?

Did we create the poster and check it?

Did we present the poster to the class and discuss our production problems?

Think About It: What strategy could you use to avoid any editing or proofreading errors in your poster?

Visual Aids

Visual aids such as charts (tables) and diagrams (graphics) help your readers to understand difficult concepts, especially technical ones. They are "snapshots" of information that must be carefully created to be effective.

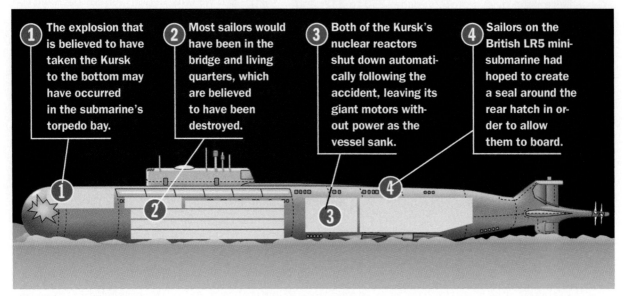

1. The explosion that is believed to have taken the Kursk to the bottom may have occurred in the submarine's torpedo bay.

2. Most sailors would have been in the bridge and living quarters, which are believed to have been destroyed.

3. Both of the Kursk's nuclear reactors shut down automatically following the accident, leaving its giant motors without power as the vessel sank.

4. Sailors on the British LR5 mini-submarine had hoped to create a seal around the rear hatch in order to allow them to board.

On August 12, 2000, the Russian submarine *Kursk* sank to the bottom of the Bering Sea. *Maclean's* used this cutaway diagram to help its readers understand this complex situation.

How to Create a Visual Aid

1. Be clear about your purpose.

- There should be just one main idea for each chart or diagram. Focus on the information that your audience needs to know.
- Think about how your audience will use the information.
- Choose your details carefully. Remove any information that will distract the viewer's attention from your main idea and purpose.

2. Design for clarity.

- Provide a descriptive title so that your readers will know what the chart or diagram is showing.
- Include any labels that will help your readers understand the purpose of the visual aid.

Try It!

Learn to use your computer applications to create visual aids. All office application suites can automatically create different types of charts and graphs.

- Use colour or shading to set apart elements that are being compared.
- Be clear about what units of measurement are being used.
- Include a legend to explain the meaning of symbols, numbers, letters, or colours.
- Consider adding a caption to summarize the main ideas in the visual aid.
- When drawing diagrams, consider different points of view: aerial view, side view, or cutaways. Decide which view would best serve your purpose and help your readers understand the material.

3. Use an appropriate type of visual aid for your purpose and information.
- Charts present numerical information in columns and rows so that viewers can interpret the information quickly and make comparisons.
- Graphs present numerical information in a way that shows comparisons, ratios, and trends over time.
- Cutaway diagrams clearly show the parts of an object.

4. Create a clear relationship between your visual aid and the text.
- Place your visual aid as close as possible to the text it explains. This makes it easier for the reader to make the connection between the text and the visual.
- Mention the visual aid in your report and briefly explain why you have included it.
- Use the same language and units in your visual aid as are used in the accompanying text. For example, if you use the word "chart" in the title of the visual aid, don't refer to it as a "graph" in your report. If you talk about "billions" in your report, don't create a graph with "millions" as the unit of measure.

5. Edit your visual aid carefully.
- Check that you have all the data you need and that all your numbers and totals are accurate.
- Make sure that your legend matches the data in the visual aid.

Aerial view

Side view

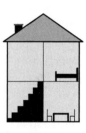

Cutaway view

Cross-Reference

For more on types of graphs, and how to view them, see pages 30 to 32.

Troubleshooting: Achieving Clarity

As you work on your visual aid, try different formats and colour schemes to make it as clear as possible. Include labels and captions even in your rough drafts so all elements are identified. Then ask others to review your visual aid and the section of text it is intended to illustrate. Ask your reviewers to comment on which of your drafts most clearly meets its goal.

Apply It!

1. Look closely at the cutaway diagram of the *Kursk* and answer the following:

   - Identify the four sections of the submarine.

   - How does this diagram show the difficulty of this situation?

   - Which parts of the diagram are most memorable? Why?

   - How do the labels and captions add to your understanding?

   - Are any details left out? If so, why are they missing?

2. The chart below was created to give the following information about ticket sales at a local movie theatre:

   - which days of the week were the biggest money-makers over the past two weeks

   - what percentage of total ticket sales took place on each day of the week

The chart is confusing. In pairs, discuss why this chart does not work, and create a different, clearer format. Remember that you may have to create more than one chart or diagram to replace it.

Checklist

- ✓ Did I examine the diagram of the *Kursk* and identify the sections of the submarine?

- ✓ Did I note how the diagram's labels and captions added to my understanding of the situation?

- ✓ Did I note why the chart of movie sales was a poor visual aid?

- ✓ Did I suggest alternatives? Did they work?

Box Office Receipts 12/1/00 to 12/14/00		
December 1 (Mon) $10 309	December 6 (Sat) $21 618	December 11 (Thurs) $10 931
December 2 (Tues) $16 834	December 7 (Sun) $18 873	December 12 (Fri) $18 432
December 3 (Wed) $12 543	December 8 (Mon) $9 611	December 13 (Sat) $23 700
December 4 (Thurs) $ 11 472	December 9 (Tues) $19 457	December 14 (Sun) $25 300
December 5 (Fri) $19 789	December 10 (Wed) $14 873	

Think About It: Which kind of visual aid do you personally find the most useful or eye-catching? Why does it work for you?

Brochures

Brochures can inform, educate, and/or persuade. Effective brochures give readers a quick overview of a subject, company, product, or service. But regardless of their content and function, brochures need to grab the reader's attention and hold on to it until they achieve their purpose.

How to Create a Brochure

1. Think about your purpose.

- Are you trying to persuade or inform? Knowing this will affect everything from layout to language.

- What points do you want to make? Usually a brochure makes no more than three or four important points. Make sure these points stand out.

- How do you want your brochure to be used? Will it be kept for future reference or read once and then thrown away? Your design should reflect this.

2. Think about your target audience.

- Who will use your brochure? What are their main interests? What attracts them?

- What type of language and tone do they expect?

3. Gather your information and choose a format.

- Write down what you already know about your subject, and then do other research to achieve your purpose.

- Sketch out rough ideas for the content of your brochure and of how you want the brochure to look. Include any graphics you think will help get your message across to your audience.

4. Find a way to capture the reader's interest.

- What is the first thing that your audience will see? Is it a caption? Is it a striking image? Make sure this element communicates your message quickly.

- Focus on your title (on the first page). How will it get people to read on? The best way to get people to read your brochure is to show how your product or information will benefit them or solve a problem.

Cross-Reference

For more on brochures, and how to view them, see pages 42 to 45.

Try It!

Many of today's word-processing programs have templates that you can use to help create brochures. You can view your different drafts on the screen, or print them out so that you can see the full effect.

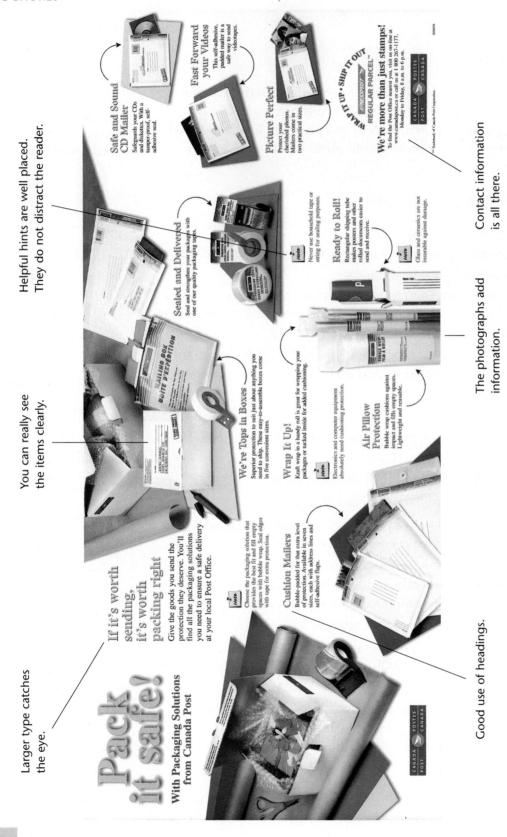

Larger type catches the eye.

You can really see the items clearly.

Helpful hints are well placed. They do not distract the reader.

Contact information is all there.

The photographs add information.

Good use of headings.

What captures a reader's interest?

- Make the information reader-friendly. Look at different type styles and sizes. Generally, text in large type (often called a heading) grabs the reader's attention first.

5. Use strategies to hold your audience's attention.

- Don't overwhelm your readers or they will stop reading.

- Make your brochure easy to read quickly. Use both text and visuals to divide your text into short, readable chunks of information. Use headings.

- Anticipate your readers' questions and give factual answers.

- Ask your reader to take action. If you want the reader to telephone, provide a phone number. If you want your reader to purchase something, provide a purchase form.

Apply It!	Checklist
1. Collect some brochures that you think work well. For each, look at the content and organization, layout, type style, and any visuals. Create a chart showing both the strong and weak points of each brochure. Use this chart to copy the strong points and avoid the weaknesses in your own brochures.	✓ Did I collect brochures that I thought were effective?
	✓ Did I examine the brochures for content and organization, layout, type styles, and visuals?
2. Work with a writing partner to plan, design, and publish a brochure advertising a tourist area. You could use your own community, a different location, or a place out of your imagination—another planet, perhaps.	✓ Did we review the design process before planning the tourist brochure? (See Checklist, page 232, for the steps.)
	✓ Did we create a brochure and check it?
	✓ Did we include all the information that our readers will need to take action: name and address, phone number, Web site, or e-mail address?

Think About It: If you used a template from a software application, how did it affect your choices of layout and content? Don't let the template guide these decisions. Make those decisions yourself depending on your purpose and audience.

Videos

Cross-Reference

For information on films, and how to view them, see pages 46 to 48.

Videos are very different from many of the other representations you've studied and created in this chapter. These moving images work in a way that cannot be copied on a flat, unmoving page. They move through time, and the printed page stays put! Remember this as you create your videos. Your audience interprets this representation in a different way from flat-page representations. The effect of your video will build through the playing of the video. So you will have to focus on this audience effect throughout your planning and production stages.

At home, at school, and in your future careers, you may be asked to create different kinds of videos: visual reports and documentaries on various subjects for school projects, home videos to record important events, and training videos to show other workers how to perform tasks. For these reasons, it is important that you learn to create videos that communicate well.

How to Create a Video

Planning

1. Always keep in mind the effect you want to create.

- Ask yourself: Will this element contribute to my goal? Will it create the right effect on my audience?
- Think about the type of video that you will create. A documentary has a different purpose than a training video or a video report, so your plan will be different.

2. Plan your video so that it has all the elements of a successful story.

- Every television show, news report, or documentary contains the elements of successful storytelling: plot and conflict, characters, dialogue, tone, and setting. Think of how these elements are used in your video.
- Use your own experience and other resources to draw up an outline of the organization of your video.

 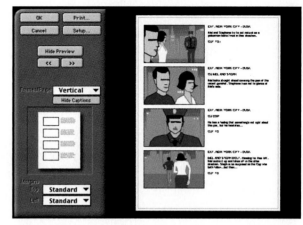

Each frame of the storyboard represents a scene of the video. Storyboards can now be created using computer software, but the elements remain the same. Left, a completed storyboard. Right, each frame of the storyboard has been scripted. Storyboards let you review the organization of your video at a glance.

3. Carefully plan your video before you pick up the camera.

- Use scripts and storyboards to map out your video. A script contains what will be said, while a storyboard shows what will be seen. There should be a clear connection between the dialogue or narration, sound effects and music, and what will be seen.

- Plan the costumes, props, lighting, and sound that you will use in each scene. Think about how these elements will help you create the effect that you want.

- Determine where and when you will be filming. Consider lighting and background noise at different locations and at different times of the day.

Troubleshooting: Teamwork

Making a successful video often requires a creative team. Use teamwork and team processes such as brainstorming. When you are in the early planning stage of your video project, meet with your team members and decide on your roles. Assign tasks based on the skills of each person in your group.

Try It!

Before you begin, decide how long your finished video needs to be. This will help you create a script and storyboard that will work within this time frame.

Cross-Reference

See Effective Group Work, pages 266 to 270.

Filming

Here are some tips for when you finally begin filming.

- It is easy to begin moving away from your plan, so refer to your script and storyboards often.

- Know how to use the video equipment. Take the time to check out all the features of your camcorder so that you can use it effectively.

- Open your video with a shot that establishes place, time, mood, and purpose for your audience.

- Since events may be filmed out of order, ask someone to keep track of continuity. For example, make sure that characters are wearing the same clothes from scene to scene.

- Listen for all the sounds that will be heard in your finished video. This means including the sounds you want to hear and being aware of other noises that do not belong.

Editing

This is an important stage of making a video. As editor, you need to work with all the different elements of the video at once and do this with images that are moving through time. This is not easy, and there are many examples of films where poor editing has introduced humorous inconsistencies. Here are some tips to help you edit successfully.

- Watch the time limit for your video. You will probably need to cut out some of your material to fit the time allotted.

- Fit the scenes and elements together so that they appear seamless to your audience. Use transitions carefully to gain this effect. For example, use cutaways to show characters' reactions to an event or to focus on things that are mentioned by the speaker in the video.

The Final Touches

Now is the time to include elements such as titles and subtitles. Include full credits so that everyone who was involved in making the video is recognized for his or her work.

Troubleshooting: Beyond the Technology

With advances in video technology, you have a wide range of choices when making a video. For example, digital technology allows you to record, change, and move any kind of message or data—print, images, sounds—using just one machine: your computer. But no matter what technology you use, you still need to focus on the basics of communication: your purpose, your audience, and the situation in which the audience will see your video.

Apply It!

1. With a partner, tape a television commercial or a brief news broadcast and study how the editor has cut and combined elements in this short production. Be prepared to present your tape and analysis to the class.

2. With a small group, choose a subject for a short video. This could be a news broadcast, a commercial, a screen adaptation of a favourite short story or poem, or a training video. As you work through your production, follow the stages described in this section. Present your final product to the class, sharing any production problems that you might have faced and how you overcame them.

Checklist

✓ Did we tape a commercial or newscast, analyze its effectiveness, and present our analysis to the class?

✓ Did we choose a subject for a video?

✓ Did we plan the elements to suit our purpose and audience?

✓ Did we create a script and storyboard to outline our video?

✓ Did we pay attention to continuity and to sound effects as we filmed?

✓ Did we edit our video carefully to be sure that all the elements work together to create the best effect?

✓ Did we present our video to the class and share any production problems we faced?

Think About It: What do you think is the most difficult part of making a video? Which strategies do you think are most helpful?

Web Sites

Cross-Reference

For more on Web sites, and how to view them, see pages 49 to 52.

Web sites are used to entertain, persuade, explain, educate, and inform. Perhaps you have already created a Web site—there are lots of software programs that can help. You can add visuals of all sorts—video clips, photographs, charts, graphs, maps, art, animation—and sound as well as text to your Web site.

However, in order for your site to be useful, you still need to know your audience and purpose. And you still need to ensure that your site can be navigated easily. Otherwise, people won't come back.

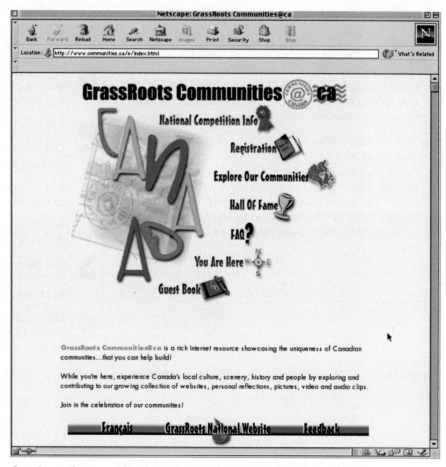

GrassRoots Communities showcases students' Web sites about their local communities. Visit the site to see what other students are doing in the field of Web design.

How to Create a Web Site

1. Take the time to plan your Web site carefully.

- Decide on the purpose and audience for your site. Tell your visitors what is on your site and why it is there.

- Ask yourself if your site fulfills its purpose and will be effective for your audience.

- Organize your information so that your site makes sense and is easy to navigate.

2. Design your Web pages carefully.

- Your site should be attractive. Although content is more important than presentation, if your site looks unprofessional or unfriendly, people will not stay long enough to read it.

- Make sure your text is easily readable. Choose your type styles and colour carefully.

- Check that each page you design is small enough that it will load quickly. Test your site on different screen types, computers, and modems to see how quickly they appear.

- Make your site easy to navigate. On your opening Web page, include a clear title for the site, a site index, menus, and links so that your visitors will know where to go and what they will find when they arrive.

- Don't put too much text on a single page. Try to limit pages to no more than three screens.

- Use links that are dependable, that have reliable sponsors, and that are related to the purpose and the audience for your site.

- Date your Web site so that visitors will know when it was last updated.

3. Edit your page carefully.

- Write clearly so that you say exactly what you intend to say.

- Check that the information on your Web site is accurate and useful for your visitors. Inaccurate information is one of the greatest downfalls of the Web.

- Make sure that your information is free of bias.

- Check your spelling and grammar. Even one spelling mistake can make the reader question how trustworthy your site is.

Try It!

Check that visitors can easily link back to your main page from any other pages on your site. A site should *never* hit a dead-end where the user has to use the "back button" to get off a page.

Try It!

Be prepared to update your Web site regularly and make sure that all your links are still working (that the linked Web sites still exist). Some programs will do this automatically.

• Respect the copyright of other artists, writers, and Web creators. Ask permission before you copy anything, and credit all your sources.

Apply It!	Checklist
1. Visit two Web sites and evaluate their effectiveness. What type of planning went into their creation? Be prepared to share your findings with a group of classmates. 2. Working with a small group, create a plan for a Web site for your school. If your school already has a Web site, evaluate its contents and suggest ways to improve it. After your planning, create the site and present it to your class.	✓ Did we visit two Web sites and evaluate their effectiveness? ✓ Did we conclude how well planned the sites were? ✓ Did we set a clear focus for our Web site based on our purpose and audience? ✓ Did we create a layout that viewers will find easy to read and to use? ✓ Did we use colour and different type styles to complement our layout? ✓ Did we organize our site so that it is easy to navigate with clear and easy-to-use menus and links to other sites? ✓ Did we present our Web site to the class?

Think About It: In your notebook, write a paragraph on any production problems that you faced while creating your Web site. How did you overcome them? Which of the strategies in this chapter will you use to create other Web sites?

Speak Out!
Listen Up!

Concentrate

"Speaking" is what you do with your friends, family, and teachers, of course. Then there's specialized speaking—speeches, debates, presentations, and so on. And, where there's speaking, there's listening! At least, there should be. Get ready to find out about different kinds of speaking and listening situations.

Give a Speech

Make Notes

Work Together

Contents

Chapter 10
Speaking and Listening   252

Speaking and Listening

The most basic of all human needs is the need to understand and be understood.

—Ralph Nichols

Does your mind wander when someone else is talking? Do you interrupt people? When you are speaking, do you ever stop to think about what your listener wants to hear or do you just keep talking?

If any of these things happen to you, perhaps you need to brush up on your speaking and listening skills. In this chapter, you will learn the skills for effective speaking and listening. You will also begin to appreciate how these skills are needed for effective group work.

Contents

Effective Public Speaking	253
Effective Listening	261
Effective Group Work	266
Types of Groups	271
Think More About It	276

Learning Goals

- use effective speaking skills
- know how to do an effective oral and visual presentation
- use effective listening skills
- understand types of groups
- understand group roles and how groups function
- relate communication skills to future school or career plans

Effective Public Speaking

Most people don't enjoy speaking in front of an audience. However, effective public speaking is a valuable skill. It can help you get your message across to many people, it can promote action, and it can foster good relationships.

Below are ways to help you learn effective public speaking for oral presentations.

Thinking About Public Speaking: What, Who, Why, How, Where, and When

To help you plan for public speaking, ask yourself the following questions.

1. Topic: *What* am I speaking about?

- What is my topic? Do I have information on the topic?
- What questions might I be asked? Do I know how to answer them?

2. Audience: To *whom* am I speaking?

- Who is my audience?
- Is my audience familiar with this topic? What information will I need to explain?
- Is my audience made up of friends and colleagues, or people that I do not know?

Knowing your audience will help you decide on the tone and the level of language to use.

Audience	How to Say It
Your own science class	• Use information known by everyone. • Highlight new information. • Be well organized, concise, and relaxed. • Use less formal language.
Members of your photography club	• Present the facts but don't give a speech. • Be relaxed and casual. • Use an informal tone and language, including slang and humour.
School officials and community members	• Respect your audience but don't apologize for your opinions. • Stick to the topic. • Be formal, concise, and well prepared. • Use formal language and presentation.

3. Purpose: *Why* am I speaking?

- What is my purpose? Am I trying to inform, persuade, or entertain my audience?

Purpose	What to Say
To present a science project	• Describe project plan and format. • Provide facts and findings. • At the end, summarize your material.
To open a meeting	• Welcome the group. • List topics to be discussed. • Follow any club procedures.
To deliver a speech to persuade school officials	• Argue a position with evidence. • Address any contrary opinions openly. • Restate your position firmly.

4. Setting: *How* is this meeting being run?

- Am I giving a speech by myself or within a group?
- Will I be expected to answer questions at the end of my speech?
- If I am part of a group discussion, is the group
  - exploring a topic and coming to a conclusion (e.g., a formal meeting)?
  - exploring different sides of an issue (e.g., panel discussion or symposium)?
  - voicing opposing viewpoints (e.g., debate)? Will I have to defend my position?
- Will roles be assigned? What role will I play? (The chairperson, for example, will have a specific role to play.)

5. Place: *Where* will I be speaking?

- What will the room be like? Will it be large or small?
- Will I need a microphone? Will other audio-visual equipment be available?
- How will the audience seating be arranged? Can I choose the setup?

6. Time: *When* will I speak?

- Will I speak after or before another speaker?
- Will there be a time limit on my comments or presentation?

Cross-Reference

See also Speeches on page 255; Committees and Formal Meetings on page 271; Panels, Symposiums, and Forums on page 273; Debates on pages 274 to 275; and The Role of the Chairperson on page 266.

What's the time limit?

Checklist for Preparing to Speak in Public

- ✅ Am I well informed about my topic?
- ✅ Am I familiar with who my audience is?
- ✅ Do I understand what my purpose is?
- ✅ Do I understand how the meeting will be run?
- ✅ Do I know where it will take place?
- ✅ Do I know when it will take place?

Writing an Effective Speech

In some ways, writing a speech is like writing an essay—both can inform, explain, entertain, persuade, and impress. When writing your speech, start by referring to the writing process outlined in Chapter 3. Here are some more tips.

Capture Your Audience's Attention

Hook your listeners' interest right away with a startling statement or image, a humorous story, a personal anecdote—anything that will make your audience sit up and listen.

Keep Your Audience with You

- Tell your audience what you will be talking about and the points that you will be raising. Pay attention to the structure of your argument, and summarize your points from time to time. This helps your listeners to concentrate.

- Use strong visual images that will help your audience to remember what you have said. Appeal to their senses: sight, hearing, smell, taste, and touch.

- Use stories and anecdotes to illustrate difficult or important ideas. They help your audience understand and concentrate.

- Keep your language simple. Avoid "speech" words such as "therefore," "in conclusion," and "nevertheless." Avoid using too many adjectives—instead, try to make your verbs and nouns do the work.

Send Your Audience Away with Your Message in Mind

Write a strong conclusion that recaps the main ideas in your speech. Don't end your talk with "And that's it" or "That's all I have to say." What message do you want to leave with your audience?

Try It!

Create a chart with six columns titled: What (Topic), Who (Audience), Why (Purpose), How (Format), Where (Place), and When (Time). Make several photocopies to keep for future public speaking opportunities.

Make your audience sit up and listen.

Here is an example of a speech written and delivered by a graduating high school student. Notice if the writer of the speech has followed the rules outlined on the previous page.

A High School Graduation Speech

by Erika Juergensen

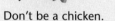

Don't be a chicken.

Good evening. I would like to begin my speech with a local fable.

Once upon a time, there was an eagle's nest that contained four large eagle eggs. One day, the nest was disturbed by a terrible storm, causing one of the eggs to roll down into a chicken farm, located in the valley below. The chickens knew that they must protect and care for the eagle's egg, so an old hen volunteered to nurture and raise the large egg.

One day, the egg hatched and a beautiful eagle was born. Now, the eagle loved his home and family, but his spirit cried out for more. Whenever the eagle looked up toward the sky and saw a group of mighty eagles soaring, he would cry, "How I wish I could soar like those birds."

This always caused the chickens to roar with laughter. "You cannot soar with those birds!" they cried. "You are a chicken now, and chickens do not soar."

But the eagle could not stop dreaming of being with the other eagles. Each time the eagle would let his dreams be known, he was told that it couldn't be done. And finally, that is what the eagle learned to believe. In fact, he died believing he was a chicken.

I believe that this story holds the greatest message any person can ever receive. That message is that you become what you believe you are. So, if you ever dream to become an eagle, follow your dreams. Don't believe what someone tells you.

Undoubtedly, each one of us may reach a point in our lives where it would be easy to settle for a career that isn't fulfilling, saying, "Hey, it puts food on the table." So my question is, why would you want to do that? We are a class so rich with potential and talent that we should not settle for something that falls below our abilities. I can't imagine a worse punishment than waking up every morning and going to work at a job that you can't stand or have little interest in.

Luckily every person in this graduating class has the potential to be something outstanding. Don't let any person tell you that you shouldn't pursue your interests because it doesn't make enough money or you shouldn't because it's too competitive or you shouldn't because it's not sensible. If it is something that you truly want to do, no matter what, you will be successful.

Stay true to yourself—follow the path of the eagle.

Apply It!

1. Analyze the sample speech according to the suggestions for writing speeches given in this section. Write notes and labels on sticky notes and attach them to the printed speech. Write a brief note describing one way the speech could have been improved. Compare your point-form analysis with a partner's.

2. Choose an essay from your portfolio and rewrite it as a speech. As you write, remember that one difference is that your audience will be *hearing* your words, rather than *reading* them.

Checklist

☑ Did I look for examples of the speech-writing tips as I read the sample speech?

☑ Did I label both strong and weak elements?

☑ Did I clearly describe one way the speech could have been improved?

☑ Did I keep my listening audience in mind as I rewrote my essay into a speech?

☑ Did I start with an attention-grabber?

☑ Did I change the tone at all?

☑ Did I keep the main points of the essay?

☑ Did I write a conclusion that will keep my message in the audience's mind?

Think About It: How did reading and analyzing a sample speech help you write your own? How did you use the tips?

Using Audio-Visual Aids

Audio-visual aids can enhance your presentation. Here are some things to think about.

1. Which aids would help me communicate my message?
2. Which ones will distract my audience too much?
3. Do I have access to the right equipment? Check in advance.
4. Is the presentation room set up practically for viewing audio-visuals? Can the seating be changed if necessary?
5. Can my visuals be seen by everyone? Can everyone hear my audio examples?

Can everyone see the visuals?

Giving an Effective Presentation

Practise, Practise, Practise

Practising your presentation is very important. The more prepared you are, the calmer you will be. Here are a few things to think about when you practise.

• Go over your speech until you are familiar with it. Then write brief notes on 7 cm x 13 cm note cards. Number the cards in order. You can refer to these cards and "speak to the points" instead of reading your speech. Practise using the cards so that you become comfortable with using them. Here is a sample cue card for a speaker talking about racism:

7
Racist hatred stems from fear.

- Ask if you can practise your speech in the room that you will be speaking in.
- Ask someone to listen to you practise and offer feedback.
- Ask your test audience to comment on your voice quality. If you are practising alone, tape-record yourself and listen to your voice.
- Practise using your audio-visual aids so that you can use them without fumbling.

Apply It!	Checklist
Take out the speech that you wrote earlier.	✓ Did I listen to myself reading my speech?
• Read it aloud as it is and/or tape it.	✓ Did I write all the main points I wanted to make on my cue cards?
• Write notes and main points on cue cards.	
• Practise your speech using the cue cards. (You could tape yourself.)	✓ Did I ask someone to listen to me practise and give me feedback?
• Note differences between reading your speech and using cue cards.	✓ Did I tape-record myself if I practised alone?
• Plan the use of any audio-visual aids you might want during your speech.	✓ Did I practise with my audio-visual aids?
• Work with a partner or family members to get feedback and polish your speech.	

Think About It: What worked best for you to make your speech sound like a speech? Write down the steps you will take the next time you prepare a speech.

Being on Stage

On the day of the presentation, arrive early so that you can check the room. Check that all the equipment you need is there, that it is working well, and that you know how to use it. Test and adjust all controls such as lighting and volume levels before you begin.

When it's time to begin, here are some things to keep in mind.

- Be relaxed and enthusiastic about your topic, even if you want to bolt from the building. If you are nervous, don't hold your notes since any hand shaking becomes noticeable. Set your notes on a table or lectern. Your audience is looking to you for cues, so if you are noticeably anxious, your listeners will feel this way too.

- Be friendly and make eye contact with different people in the room.

- Respect the listener. Allow listeners to have their own points of view, to ask questions, and to give you feedback. *Never* argue with an audience member.

- Keep your language at the level suited to your audience. Don't use language that is too high or formal or "talk down" to your audience.

- Watch your audience for feedback. If your audience looks confused, distracted, or bored, take steps to bring them back. Clarify an issue, ask them a question, or just "shift gears."

- Keep your sense of humour. Your audience will probably laugh with you, even if something unexpected happens.

Help Your Audience to Follow Your Argument

- Begin by telling your audience what you will be speaking about.

- Use gestures, eye contact, and tone of voice to alert your listeners to important statements or to indicate when you are moving to a new point.

- Review what you have said and preview where you are going.

- Keep your listeners involved. Ask questions even if you don't expect an answer. This keeps your audience members thinking.

Remove Barriers to Listening

- Make sure that all your listeners can hear and see you clearly.

- Be enthusiastic but don't use body language that could distract your audience.

Try It!

Make a conscious effort to keep your shoulders down rather than hunched up and tense. This will help you to look and feel relaxed.

Don't be afraid to laugh.

- Be aware of your speaking pace. Most people tend to talk too fast. Pause occasionally to give your listeners time to digest an important point.
- Use your visuals at the appropriate point in your speech. Ensure that everyone can see them.

Here is an example of what not to do when making an oral presentation.

Apply It!

1. Study the cartoon above. With a partner, identify what the speaker is doing wrong based on what you have learned about effective speaking.

2. Deliver the speech you have been preparing to your classmates. Consider all the hints that you have learned in the previous pages to help you deliver an effective speech.

Checklist

- Did we identify the cartoon speaker's errors based on what we've read?
- Did I feel well prepared for making my speech?
- Did I stay on topic during my speech? Was I concise and to the point?
- Did I watch for cues from the audience and react to them?
- Did I sound and act interested in my topic? In my audience?
- Did I speak loudly and slowly enough?
- Did I use the room effectively? Were my audio-visual props effective?
- Did I stay within the time limit?

Think About It: Use the checklist to help you evaluate how you delivered your speech. Identify three things you could have done better and what you will do better next time.

Effective Listening

We spend over 45 percent of our day just listening to others. But we often hear without really listening. Effective listening is an active process.

Preparing to Listen: What Are Your Expectations?

Before you listen, ask yourself:

1. What is the topic of this discussion?

Knowing the topic lets you determine if the speaker is on topic.

2. Who is the speaker?

The identity of the speaker could give you a clue as to the speaker's opinion.

3. What are your feelings about the person who is speaking?

What would you think of this same message if your best friend said it?

4. What are your opinions about this topic?

We often listen for the information that supports our personal views. Listen to learn something new.

The following story shows a listener who just wasn't prepared to listen.

"Hey Kelly, we're going down to the rink to play some shinny. Want to come?" Adam asked.

"No, I can't. Our computer teacher said we have to go listen to this guy talk about careers in the computer field."

"What!? On a Saturday? Come on. Skip it."

"I can't. My teacher says that she's going to ask us a bunch of stuff on Monday."

"Well, okay. See you later!" Adam laughed as he poked her with his stick and ran off toward the rink.

Kelly sighed as she turned toward the grey building about a block away. Now she was more than a little angry about having to go to the presentation. As she entered the hall, she noticed a large gathering of people, but none of her friends. The speaker was about to start so she slipped into the back corner and slunk down into the seat.

Why is Kelly bored?

While waiting, she examined the graffiti on the back of the seats in front of her. She barely even noticed the man beginning to speak. When she looked up, her reaction was, "Oh man, look at that guy. He can't even dress himself!" The next hour and a half felt like a day and a half. At least she had the graffiti to keep her attention. She also scored about two dozen goals in her mind as she waited for the presentation to end.

Finally the lights came on. Was her torture over? Nope. Someone in the front row had about a hundred questions so she was stuck there for about another half hour. When the speaker finally said his thanks, Kelly could hardly wait to get out of there. She took a quick glance to see who had asked all the stupid questions and was amazed to find that it was her friend Cyndi. At that moment, Cyndi turned and, seeing Kelly, she excitedly waved hello and bounded toward Kelly.

"Hey, Kel. That was pretty interesting, eh? I can't believe what he said about the trends. And how about the money you can make? Awesome! I have so many more questions. What did you think?"

Apply It!

1. Create a three-column chart. In the left column, write the four basic questions from Preparing to Listen on page 261. Add one or two more questions of your own. In the role of first Kelly, then Cyndi, write "their" answers to the questions in the other columns.

2. With a partner, discuss why Kelly had such a different experience from Cyndi. List suggestions for how Kelly's experience could have been better.

Checklist

- Did I rewrite the questions from Preparing to Listen in chart form?
- Did I add any that I thought of myself?
- Did I answer the questions as if I were first Kelly, then Cyndi?
- Did I notice differences in how "they" responded to some questions?
- Did my partner and I agree on why their experiences were so different?
- Did we list some things Kelly could have done to make her experience better?

Think About It: In your notebook, list at least four strategies that help you to be a good listener. Which is the most difficult for you? How can you improve?

Listening: Concentration and Active Participation

The key to listening is concentration and active participation. Here are some tips.

1. Listen with your whole body.

- Keep your eyes focused on the speaker, not on the room.
- Be relaxed, but alert. Don't slouch! Lean toward the speaker.
- Take notes.

When it is clear that you are listening, the speaker becomes more relaxed and comfortable presenting his or her ideas to you.

2. Listen for a reason.

You can listen for all sorts of reasons: to understand, to be entertained, or to get closer to a friend. Here are a few reasons you might listen to another person, and some actions you can take to keep yourself focused on your goal.

Cross-Reference

See Taking Notes in Lectures or Discussions on page 265.

Reason for Listening	Example	Plan for Active Listening
To gather information	science lecture	• Write down main ideas. • Write down your questions. • Review notes soon after the event.
To get help in forming an opinion	a political debate	• Make notes of main ideas. • Analyze the validity of each point. • Be prepared to ask questions.
To develop closeness	a friend	• Listen to the other person's needs and viewpoint. • Ask questions that show interest in the person's views.

3. Listen critically.

- Is the speaker trying to entertain you, give you information, or persuade you?
- Don't let the speaker lead you. Question each point made by the speaker.
- Question the speaker's conclusions. Has he or she given evidence? Where did it come from? Is it accurate? Does it really support the conclusions?

- Listen to the speaker's language. Is he or she using "absolutes"? There are very few absolutes in life. Be suspicious when you hear words or phrases such as "all," "every," "not one," "of course," or "everyone knows."

4. Listen to get the big picture.

- Watch for the "building blocks"—the main ideas that create the big picture. Like an essay, a speech has a definite structure and your job is to discover it.

- Watch for changes in tone or body language—they can signal an important point. Also watch for words or phrases that indicate points are being made, such as "first," or "finally," or "I will present four reasons why...."

- Try to determine why the speaker is speaking and where he or she is going to take you. This will help you to concentrate on the discussion and listen critically.

Here is a listener who hasn't understood what it means to be a good listener.

Try It!

Even if you are listening to a speech in a huge auditorium, try to listen as if you and the speaker were alone in the room, having a private conversation. Think about how you would respond to each point being made.

Apply It!

1. With a partner, study the above Peanuts comic strip. Discuss the message of the comic strip. How has Peppermint Patty shown that she is not listening?

2. Go over what you have read so far in this chapter about effective listening. Write down at least six specific actions you will take the next time you are in a listening situation. Turn them into a checklist so you can assess your success.

Checklist

✓ Did my partner and I "get" the message of the comic strip?

✓ Did we recognize the signs that Peppermint Patty wasn't listening?

✓ Did I review the section about effective listening?

✓ Did I make a checklist of at least six actions I will take when I am in a listening situation?

Think About It: In your journal, write in point form an evaluation of your listening behaviour and skills. Identify areas you could work on to improve your listening.

Troubleshooting: Overcoming Barriers to Listening

Being an effective listener also means not letting barriers interfere with your listening.

- Try to block out all distractions.
- Listen for the main ideas (the big picture) and note the details later.
- Avoid getting upset and presenting arguments before the speaker is finished.
- Evaluate *what* is said, not *how* it is said. Avoid criticizing the speaker's personality or manner of presentation.

Taking Notes in Lectures or Discussions

Some people have trouble taking notes in lectures or discussions because they try to write down everything a speaker says. These key points are worth remembering.

- Write down just the main ideas.
- Limit details to one or two words that will jog your memory later.
- Spend more time listening than writing. Listen, think, then write.
- Use headings and charts to help organize your thoughts.
- Fill in your notes immediately after the discussion.

The next time you take notes during a lecture or discussion, use this checklist.

Checklist for Effective Note Taking

- ✔ Did I write down keywords and phrases?
- ✔ Did I listen, think, then write?
- ✔ Did I include headings to help organize my notes?
- ✔ Did I create charts or other visual shortcuts?
- ✔ Did I fill in my notes with details later on?
- ✔ Are my completed notes readable and helpful?

Think About It: What is most difficult for you about taking notes while you listen? What can you do to make it easier?

Effective Group Work

When you come together as a group, make sure that you work together to achieve your goals. Start by asking:

- Why has this group been formed? What is our purpose? What do we hope to achieve?
- What knowledge, expertise, and strengths do we have?
- What procedures would help us stay on topic and on schedule?
- How will we deal with disagreements and reach consensus?

Once you have determined the purpose of your group, you can use roles and procedures to help you be more effective.

Roles

Some groups have formal roles that help the group run better. In a formal setting, there is usually a chairperson and a secretary.

The Role of the Chairperson

The chairperson

- prepares and distributes an agenda or outline in advance
- communicates the format and time restrictions well in advance of the meeting
- makes an opening statement explaining the purpose of the discussion
- ensures that participants stick to the subject
- makes sure that each person gets a chance to participate
- ensures that participants show courtesy and respect for others

Even if the role of chairperson is not formally assigned, it is important that someone assume this role. Usually, this role falls to the person who calls the meeting.

The Role of the Secretary

The secretary

- records and condenses the information from the meeting into key points
- records decisions, actions, and important information
- provides a summary at the end of the discussion or during the discussion
- produces the minutes (notes) from the meeting, has them approved by the chairperson, and distributes them

Formal meetings need a chairperson.

Try It!

If a group member is taking up too much time or going off topic, it is the chairperson's responsibility to step in politely. Try saying something like, "Excuse me, but I think we need to concentrate on the main point of the discussion."

Working Together

Brainstorming

Brainstorming is a great way to open a meeting because it encourages creative ideas. The goal of brainstorming is to produce more ideas than are actually needed. Brainstorming is especially helpful in showing all the issues that are linked to a topic.

Here is how to brainstorm:

1. The chairperson introduces the topic or problem.

2. Someone stands at the front of the group and writes down all the ideas that the group can think of. Make sure all members can see the ideas that are written down.

3. Don't judge or reject *any* of the ideas. Even if an idea sounds silly, it may help someone else think of a better idea. It is up to the chairperson to catch anyone who starts to criticize or analyze an idea at this stage.

4. Aim for quantity, not quality. Build on other members' ideas.

5. After you have created as many ideas as possible, have your own group or another group narrow down the ideas and analyze each remaining idea in detail.

Apply It!	Checklist
Work in a group of four or five. Choose one of the suggested topics (or one of your own) and do a brainstorming session for ideas. • raise money for a school activity (such as a trip or a dance) • reduce conflict on school grounds • create a dress code • find part-time jobs • decorate the gym	✓ Did we choose a chairperson to introduce the topic? ✓ Did someone write down all the ideas? ✓ Did we accept all ideas without judging them? ✓ Did we aim for quantity rather than quality? ✓ Did we narrow down the ideas and analyze those remaining? ✓ Did we end up with a list of solid ideas to continue discussing?

Think About It: In your notebook, write down what worked well in your brainstorming session and what didn't. Write two suggestions for making the next session more effective.

Troubleshooting: Impractical Ideas

Before you reject the more impractical ideas, see if they have any value. Try making them into something more practical. For example, if a student suggests you get Bryan Adams to do a benefit concert for the school, someone else could follow up by saying, "Maybe we can't get Bryan Adams, but we could have an 'air band' contest where people imitate him." This is how an impractical idea leads to a practical one.

Dealing with Disagreements

Most groups go through a growth period when members feel dissatisfied with the way things are going. In most cases, this stage passes and the group starts to work well together. If you are having difficulty working together, remember the following:

- Don't take discussions personally. When someone disagrees with you, listen to what they have to say and keep an open mind. Don't decide that they just don't like you.

- If you disagree, be friendly. Make friendly eye contact with the person who presented the idea, keep your voice calm, and discuss the idea. Avoid confrontational words or body language such as leaning away or crossing your arms. Do not verbally attack the person. For example, never say, "I disagree with *you*." Instead say, "I disagree with *the idea* that…." Then, be prepared to listen. Maybe the other person was right after all.

- Do use sentences that start with "I feel." This takes some of the responsibility for the disagreement away from the speaker. Also, most people are sensitive to others' feelings. The person you are disagreeing with may be more open to your views as a result.

- Find common ground. Without a common goal, you would not be together as a group. Remind yourselves of what that goal is. Focusing on what you have to do together to accomplish it may help you to set aside your differences, at least temporarily.

- Split into subgroups. Research has shown that groups tend to work best when they are small (three or four members). If you find that some group members are not working as hard on a project as others, consider breaking up into smaller groups with specific tasks assigned to each.

Don't take it personally.

Try It!

Give praise where praise is due. Acknowledge individual efforts, encourage members who come up with ideas, and never make fun of what another member says. We all like to have our talents and contributions recognized.

Apply It!

In your original group, think about a situation that led to disagreements (or create one that might). Together compose a one- to two-page script showing how best to deal with a disagreement. Be prepared to each take a role and present your script to the class.

Checklist

✓ Did we work together to create different approaches and possible solutions?

✓ Did we respect each other's input and consider each other's ideas carefully?

✓ Did we resolve differences by using tactful language to respect others' feelings?

✓ Did we make sure that we did not make the discussion personal or take any of the comments personally?

✓ Did we come up with and agree upon an interesting, workable solution?

Think About It: How did you contribute to the group task? How might you improve in your next group work? What did you learn about dealing with disagreements from writing the script and playing your role in the script?

Achieving Consensus

Consensus is the general agreement arrived at among group members. General agreement about a topic, issue, or goal may not always be achieved. In this case, the goal of consensus is to follow a fair process and reach a decision that all members can live with.

To achieve consensus, it is important that some basic ground rules be followed:

A decision everyone can live with!

- Each person must understand and believe in the group's purpose. A strong agenda, which all members agree with, must reflect this purpose.

- There must be mutual respect among group members.

- All group members must be considered equally important. If any member, even secretly, believes that there are more and less important people in the group, arriving at consensus will be difficult.

- Every member is responsible for offering input. To be silent is to show agreement!

- It is important to have a facilitator (the chairperson may fill this role). The facilitator draws the best from each group member by being open and fair to everyone.

- When it comes time to make a decision, every member has three options:
  - to block the conclusion by refusing to agree
  - to stand aside, which means that though the member does not agree with the conclusion, it is something that he or she can live with
  - to give consent to, or agree with, the conclusion

Apply It!	Checklist
Revisit the list of ideas from your brainstorming session. With the same group, continue the discussion and arrive at a consensus about what action to take.	✓ Did we understand the group's purpose? ✓ Did members show mutual respect for each other? ✓ Did we consider all members as equal? ✓ Did everyone offer input? ✓ Did a fair facilitator help to resolve disagreements and guide the group to an agreement? ✓ Did everyone give consent?

Think About It: What posed the largest problem to reaching consensus? List some ways of making the process easier the next time.

Troubleshooting: Achieving Consensus

To make sure that your group achieves consensus smoothly, consider using a facilitator who will not participate in the discussion so that he or she doesn't show any favour toward one argument over another.

Types of Groups

People form groups for different reasons. They might come together to discuss problems and propose solutions, to explore ideas, or to achieve a task. Let's look at some types of groups and the speaking and listening skills involved in them.

Groups That Form to Achieve a Task and Solve a Problem

Committees and formal meetings are formed to accomplish tasks and find solutions to problems. It is important that the roles of chairperson, secretary, and timekeeper be assigned to keep the meeting on track.

Committees

A committee is made up of a small group of people who have been asked to work on behalf of a larger group. You might want to form a committee

- to solve a problem
- to gather information
- to monitor an ongoing situation
- to initiate and carry out a specific task (such as selling tickets)

Each time a committee meets, there is a group discussion. It helps if the committee has a chairperson and if each member has a specific area to report on.

Formal Meetings

A formal meeting is usually a regular gathering of people who belong to a company, a club, or an organization. The meeting is conducted by a chairperson according to the rules of parliamentary procedure. It follows a specific plan, or agenda, prepared and distributed in advance. Most formal meetings follow this pattern:

1. Call to order by the chairperson
2. Reading or distribution of the minutes of the previous meeting. (The minutes are the official record of what happened at the meeting.)
3. Reports of various committees
4. Unfinished business from previous meetings
5. New business

> **Cross-Reference**
>
> See also The Role of the Chairperson, page 266.

6. Announcements

7. Adjournment by the chairperson

All remarks in a formal meeting are directed to the chairperson. Decisions in a formal meeting are made by motions, followed by voting. A motion is a formal suggestion put before the group for consideration, such as "I move that we adopt a pet rat as our school mascot."

Here is the process by which a motion leads to a decision by the group.

1. The person making the motion begins his or her statement by saying, "I move that...."

2. A motion requires a seconder, a person who agrees that this motion is a good idea. The seconder says, "I second the motion."

3. A discussion of the motion follows. Those wishing to speak, raise their hands to address the chairperson.

4. When discussion seems near an end, the chairperson will ask, "Is there any further discussion?" If not, voting follows. Generally, motions are voted on by a show of hands. The chairperson only votes if there is a tie.

For more information on parliamentary procedure, look over a copy of *Robert's Rules of Order*. Most libraries have this book.

A show of hands.

Checklist for Committee and Formal Meetings

When listening at a committee or formal meeting:

- ✅ Did we actively listen to other participants?
- ✅ Did we listen without interrupting?
- ✅ Did we ask relevant questions?
- ✅ Did we show respect to all participants when voicing different opinions?
- ✅ Did we respect the direction of the chairperson, secretary, and timekeeper?
- ✅ Did we respect the decision made by the group?

When speaking at a committee or formal meeting:

- ✅ Did we make sure that everyone understood how the meeting would proceed?
- ✅ Did we begin by defining the purpose of the discussion?
- ✅ Did we come to the meeting prepared to contribute to the discussion?

Try It!

To find out what a formal meeting is like, attend a local city council meeting.

✔ Did we stick to the topic?

✔ Did we give each member a chance to speak?

✔ Did we come up with a workable plan or solution?

Groups That Form to Explore Ideas

Panel discussions, symposiums, and forums are types of gatherings that are formed to explore ideas.

Panels

A panel is made up of three to seven people who are knowledgeable about a specific topic. Most panel discussions have a chairperson or moderator.

A comedians' panel discussion.

In a panel discussion, the panellists sit before an audience and talk among themselves in voices loud enough to be heard by the audience. The audience has the opportunity to hear different points of view on a topic.

Many panel discussions allow for a question period at the end. During the question period, audience members ask questions directed either at an individual panel member or at the panel as a whole.

Symposiums

A symposium is a gathering of well-informed individuals, each of whom is prepared to give a formal presentation on a specific aspect of a chosen subject. The presentations are usually given in front of an audience; however, participants in a symposium don't necessarily discuss the issue among themselves in front of the audience.

A symposium is usually chaired by one person who introduces the participants and explains their areas of expertise. There is usually a question period after each presentation.

Forums

A forum is a group discussion in which everyone has an opportunity to express views or ask questions on a topic. A forum often begins with a panel discussion, followed by questions and comments from the audience. The chairperson calls upon the audience members and directs their questions to the appropriate panel members.

Checklist for Panels, Symposiums, and Forums

When listening to a panel discussion, symposium, or forum:

✔ Did we listen attentively to each speaker and try to separate fact from opinion?

✔ Did we come prepared to ask questions of the panel members?

✔ Did we try to compare and evaluate the different opinions of the participants?

When speaking in a panel discussion, symposium, or forum:

✔ Did we come well informed about the topic?

✔ Did we stick to the assigned topic?

✔ Did we speak loudly enough for the audience to hear?

✔ Did we respect each other's opinions and avoid interrupting?

✔ Did we respect the instructions of the chairperson and time-keeper?

Groups That Form to Argue Viewpoints

Debates are very structured types of meetings. Their success relies on following the structure and keeping within time limits. It is important to assign the roles of a chairperson and timekeeper.

Informal Debates

In a debate, people present arguments for and against a point of view. When you take part in a debate your aim is to defend a position, regardless of your personal views. Here is a five-stage plan for an informal classroom debate.

Stage 1: Decide on a Topic or Resolution

Present the topic (often called a resolution) as a statement, preceded by the words "Be it resolved that...." Make the resolution as specific as possible. For example: "Be it resolved that people who smoke should pay for their own health-care costs."

Stage 2: Present the Opposing Views

Choose four students to present the arguments in the debate. These students will have to research and prepare their statements before the debate. Two of them will take the affirmative side (agree with the statement made in the resolution). The other two will take the negative side (disagree). The two sides alternate, each member presenting a five-minute speech, while the audience listens and evaluates their arguments.

Stage 3: Refute the Arguments

Each member of the debating team has a few minutes in which to refute (prove incorrect) the arguments put forward by his or her opponents.

Stage 4: Question Period

For 10 minutes, members of the audience are given a chance to ask questions of the debaters. The chairperson should call on those who want to ask questions.

Stage 5: Vote

At the end of the question period, the chairperson asks the audience to vote by a show of hands to decide which side has won the debate.

Formal Debates

Formal debates follow parliamentary procedure—very strict guidelines for how an argument should be presented and refuted. The process is much like the informal debate, but the procedures are more complex. If you want to know more about formal debates, visit your library or search the Internet.

Follow parliamentary procedure.

Apply It!

With your classmates, brainstorm debate topics. Come to a consensus on which one to debate. Plan and hold the debate, using skills you have learned in this chapter.

Checklist

As the audience of the debate:

- ✓ Did we listen objectively?
- ✓ Did we listen to the language to see how it was trying to persuade us?
- ✓ Did we come with prepared questions?
- ✓ Did we make a decision based on the arguments, rather than on personalities?
- ✓ Did we consider the accuracy of the evidence and the logic of the arguments?

As participants in the debate:

- ✓ Did we anticipate the opposing arguments in our planning meeting?
- ✓ Did we present our side and refute the opposing side?
- ✓ Did we rely on facts and sound reasoning?
- ✓ Did we stick to the topic and respect the time limits?
- ✓ Did we use our body, voice, and language in a persuasive manner?

Think About It: Which skills developed in this chapter did you have an easy time mastering? Which skills were more difficult to acquire? Write down one or two reasons for each difficulty.

Think More About It

Cross-Reference

See A Career Planning Tool, page x.

You have been thinking about the occupation or college program that you would like to pursue.

Review the list of communication skills that you made for the occupation or program. Think about what you have learned in this book. Then ask yourself:

- Which skills do I need to develop further?
- How should I go about developing them?

With your teacher, create an action plan to address these needs.

Study Skills

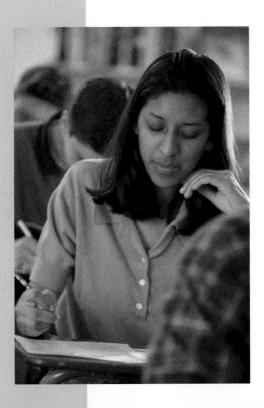

Living in the Age of Information means that you will always be receiving new information and gaining new skills. Learning how to learn—developing good study habits—is one of the most important skills you can acquire. The tips in this Appendix will help you use your time effectively, and improve your reading, note-taking, and exam-writing skills.

Contents

Managing Your Time   278

Effective Studying   279

Tests and Exams   282

Learning Goals

- plan and schedule study time effectively
- review a variety of reading strategies and understand how they are used with different texts
- use the elements of texts to skim for meaning
- organize information to summarize lectures, books, and media

Managing Your Time

Knowing how to use your time is an important skill. Here are a few tips to help you use your day effectively.

Planning

Cross-Reference

See page 162 for planning and scheduling research projects.

1. Break large projects down into smaller tasks.

   • It is better to plan a small task that you know you will be able to finish than to do nothing because you can't finish the whole thing in one try. If you are having trouble getting started on a history project, for instance, set yourself the task of going to the library to look up books on your topic, or plan to read your notes to get ideas for a topic.

2. Make lists.

Try It!

If you have seven things on your list and three are quick and easy, do the three easy things first. This strategy will cut your list almost in half.

   • Lists let you record "the big picture" and keep track of what you have to do. No one expects you to get through your lists right away, but just having them will remind you of your tasks.

   Here are some ways you can use lists in school.

   • Regularly make a list of things to do, especially when you feel pressured for time. Then use the list to set your priorities.

   • Make a list of questions to ask your teacher if you are not sure about an assignment.

Cross-Reference

See Commonly Confused Words, pages 101 to 102.

   • Keep a list of words that you often misspell or confuse. Refer to this list whenever you are revising or editing a paper or assignment.

Scheduling

Get an appointment book, and keep it close by all the time. At the beginning of every week, look ahead to see what you have planned that week. Every morning, check your appointment book, and make a list of all the things you have to do that day. As you do them, cross them off the list. If something on your list doesn't get done, don't give up. Just move it ahead to the next day.

   • Work in small blocks of time. If you are feeling pressured, try breaking your day into 15-minute segments. Studying a subject for 15 minutes every day is better than waiting until the day before a test and cramming.

- List all the tasks you have to accomplish in the next 24 hours. Decide if you can take care of any small tasks right away. Then set a schedule for accomplishing the rest of your goals. Cross each item off the list as you do it.
- Be realistic. Don't schedule study time on Friday night if you know you will want to go out with your friends then. Think about when you work best, and try to work on your most important projects at that time.

Cross things off your list.

Effective Studying

Effective studying involves using reading and writing strategies, as well as scheduling and planning.

Reading

By now you have learned different strategies for reading both fiction and nonfiction. Many of these strategies involve getting to the important information first. Knowing how to "cut to the chase" can save you study time.

Skimming Material

The way to get the most out of what you read in the shortest time is to skim. This method will give you a general sense of the material you have to read and tell you whether the material is useful. Here's how to skim a book.

1. Start with the title. It will give you a clue to the subject matter.

2. Check the copyright page. It will tell you the date and place of publication.
- Is the book too old?
- Is the book relevant to your topic? For example, would a book published in England have information on Canadian law?

3. Read the table of contents to preview the subjects, maps, tables, and appendices.

4. Read the preface, foreword, or introduction to find the purpose of the book.

5. Look at any appendices at the back of the book. These contain additional materials that may be useful.

> **Cross-Reference**
>
> See Chapter 1 for reading strategies for short stories, poetry, plays, novels, and newspaper articles.

> **Cross-Reference**
>
> See pages 170 to 171 for how to skim library materials.

Is the material useful?

6. Check to see if there is an index. It may help you to find specific information later.

7. Read the chapter headings and quickly flip through the pages to get the main ideas. Occasionally, read a short section that looks important. It may deal with what you really want to know.

Reading to Remember

Here are some tips to help you remember what you read.

- Read with a purpose. If you know what you are looking for, it is much easier to remember what you read. If you are doing research for a paper, your purpose is to gather information on the topic you have chosen. However, if you do not have such a clear reason for reading, try turning chapter headings into questions to guide you. For example, the heading Reading to Remember might encourage you to ask: "What do I want to remember?" You can do the same for each subhead in the chapter.

- Before you start reading, ask yourself what you expect to find. As you read, visualize the material, predict what is to come, and revise your interpretations as you go.

- Put the information in your own words. When you have read through a section of the material, stop for a minute and summarize in your own words what you have just read.

To Skim or to Read?

To decide how closely you need to read a particular text, consider the following questions.

- How much do you know about the subject? If you are not familiar with the topic, you might find skimming lightly over a few books is a good way to get a general sense of the issues involved.

- How difficult is the subject? Books on difficult topics will require more concentration and more focused reading than easier subjects.

- Why are you reading? If all you need to know are general details on a subject, you don't need to read a 400-page book from beginning to end. You can skim the material to find the relevant dates and events. However, if you need a more detailed account, you might need to tackle the whole book. If you are interested in only one specific aspect of a larger topic, skim to find the related chapters and then read those pages more slowly.

Whether you are skimming or giving a text your full concentration, always read with a purpose. Before you pick up the book, ask yourself what you hope to get out of reading it. Reading with a purpose makes it easier for your brain to distinguish important information from unimportant details.

Taking Notes

Take a lot of notes. Notes are a good way to remember things that are important. You can take notes from many sources, including books, lectures, speeches, or films. Here is a summary of how to record your notes.

- At the top of the page, identify the source of information (the title of the lecture or book, including pages or sections covered) and the date the notes were written.

- Write neatly and leave space for more information. Keep all notes for a single subject together and in order by date or topic.

- Write the ideas in your own words. This technique forces you to think about what is being said.

- Be selective. Write down the main ideas, important supporting ideas, and facts. If you try to write down every idea and example, you will probably get confused.

- Use symbols and abbreviations that will make sense to you later.

- Whenever possible, take notes in point form. This method organizes your material and thoughts as you go along.

Here is an example of how your notes might look for the first section of this Appendix.

Cross-Reference

See Taking Notes, pages 174 to 176.

12/12/02

COMMUNICATE!
Notes on Appendix: Study Skills

1. Time Management
   - break lge projects down to <er tasks
   - divide time into short segments (15 mins.?)
   - don't try to do everything
   - make lists
     - appt book
     - daily list
     - do easy things first
   - balance work/leisure times

Don't just sit there—write it down!

Taking notes about your own interests as they relate to a school subject can give you many ideas for projects. For example, you might find yourself intrigued by a certain character in a novel or short story. If you keep jotting down why that character seems interesting, you could have the beginnings of an essay on character, such as the one you read in Chapter 6. Don't think that you will remember all those details—even professional writers don't trust their memory. They keep notebooks with them to jot down all their insights and questions.

Tests and Exams

If you manage your time and practise your study skills throughout the year, you will be prepared for your exams. Here are some more tips.

Preparing for an Exam

- Choose a regular place and time for studying. The place should be quiet and comfortable (not the TV room). Choose the time carefully so that your other activities will not interfere. Take regular breaks but keep them short.

- Start studying for an exam several days before the date it is scheduled. Then review the material again the evening before. This plan will give you time to find out about something you don't know and makes the night before a lot less frantic.

- While you study, note the main ideas and organize the details and examples under these ideas. Make note of any questions that you need answered before the exam.

- Select a number of potential exam questions and practise answering them in outline form. Then choose one question and write a full answer for it.

Writing an Exam

Exams come in all types and sizes. Here are some guidelines that apply equally to all types of exams, from multiple-choice and true-false questions to essay-style questions and problems.

- Make a quick survey of the entire exam.

- Note any specific directions, such as "Write on one side of the paper only," or "Do all scratch work on the exam paper."

- Take note of each section in the exam. How many points is each worth? Which sections can you do quickly? Which will take more time?

- Figure out how much time you have to complete the exam, and then allot a portion of that time to each section. Write your time allocations in the margin beside each section heading.

- Do the easy sections of the exam first. If you don't know an answer, or think it will take you a long time, go on to the next question. Then return to the first question later.

- Write neatly and clearly. A "T" that looks like an "F" in a true-false section will cost you marks.

- Identify precisely what the question is asking and answer accordingly. If the question asks, "What is the quotient of 752.8 divided by 27.62, rounded off to the nearest hundredth?" you won't get full marks for simply performing the calculation. You need to remember to round off your answer as well.

- Check over your completed exam. Make sure you have answered everything that you can. Look for grammar, punctuation, spelling, arithmetic errors, and any words that are hard to read because you were writing fast. Write your name on each page.

Essay-Style Questions

When writing essay-style answers to exam questions, it is tempting to launch right into the writing so you get all the information down on paper. But a few minutes spent organizing your ideas can mean the difference between average and excellent work. Here is how to approach essay-style questions:

- Look for keywords in the question, such as explain, compare, contrast, discuss, and define.

- Spend a few moments gathering your thoughts. On scrap paper, list what you know and write a brief outline, cluster, or tree diagram before you start writing.

- Use a formal writing style for your answers. Unless you are told otherwise, always write in full sentences.

- In your introduction, write a thesis statement and summarize the main points you intend to make in the essay. As a result, if you do

Cross-Reference

See Keywords in Essay Topics, page 149.

Cross-Reference

See pages 145 to 146 for more on thesis statements.

not have time to finish, your teacher will at least know what you intended to write. In the paragraphs that follow, focus on explaining each main point. Keep your supporting details simple and concise.

- Watch out for spelling and punctuation errors. If you do not know how to spell a word, avoid using it. Think of another word instead.

Multiple-Choice Questions

Here are some tips for taking multiple-choice tests.

- Read the instructions carefully to find out if you are looking for the right answer or the best answer. In the first case, all the other answers will be at least partly wrong. In the second case, any or all the choices may be right; your task is to decide which is the most accurate.

- Try to answer the question in your head before reading the answers.

- Look over *all* the answers before choosing one.

- Narrow your choices: cross out all answers that are obviously incorrect.

- Watch out for negatives. It is easy to overlook words like "not," "never," and "don't" that change the meaning of the question completely. (If the statement contains strong positive words such as "always" and "forever," be careful that the answer you choose is not true just sometimes or for a while.)

- Don't change your first answer unless you are absolutely sure it is wrong.

Glossary

acronym A word formed from the first letters of other words. Example: NATO (North Atlantic Treaty Organization).

alliteration The repetition of sounds, usually at the beginning of a line or series of words. Example: zany zone.

appendix The material at the back of a book or article that supplements the main text.

assonance The repetition of vowel sounds in a line or a series of words. Example: being and ideal.

atmosphere The main feeling created by a text that causes the reader to expect certain things to happen. Atmosphere is another term for "mood."

audience The intended readers, viewers, or listeners of a work of fiction or nonfiction.

bias Prejudice that prevents a person from looking at something objectively.

bibliography A list of all the reference works you read in your research, whether or not you mention them in your report or essay.

brainstorming Sharing many thoughts about a topic without thinking too much about each one.

caption Words that go with a photograph, picture, or cartoon.

character A person who is represented in a work of fiction, such as a novel or play.

conclusion The end of a text, often summarizing the main ideas in a text.

conflict The struggle between opposing characters or forces.

connotation The meaning of a word that comes from its associated meanings. Example: "clown" could connote any funny person, not just a circus clown.

consonance The repetition of consonant sounds at the beginning or end of a line or a series of words. Example: think tank.

context The spoken or written text that surrounds a particular word or passage and determines its meaning.

contraction A word that is shortened with an apostrophe. Example: "don't" for "do not."

contrast A striking difference or differences between two things being compared.

copyright A right granted by law for a certain number of years to an artist, writer, or composer making him or her the only person who can sell, print, publish, or copy a piece of work.

denotation The most direct or literal meaning of a word (in contrast to its figurative meaning).

dialogue Any conversation between characters or people.

editorial A personal opinion piece written on an issue of interest.

euphemism The substitution of a harsh word or phrase with a more gentle one. Example: "passed away" for "died."

fiction Imaginative literature, such as novels and short stories, featuring made-up characters.

font In printing, a complete set of type of one style.

form The way in which a text is put together; how it is organized.

formal In speech or writing, a style that is serious and correct.

genre A type of text such as poetry, short stories, film, and so on.

headings On a printed page, the larger type that announces what the text below is about.

hyperbole An exaggerated statement that is not meant to be taken at face value.

imagery The language used by a writer that allows the reader to picture or form a sense impression of what is being said.

index The alphabetical listing of all the topics and proper names in a book, with page references. The index appears at the back of a book.

informal In speech or writing, a style that is conversational or sometimes uses slang.

introduction The beginning of a text, often indicating the topic or thesis of a text.

irony A literary device used to achieve a meaning opposite to what is actually being said.

jargon Language that is unique to a trade or profession, sometimes used to hide meaning.

layout Visual organization of a text, or text combined with graphics.

lead The first paragraph of a news story that gives key information so that the reader wants to read further.

literary device The technique of using words to achieve a specific effect and an emotional impact on the reader, sometimes called a rhetorical device.

media All-inclusive terms referring to means of mass communication, such as television, movies, newspapers, radio, magazines, and books.

metaphor A direct comparison by stating that something *is* something else. Example: That baby is the sunshine of his life.

modifier A word that adds to the meaning of another word, often by describing it. Example: a *small* dog.

parallel structure In speech or writing, the repetition of an identical grammatical or stylistic structure for the sake of clarity. Example: The window, *which is open just a crack*, and *which is facing south*, provides the best view from the second floor.

personification Giving human characteristics to things or non-human creatures.

plot What happens in a story—the storyline or the series of episodes.

point of view The perspective of the character or person telling the story, or the perspective of the author in nonfiction. In media texts, point of view is usually understood as the position from which something is viewed or filmed.

prefix Letters that are placed before a word that change its meaning. Example: *un*kind.

proofread To read for and correct mechanical errors in grammar, spelling, punctuation, capitalization, and so on.

purpose The reason the author or artist created the text.

quotation A passage in a book or article that repeats directly what someone said or wrote elsewhere.

reading strategy A way of reading that adds to your understanding of the text.

rhyme The agreement of the ending sounds in two or more lines of verse. Example: height and plight.

script The text of a drama, including all the dialogue, and the stage or shooting directions.

setting The time and place of the book, story, or drama.

simile An indirect comparison using "like" or "as." Example: The pond was as smooth as glass.

situation The reason for an audience coming together, such as a symposium or an informal club meeting. In literature, "situation" refers to a character's living circumstances, issue, or predicament.

stage directions Text in a script that tells the actors how to speak, stand, and move, and indicates how the sets and props should be arranged.

storyboard A graphic organizer used to show the integration of visual, textual, and audio material in a video production. It helps the director visualize how a completed video will be constructed.

style How a writer or speaker says something, including sentence length, literary devices, rhyme, and so on.

suffix Letters that are placed at the end of a word that can make it a new part of speech. Example: kind*ly*.

supporting detail A specific detail, often an example, that supports the main thesis.

suspense A feeling of anxious uncertainty set up in the reader about a character or situation. Suspense is an element of atmosphere.

symbol Something that stands for or represents something else.

table of contents A listing of the contents of a book with page references. The table of contents appears at the front of a book.

text Work that has been created. "Text" may refer to fiction and nonfiction, as well as paintings, drawings, and photographs.

theme A central idea of a text that is often implied rather than directly stated.

thesis A main idea or argument of an essay found in the first paragraph.

title page One of the first pages in a book that gives the title of the work, the author(s) of the work, and the publisher of the work.

tone The attitude of the writer or speaker toward his or her topic or audience.

topic What the text is about.

transition Movement from part of a text or argument to the next part.

voice The person who is talking to the reader. In grammar, active voice indicates that the subject acted upon the object. Example: Todd ate the bread. Passive voice indicates that the object was acted upon. Example: The bread was eaten by Todd.

Web site On the World Wide Web, a home page and other electronic files maintained by a particular organization or person.

works cited A list of the reference works you have mentioned in your report or essay.

Index

A

Abbreviations, 119–120, 224
Acknowledgments, 177–178
Active voice, 93, 224
Adjective clauses, 80–81
Adjectives, 100, 118
    comparative, 100
    superlative, 100
Adverb clauses, 81
Adverbs, 80–81, 100
    comparative, 100
    superlative, 100
Advertisements, print. *See* **Print advertisements**
Advertising, 36–41
Alliteration, 8, 103, 285
Almanacs, 164
Analogies, 224
Apostrophes, 128–129
Appendices, 141–142
Assonance, 8, 285
Atlases, 164
Atmosphere. *See* **Mood; Tone**
Audience:
    of brochures, 42, 241, 243
    of business writing, 185
    of debates, 274, 275
    demonstrations to, 228
    editing for, 74
    of feature films, 46
    language and, 75
    of photographs, 233
    plays, 12
    posters, 235
    presentations to, 259
    of public speaking, 253
    of representations, 230–231
    of speeches, 255
    of technical writing, 224, 225
    television, 46
    videos, 244
    of visual aids, 30, 238
    Web sites, 248, 249

    of writing, 57–58, 68
Audio-visual aids, in presentations, 257, 258
Audio-visual materials, in libraries, 166
Authors:
    of newspaper opinion pieces, 24
    of novels, 18
    of short stories, 3–4, 5

B

Back matter, 141–142
Bar graphs, 31
Bias:
    gender, 90–91
    in newspapers, 24
Bibliography, 141, 170, 179–180
Blocking, 12
Block method, of comparison, 150
Boldface, 44, 134–135, 138
Boxes, 135–136
Brainstorming, 56, 267
Brochures:
    creation of, 241–243
    viewing, 42–45
Bulletin boards, 167–168
Bullets, 44, 136
Business letters, 127, 187–195. *See also* **Letters**
Business reports, title page for, 139
Business writing, 183–186
    e-mail, 198–199
    job applications, 200–210
    letters. *See* **Business letters**
    memos, 196–197

C

Camera angles:
    in feature films, 47
    in photographs, 33, 35

Capital letters, 123–125, 136, 138
Captions:
    brochures, 44
    editorial cartoons, 28
    visual aids, 239
Caricatures, 28
Cartoons, editorial, 28–29
Cause and effect, transitional phrases, 59, 77
Chairpersons, 266, 267, 269, 271, 272, 274, 275
Chambers of commerce, 169
Characters:
    of feature films, 47
    of novels, 18
    of plays, 11, 12
Charts, 30–32, 239. *See also* **Visual aids**
The Chicago Manual of Style, 177
Chronological order, 59, 70
Circle graphs, 30
Clauses, 80–81
Clichés, 75, 104
Clustering, 56, 170
Collective nouns, 89
Colons, 127–128
Colour:
    in feature films, 47
    in photographs, 35
    in print advertisements, 39
Commands, sentences as, 79
Commas, 126–127, 130, 136
Committees, 271, 272–273
Community resources, for research, 168, 169
Comparison(s):
    contrast and, 59, 150–153
    in technical information, 224
    transitional words, 77
Complaint, letters of, 190–192
Complex sentences, 78–79, 84
Compound adjectives, 118

Compound modifiers, 118
Compound sentences, 78–79, 84
Compound subjects, 89
Computer networks, 167
Computers:
    formatting on, 134–135
    revising writing and, 68. *See also* Spell checkers
Conjunctions:
    coordinating, 78, 84
    correlative, 88
    subordinating, 78, 84
Connotations, of words, 98
Consensus, group, 269–270
Consonance, 8, 285
Consonants, doubling the final, 115
Contractions, 63, 108, 129
Contrast:
    comparison and, 59, 150–153
    in transitional phrases, 77
Coordinating conjunctions, 78, 84
Copyright. *See also* Plagiarism
    Web sites and, 250
Correlative conjunctions, 88
Cue cards, 258

D
Dangling modifiers, 86
Databases, 166
Debates, 274–275
Defining terms, 224–226
Demonstrations, to audience, 228
Denotations, of words, 98
Design:
    process, 230–232
    of Web sites, 249
Diagrams, 239. *See also* Visual aids
Dialogue, 129–130
Dictionaries, 164
Digital technology, 247
Directions, capital letters in, 125
Direct speech, 129
Disagreements, in group work, 268–269
Discriminatory language, 90–92
Domains, of Web sites, 49

Double negatives, 100
Drafts:
    of representations, 231
    revision of, 66–69
    in writing, 59–64
Dramatis personae, 11

E
Editing. *See also* Proofreading; Revising
    of representations, 232
    of videos, 246
    of Web sites, 249–250
    of writing, 69–74
Editing symbols, 72–73
Editorial cartoons, 28–29
Editorials, 23
E-mail messages, 167, 198–199
Emphasis:
    in feature films, 47
    italics with, 132
    in literary essays, 150–151
    underlining with, 132
Encyclopedias, 164
Endnotes, 178
Essays:
    literary, 150–153
    persuasive, 154–156
    research, 156–160
    title page for, 139
    writing, 143–149
Euphemism, 105
Evaluative reports, 215–218
Exclamation marks, 79, 125
Exclamations, sentences as, 79
Explanations, transitional phrases, 77

F
Fax transmission, 195
Feature films, 46–48
Figures, 137
First person, writing in, 63, 108
Focus:
    editing for, 69, 107
    of paragraphs, 69, 107
    of photographs, 233
    of posters, 235
    revising for, 67–68, 107
    in writing, 108

Fonts, 42, 134
Footnotes, 178
Formal writing, 63, 108
Formatting:
    of brochures, 241
    of writing, 133–137
Forums, 273–274
Framing, in photographs, 33
Freewriting, 56
Frequently Asked Questions (FAQ), 50
Front matter, 138–141

G
Gender:
    bias, 90–91
    pronouns and, 91–92
Generalizations, 145
Genres:
    of feature films and TV, 46
    of fiction, 3
Gerund phrases, 82
Gerunds, 82
Government departments, for research, 169
Grammar, 75
Graphics. *See also* Visual aids
    in technical writing, 228
Graphs, 30–31, 137, 239. *See also* Visual aids
Groups:
    consensus in, 269–270
    disagreements in, 268–269
    roles within, 266
    subgroups, 268
    types of, 271–276
    work, 266–270
    writing, 106–107

H
Headings:
    of presentations, 135
    in reports, 211–212
    in technical information, 223
Headlines:
    newspaper, 24
    of print advertisements, 40
History references, 124
Hook line, 40
Hyperbole, 104
Hyphens, 118–119

I

Imagery, poetry, 8
Images:
    in brochures, 44
    visual, 229, 255
Informal writing, 63, 108
Information retrieval, 167
Interlibrary loan, 166
Irony, 104
Italics, 132
Items in series. *See also* **Lists**
    commas with, 126–127
    parallelism in, 87–88

J

Jargon, 104–105, 224
Job applications, 200–210
Job interviews, 205–208
Journal entries, 56

K

Keywords:
    in clustering, 56
    in topics, 149
    in transitions, 76

L

Language. *See also* **Word choice**
    discriminatory, 90–92
    formal, 108
    informal, 108
    meaning and, 75
    plain, 105
    of presentations, 259
    of public speaking, 253
    of speeches, 255
    in technical writing, 224–228
    tone and, 75
    in visual aids, 239
Layout, 133–134
Letters:
    of application, 200–202
    business. *See* **Business letters**
    capital letters in, 124
    of complaint, 190–192
    to editors, 192–194
    faxing, 195
    follow-up, 209–210
    to members of parliament, 192–194

    requesting information, 188–190
Libraries:
    catalogues, 163, 170
    reference resources, 163–165
    researching in, 163–167
Lighting:
    in feature films, 47
    in photographs, 35, 233
    stage, 12
    of videos, 245
Line graphs, 31
Listening, 252, 259, 261–265
Listing, of ideas, 56
List of works cited. *See* **Works cited**
Lists. *See also* **Items in series**
    punctuation with, 126, 127, 136
Literary devices, 8, 103–104
Literary essays, 150–153

M

Magazines, 165
Meaning, language and, 75
Measurement:
    abbreviations with, 120
    with visual aids, 239
Media, 27
Meetings, formal, 271–273
Memos, 196–197
Metaphors, 8, 103
Metric symbols, 120
Metric units, 122–123
Misplaced modifiers, 85
MLA Style Manual, 177
Modifiers, 85–86
    compound, 118
Money, sums of, 120
Mood. *See also* **Tone**
    colours and, 39
    in photographs, 35
    in plays, 12
Motions, in meetings, 272
Movies. *See* **Feature films**
Music:
    in feature films, 47
    in plays, 12

N

Negatives, double, 100

Newspapers, 22–26, 165
Note taking, 17, 174–175, 265, 281–282
Noun clauses, 80
Nouns:
    collective, 89
    with plural-sounding endings, 88
    possession of, 128
Novels, 3, 17–21
Numbers and numerals:
    hyphens with, 118
    spelling out, 121

O

Opinion pieces, 23–26
Oral presentations, 253–260
Order:
    chronological, 59, 70
    of ideas, 59–60
    of paragraphs, 106
    within reports, 211
    of sentences, 69–70
Outline, of writing, 60

P

Panels, 273, 274
Paragraphs:
    editing, 69–70, 73–74
    structure, 62
Parallelism, 87–88, 224
Paraphrasing, 181–182
Parliamentary procedure, 271, 272, 275
Participles, 81
Passive voice, 93–94, 227
Past participles, 81
Periodical indexes, 165–166
Periods, 125, 136
Personification, 8
Persuasive essays, 154–156
Photographs:
    creation of, 233–234
    viewing, 33–35
Phrases, 82
Pie graphs, 30
Place:
    order by, 59
    transitional words, 77
Plagiarism, 181–182. *See also* **Copyright**

Plain language, 105
Plays, 11–16
Playwrights, 11
Poetry, 7–10
Point-by-point method, of
    comparison, 150
Possession, 128
Posters:
    creation of, 235–237
    viewing, 36–38
Predesigning, 230–231
Prefixes, 98, 118
Prepositional phrases, 82
Presentations:
    listening to, 261–265
    oral, 253–260
Presenting, of writing, 111–112
Present participles, 81
Prewriting, 56–60
Print advertisements, 39–41
Progress reports, 212–214
Pronouns:
    antecedents of, 94
    gender and, 91–92
    indefinite, 89, 95
    personal, 95–96, 128
    relative, 80, 94–95
    in transitions, 76
Proofreading, 113–114. *See also*
    Editing; Revising
    posters, 235
Proper names, 119–120
Proposals, 218–222
Public speaking, 253–260
Punctuation, 125–131
Purpose:
    brochures, 44, 241
    editing for, 74
    feature films, 46
    photographs, 233
    plays, 12
    poetry, 8
    posters, 235
    public speaking, 254
    representations, 230
    sentences, 79
    short stories, 3, 4
    television, 46
    videos, 244
    visual aids, 30
    Web sites, 49, 248, 249

in writing, 57–58

Q
Qualifiers, in advertisements, 40
Question marks, 125
Questions:
    for focusing research, 172–174
    in job interviews, 205–207
    rhetorical, 104
    sentences as, 79
Quotation marks, 129–131, 181
Quotations, 130
    acknowledging, 178
    books of, 164
    capital letters in, 124
    colons with, 127
    indentations of, 130
    within quotation marks,
        181–182
    within quotations, 130

R
Radio, for research, 169
Reading, 2
    newspapers, 22–26
    nonfiction books, 279–281
    novels, 17–21
    plays, 11–16
    poetry, 7–10
    schedule, 17
    short stories, 3–6
Redundancy, 97
Repetition, 97–98
    in feature films, 47
    in technical writing, 227–228
Rephrasing, of borrowed
    material, 181
Reports, 211–222
    business, 139
    evaluative, 215–218
    progress, 212–214
    proposals, 218–222
Representations, 229–250
Research:
    evaluating information,
        173–174
    focusing, 172–174
    organizing information,
        175–176
    plans, 161, 162
    resources for, 163–171

Research essays, 156–160
    acknowledging sources in,
        177–178
    title page for, 139
Resolutions, in debating, 274
Résumés, 202–205
Revising, 66–69, 106–110. *See*
    also **Editing; Proofreading**
    of representations, 232
Rewording, of borrowed
    material, 181
Rhetorical questions, 104
Rhyme, 8
Robert's Rules of Order, 272
Root words, 98
Run-on sentences, 84

S
Satire, 28
Scripts, of videos, 245
Secretary, of group, 266
Semicolons, in lists, 136
Sentence fragments, 83–84
Sentences:
    awkward, 86–87
    beginning with verbs, 227
    clarity, 71
    complex, 78–79, 84
    compound, 78–79, 84
    editing, 71–72, 73
    order of, 69–70
    purpose, 79
    run-on, 84
    simple, 78–79
    simplicity, 71
    tone, 79
    types of, 78
    variety in, 78–79, 107
Settings:
    novels, 18
    public speaking, 254
    short stories, 4
Sexist words, 91
Short stories, 3–6
Similes, 8, 103
Simple sentences, 78–79
Slang, 63
Sound effects, in plays, 12
Sources:
    crediting, 177–182

recording information about, 170

of visual aids, 32

Speaking skills, 252

Specialized terms, 99

Speeches, 255–257

Spell checkers, 113

Spelling, 114–117

on Web sites, 249

Stage directions, 11

Statements, sentences as, 79

Statistics Canada, 169

Storyboards, 245

Style, writing, 5, 69, 75, 107

Subjects. *See also* **Topics**

compound, 89

of editorial cartoons, 28

of photographs, 33

Subject-verb agreement, 88–89

Subordinate clauses, 80

Subordinating conjunctions, 78, 84

Subtitles, colons with, 128

Suffixes, 98, 115–116

Summarizing, transitional phrases, 77

Suspense, 12

Symbolism:

in editorial cartoons, 28

in feature films, 47

Symposiums, 273, 274

Synonyms, 97

in technical writing, 227–228

in transitions, 76

T

Tables of contents, 140–141

Technical information, 223–228

Technical writing. *See* **Business writing**

Techno transfer, 223

Television, 46–48, 169

Thesauruses, 75, 97

Thesis statement, 106, 145–146

Time:

abbreviations with, 120, 122

colons with, 127

hyphens with, 118

order of, 59, 70

of public speaking, 254

transitional phrases, 77

Timekeeper, in debates, 274

Title page, 138–139

Titles:

of brochures, 241

capital letters with, 124, 138

italics with, 132

of presentations, 135

quotation marks with, 131

of short stories, 3

underlining with, 132

of visual aids, 238

Tone. *See also* **Mood**

language and, 75

of novels, 18

in public speaking, 253

of sentences, 79

of short stories, 4, 5

of writing, 62, 107

Topics. *See also* **Subjects**

of debates, 274

of presentations, 259

public speaking, 253

of writing, 56–57, 106, 107, 149

Transitions, 76–77, 107

Tree diagram, 147

Type sizes, 135

U

Underlining, 132

URL (Uniform Resource Locator), 49

V

Verbs:

agreement with subject, 88–89

to begin sentences, 227

Videos, 244–247

Viewing, 27–52

Visual aids, 30–32, 137, 223, 238–240

Visual images, 229, 255

Vocabulary, in writing, 98–99

W

Web sites:

acknowledging sources on, 178

creation of, 248–250

viewing, 49–52

Word choice. *See also* **Language**

editing, 75, 98–99, 107

in short stories, 5

Words:

commonly confused, 101–102

connotations of, 98

denotations of, 98

hyphenated, 118–119

root, 98

sexist, 91

as words, in quotation marks, 131

Works cited, 141, 179–180

Writer's block, 64

Writing:

audience of, 57–58

body in, 61

clarity in, 108

conclusion in, 61, 106

drafting, 59–64

essays, 143–160

first draft, 61–64

focus in, 108

formal, 63, 108

form of, 58

groups, 106–107

informal, 63, 108

of instructions, 226–228

introduction in, 61

main vs. supporting ideas, 60

order in, 59, 69–70

outline of, 60

for power, 75

process, 54–64

purpose of, 57–58

revising of, 66–69

speeches, 255–257

style, 69, 75

tone of, 62

topic of, 56–57, 107

troubleshooting, 107–109

vocabulary in, 98–99

Y

Yearbooks, 164

Acknowledgments

Visuals

Page iii Superstock; Page vi (top) Superstock, (bottom) Thomas Brummett/Photodisc; Page vii CP Archive; Page 1 (left centre) Photofest, (right centre) Jonnie Miles/Photodisc, (bottom) Superstock; Page 2 Superstock; Page 4 SW Productions/Photodisc; Page 9 Comstock; Page 12 Comstock; Page 14 C Squared Studios/Photodisc; Page 20 Marty Honiq/Photodisc; Page 22 Dick Hemingway; Page 26 Ryan McVay/Photodisc; Page 27 Ryan McVay/Photodisc; Page 28 Reproduced by permission of Dave Elston; Page 33 Comstock; Page 34 Eugene Smith/Black Star; Page 37 Reproduced by permission of StudentCounsellor.com; Page 40 Reprinted with permission of Bozell Worldwide, Inc.; Page 43 Reproduced with kind permission of Canada Post; Page 46 Comstock; Page 47 Archive Photos; Page 51 Reproduced by permission of HowStuffWorks.com; Page 53 (left centre) Superstock, (bottom) Thomas Brummett/Photodisc; Page 54 Ryan McVay/Photodisc; Page 57 (top) CP Archive, (bottom) Corbis Royalty Free/Magma; Page 58 (right) Reproduced by permission of Bell Mobility;

Page 62 Antonio Mo/Photodisc; Page 63 (top) Corbis Royalty Free/Magma, (bottom) Corbis Royalty Free/Magma; Page 64 Corbis Royalty Free/Magma; Page 65 EyeWire; Page 68 Vicky Kasala/Photodisc; Page 70 Ryan McVay/Photodisc; Page 71 NASA; Page 75 Ryan McVay/Photodisc; Page 76 Dick Hemingway; Page 79 CMCD/Photodisc; Page 82 Michael Matisse/Photodisc; Page 83 Photodisc; Page 84 Glen Allison/Photodisc; Page 86 Karl Weatherly/Photodisc; Page 88 Sami Sarkis/Photodisc; Page 89 Michael Matisse/Photodisc; Page 91 C Squared Studios/Photodisc; Page 92 Comstock; Page 94 Comstock; Page 97 C Squared Studios/Photodisc; Page 103 Photomondo/Photodisc; Page 106 EyeWire; Page 110 © Argus Communications, Allen, TX 75013, USA; Page 111 Superstock; Page 115 Ryan McVay/Photodisc; Page 117 S. Meltzer/Photolink/Photodisc; Page 121 CP Archive; Page 126 (top) Barbara Penoyar/Photodisc, (bottom) Superstock; Page 128 Corbis Royalty Free/Magma; Page 129 Corbis Royalty Free/Magma; Page 131 Siede Preis/Photodisc; Page 132 Reproduced by permission of John Robert Colombo and Canadian Geographic; Page 135 Superstock; Page 143 Superstock; Page 146 CP Archive; Page 148 Corbis Royalty Free/Magma; Page 149 Corbis Royalty Free/Magma; Page 151 (left) Don Farrell/Photodisc, (right) Comstock; Page 154 CP Archive; Page 158 CALVIN AND HOBBES © 1989 Watterson. Reprinted with permission of UNIVERSAL PRESS SYNDICATE. All Rights Reserved; Page 161 Michael Newman/Photo Edit; Page 163 (top) John A. Rizzo/Photodisc, (bottom) CP Archive; Page 164 Archive Photos; Page 165 CP Archive; Page 167 Corbis Royalty Free/Magma; Page 168 Steve Mason/Photodisc; Page 169 CP Archive; Page 170 Keith Brofsky/Photodisc; Page 172 Superstock; Page 173 Joshua Ets-Hokin/Photodisc; Page 176 Corbis Royalty Free/Magma; Page 177 Hisham F. Ibrahim/Photodisc; Page 183

(top left) Jess Alford/Photodisc, (top right) Geoff Manesse/Photodisc, (bottom left) John A. Rizzo/Photodisc, (bottom right) SW Productions/Photodisc; Page 185 Keith Brofsky/Photodisc; Page 186 Andy Sotiriou/Photodisc; Page 188 Reprinted with permission of UNIVERSAL PRESS SYNDICATE. All Rights Reserved; Page 190 Ryan McVay/Photodisc; Page 192 TW Image Network; Page 198 Ken Usami/Photodisc; Page 200 Comstock; Page 203 SW Productions/Photodisc; Page 205 Dick Hemingway; Page 207 Antonio Mo/Photodisc; Page 208 Grantland Cartoons; Page 209 Corbis Royalty Free/Magma; Page 215 Thomas Brummett/Photodisc; Page 218 Ryan McVay/Photodisc; Page 225 Ryan McVay/Photodisc; Page 227 Siede Preis/Photodisc; Page 229 Superstock; Page 233 Comstock; Page 234 Corbis Royalty Free/Magma; Page 236 (left) Corbis Royalty Free/Magma, (right) John A. Rizzo/Photodisc; Page 238 Reproduced by permission of Maclean's; Page 242 Reproduced with kind permission of Canada Post; Page 245 Reproduced by permission of Power Production Software; Page 248 Reproduced by permission of GrassRoots@ca; Page 251 (top right) CP Archive, (bottom left) Steve Mason/Photodisc; Page 252 Superstock; Page 254 Corel; Page 255 CP Archive; Page 256 Alan and Sandy Carey/Photodisc; Page 257 Ryan McVay/Photodisc; Page 259 Barbara Penoyar/Photodisc; Page 260 Used by permission of Grantland Cartoons; Page 261 SW Productions/Photodisc; Page 264 PEANUTS reprinted by permission of United Features Syndicate, Inc.; Page 266 Jacobs Stock Photography/Photodisc; Page 268 Monica Lau/Photodisc; Page 269 Ryan McVay/Photodisc; Page 272 CP Archive; Page 273 CP Archive; Page 275 CP Archive; Page 276 (left) © Michelle D. Bridwell/Photo Edit, (bottom centre) First Light, (top right) © Michael Newman/Photo Edit; Page 277 SW Productions/Photodisc; Page 279 (top) Ryan McVay/Photodisc, (bottom) Jeff Maloney/Photodisc; Page 282 Corbis Royalty Free/Magma

Front cover: (top left) Superstock, (centre) Superstock, (bottom left) Thomas Brummett/Photodisc

Text

Page 5 From "Blood Knots" by Mallory Burton. Reprinted by permission of the author. Page 13 From *Trifles* by Susan Glaspell, © Dodd, Mead and Company 1920; Page 19 From *Fish House Secrets* by Kathy Stinson © 1992. Reproduced by permission of Thistledown Press; Page 25 Reprinted with permission from The Globe and Mail; Page 63 (top) From *The Moviemaker: Steven Spielberg* by Roger Ebert. Reproduced by permission of Roger Ebert; Page 155 Adapted and reproduced by permission of The Telegraph; Page 219 Reproduced by permission of The Ontario Public Interest Research Group – Guelph; Page 256 Adapted from a speech by Erika Juergensen, The Daily Herald Co.